NOT BY SIGHT

NOT BY SIGHT

Only Faith Opens Your Eyes

CASH LUNA

EMANATE
BOOKS

Published in Nashville, Tennessee, by Emanate Books, an imprint of Thomas Nelson. Emanate Books and Thomas Nelson are registered trademarks of HarperCollins Christian Publishing, Inc.

Published in Spanish as *No es por Vista*, Editorial vida, Nashville, Tennessee.

Thomas Nelson titles may be purchased in bulk for educational, business, fund-raising, or sales promotional use. For information, please e-mail SpecialMarkets@ThomasNelson.com.

Scripture quotations are taken from the *Holy Bible*, New Living Translation. © 1996, 2004, 2007, 2013 by Tyndale House Foundation. Used by permission of Tyndale House Publishers, Inc., Carol Stream, Illinois 60188. All rights reserved.

Any Internet addresses, phone numbers, or company or product information printed in this book are offered as a resource and are not intended in any way to be or to imply an endorsement by Thomas Nelson, nor does Thomas Nelson vouch for the existence, content, or services of these sites, phone numbers, companies, or products beyond the life of this book.

ISBN 978-1-4002-0831-9 (eBook)
ISBN 978-1-4002-0830-2 (TP)

Library of Congress Control Number: 2018932107

Printed in the United States of America
18 19 20 21 22 LSC 10 9 8 7 6 5 4 3 2 1

Here is my secret, a very simple secret: It is only with the heart that one can see rightly; what is essential is invisible to the eye.

—Antoine Saint-Exupéry,
The Little Prince

To the author and finisher of our faith,
Jesus,
our Lord and Savior

Acknowledgments

Thank you so much . . .

To Sonia, my beloved wife and faithful friend, who is always with me to take on every new challenge we believe God for.

To my children, for all the love and support they have provided in my calling to travel to other nations, taking the Word and power of God, sometimes at the expense of being away for long periods of time.

To my mother and her unwavering trust in me. She never doubted for a second that I would one day fulfill my call to be a missionary, even when neither of us really knew what that would entail.

To my pastor, Jorge H. López, who showed me the way of faith.

To my wonderful team, the greatest gift God has given me in the ministry, after His Holy Spirit. Thanks to their constant work and unbridled support, we have been able to go as far as God has granted us.

To the faithful members of Casa de Dios, the church I founded and pastor, for the love and respect they provide to me and my family. Thank you for joining me in these faith endeavors!

CONTENTS

INTRODUCTION

The great day had finally arrived! All those sleepless nights, missed meals, loans for textbooks, and long treks to college because he couldn't afford bus fare had finally paid off. With diploma in hand, Carlos tearfully embraced his mother, who was as proud as any mother could be of a son who was now a doctor. "I always believed in you, son," she whispered. Could there possibly be any greater reward than hearing those words? Just starting his new life, that young man was facing a crossroads between getting a job as a general practitioner or pursuing further studies, and the word *faith* meant everything! That word described his greatest asset—trust, assurance, and a vision of the future. This was all he had available to him, as finances were certainly not in his reach. But the conviction he heard in his mother's words continually echoed within him, motivating him to press on toward his dreams. Despite circumstances and limitations, Carlos was always optimistic, sure that he would reach his purpose and fulfill his life goals. He had faith!

We all have faith in something or in someone. We all believe, or we are at least convinced about something in life. The question is in whom and in what do you believe? This question is quite significant because our lives are defined by where we place our trust. Carlos had faith in his abilities, and his mother had faith in him. These were truths that defined his life. For example, I believe in my wife and my kids, and I trust in them. I have faith in them. But above all else, I believe in God. That truth alone has helped shape my life, more so than any other. After all, I am a pastor and founder of a ministry, which makes my Christian faith a pillar without which Cash Luna would not be Cash Luna.

One does not need to be a pastor, however, for the truth of God's Word to have an impact in a deep way. Inevitably, our human nature intertwines with a divine one, searching for a sense of existence, desiring to create, transcend, understand, and enjoy the beauty and perfection of the universe. Consequently, faith and belief are part of our very essence. It's an ability, a gift to be maximized. That, in and of itself, is the entire reason we possess it. It's not about leaning on a blind type of faith, but rather about sharing in the joy of relying entirely on the One who has loved us even before we were born. That's what I want to write about—the incredible potential that your faith has, especially the power that you can unleash when you place your potential of faith in God's hands.

As members of humanity as well as passionate believers fully convinced of the existence of God and of his infinite love toward us, it would be nothing short of futile to remain silent before so much evidence of his grace in our lives. So, where do I start? How about by sharing the lessons I have learned through personal experiences. The before and after of accepting God as my Father, Jesus as my Lord and Savior, and the Holy Spirit as my counselor, my intercessor, my comforter, and the giver of power to fulfill his work. These basic truths of the Christian faith have been the basis for how I have faced life's challenges.

Time and time again, the Lord has led me throughout all these years to share about him and his passionate love for us. But there was a time when I wrestled with the whole dilemma of religion. How to share having faith in God without sounding religious or fanatical? It seemed like an impossible task, yet this was my desire. The faith I want to share is one that flows naturally like a river; one in which you can immerse and whose waters will refresh and reinvigorate you. Moreover, if we choose to flow in that mighty current, it will lead us to a vast ocean—our purpose in life! This is exactly what the Lord desires: to renew us and give us a new life, through the eyes of faith. And it is designed to change everything, to strengthen and guide us.

I was raised in a Christian home, but it was just my mother and me. My father was never in the equation, and I have had to accept the fact that this made a huge difference in me. Why do I say this? Because it's not the same thing for a man who grows up in a traditional home to speak to you, as it is for one who has had to live first-hand his faith in God through unique circumstances. However, my mother taught me the Christian creeds, the Ten Commandments, basic prayers, and yes, even about faith! Now, looking back, I can see how God always played an important role in my life.

I was one of those neighborhood kids who never missed mass at the Catholic church. I'd even go around picking up my friends for church every Sunday. Even at the early age of ten, I had already made up my mind that I wanted to be a missionary, although I had no idea what that meant. I lived my faith out the way I was taught. However, it wasn't enough to keep me from the typical teenage risks we all go through. I tried marijuana and challenged the rules. In the end, it was the way my mother steadfastly raised me that won the battle during those quite challenging years. It was around that time I discovered that faith was a formula that had not yet deeply impacted my life. Then came the breaking point. In 1982, during a Sunday-morning service at a church known as

Fraternidad Cristiana de Guatemala, in a totally natural and spontaneous moment, I accepted Jesus Christ as my Lord and Savior. That was the instant I can truly say my faith-walk started. I went from just saying it to doing it. And that's the challenge for all of us who claim to have faith in God!

Little by little, step by step, I began to discover the vast dimension of the fatherhood of God and to engage in a deep and intimate relationship with him. It was simple, but intense at the same time. Although I had always experienced God's presence in my life, every moment, even supernaturally, it wasn't until I chose to obey his call to ministry that I truly learned to trust in his promises. In fact, I can say that was the moment I truly started walking with my eyes closed, led only by my faith in him.

As I started to read God's Word, I learned powerful and priceless truths that triggered a deep change in my life, which I'm sure will happen in yours as well. These truths are designed to broaden our view by making faith a foundational pillar in everything we say, think, and do. This is not about religion! In fact, I want to pull you as far away as possible from religious stereotypes and draw close to you as an individual. Being a person of faith isn't about shouting aloud one's belief in God, reciting certain creeds, or beating one's chest in repentance, ever fearful of divine judgment. It is about demonstrating faith every step of the way, yes, even in the simplest and most mundane things in life. You see, our faith in God is designed to sustain us in everything. So let's embark on this journey of what it really means to live by faith. I promise that you will not regret it!

THE KING'S SPEECH

George never imagined that he would be crowned king of England by the age of forty-one. His brother, Edward, the legitimate heir in the line of succession, had abdicated that immense honor and responsibility due to his emotional life drawing him in a different direction. He had fallen in love with an American commoner, Wallis Simpson, who was twice divorced, and as king, he would not have been allowed to marry her.

Sounds unprecedented, right? But it is not uncommon for reality to outdo fiction. There are also times when reality sets the stage for fiction, as in this case that provided the basis of *The King's Speech*, a drama depicting a frightened and insecure prince facing the daunting task of overcoming his speech impediment to take on the role of King George VI. His world was totally shaken. You see, George was a devoted husband and father who had settled into his role as part of royalty but with no prominence whatsoever. He knew he was in the line of succession, but since he wasn't the firstborn, the likelihood was distant. His destiny, however, took a dramatic turn.

With the country engulfed in war, the winds of change and independence were blowing to and fro. George had to open his mind and heart to overcome his childhood ordeals and assume his unintended identity as king. All his inner conflicts seemed to entangle his vocal chords. However, his stammer wasn't a luxury a man who overnight had to transmit his faith and courage to a nation that was leading the Second World War could afford.

This emerging king, burdened with so much responsibility upon his shoulders, had to project security, confidence, and power, not only in his decisions, but also in the tone, rhythm, flow, and meaning of his words. This is precisely what we, as children and heirs of a King who so deeply loves us, are also required to do. Moreover, it's also the reason why it's so vital we discover our identity, trust in our Father, and learn to live by the principles of the kingdom to which we belong. Our entire lives and futures depend on it.

One of George's first challenges was to prepare for that initial speech he would give upon ascending to the throne, an address intended to inspire a nation and the world to tackle those coming difficult years of war. To achieve this, he underwent an effective therapy designed to reconfigure his mind and his heart, one which you are about to embark on as well—in essence, a renewal of your identity to realize that you truly belong to a royal lineage. We are children of the King, heirs of his throne, and called to live according to his kingdom's principles. Let the King's discourse become our own.

1 SUPERNATURAL

God is our
loving Father
and he asks
us to believe
in him
wholeheartedly
because he
loves us.

When a twenty-three-year-old decides
to marry the woman he loves, his beautiful nineteen-year-old girlfriend, he
has everything going for him: his ability
to start a new company, his creativity,
his ironclad will, his passion, and especially his clear desire to serve the Lord.
One could say he's not missing anything
and a bright and fulfilling future awaits
him. Years later, that young man would
say, beyond a shadow of a doubt, that his
dreams had come true. He raised a beautiful family, followed the vision God gave
him, and established a ministry that gives
all the praise and glory to God. However,
the road there wasn't easy. Despite the

clarity concerning his calling and all the Lord's support, there were moments of uncertainty he had to battle, as well as heartaches in every area, from the simplest ones, such as providing for his home, to more sensitive ones like character assassination.

Just recently married and in the process of starting a new life together, the young couple rented a small house. Their wedding had been nothing short of a true miracle of provision from start to finish, blessed with many gifts. Their excitement overflowed at the sight of all those different packages. There were large boxes as well as small ones, all wrapped in white paper with beautiful designs. It was like a special Christmas and hand in hand the new couple gave thanks for so much blessing. Some presents were exceptional. For example, the parents of the bride had given them a set of cutlery made of sterling silver. Wow! Yes, I know. They couldn't imagine when they would ever use them, but they would. However, putting first things first, they needed food on the table, and that's exactly what he focused on. In fact, when he decided to get married after hearing the Lord tell him, "It's time to get engaged and start your life as a couple," a knife salesman visited his workplace and in faith he bought a set of knives for his future household. Upon receiving them, he said, "Okay, Lord, I'll obey. I'm going to get married. I've bought the first thing for our home. Could you please provide everything else."

Being a young husband, he decided to become an insurance broker, which would allow him a flexible schedule that wouldn't interrupt his service for the Lord. And indeed, he did well, convincing potential customers of his product with a special grace. In time, he became the best salesman on the team, to the point of winning awards. However, even these achievements didn't do away with a measure of doubt, or perhaps an anxiety, for wanting things to happen more quickly.

I'm not sure, however one day I left home . . . that is, this young man left for work greatly distressed over his finances, wondering how he could provide his wife the home he had promised her, and how the dreams they had visualized together would become a reality. Right at that moment he heard the Father say, "If I gave you a set of sterling silver cutlery, can't I also provide the food to eat with it?" It was such a logical question and loving promise at the same time, that the young man—that is, I—lost it and started weeping uncontrollably. Of course! Perhaps I didn't understand the full extent of what God was saying, but it was a lesson in faith, just like many more that were on the way.

People often ask me how to live by faith in God. And my reply is simple and complex at the same time. I always sum it up with this phrase: "Give yourself to the Lord," because it covers many areas, from knowing His Word—where we find our identity and code of conduct—to our attitude in every situation in life, be it large or small. For example, the well-known Lord's Prayer is a complete declaration of faith. Right from the opening statement—Our Father—we understand that we are his children, his heirs, and official citizens of a kingdom that operates under different laws and standards than those of this world. That is the key!

It is along with the model prayer left by Jesus that we declare, "Thy kingdom come, thy will be done, on Earth as it is in heaven." Many times, however, we fail to grasp the sheer magnitude of what this request encompasses: that we might have

We are his children, his heirs, and official citizens of a kingdom that operates under different laws and standards than those of this world. That is the key!

peace, that good might prevail over evil, that justice be established, and to be free of all worries and anxieties. In short, to live our life on Earth as we would in heaven. Right?

To live out these ideal, supernatural conditions, we must first learn something about God's system, which obviously is totally different from this world's system. It's not simple to achieve because it implies a willingness to renew our understanding and do away with what this world has taught us, first and foremost with the total conviction in our minds and hearts that he truly does love and care for us. Having faith in God means that the wonderful truth of his Fatherhood must become the foundation of our lives to such an extent that it totally transforms how we see things around us. As his children, just like in any other family, we have both benefits and responsibilities to fulfill.

God lays out a totally different system in his Word than the one this world offers. He asks us to totally rely on him before any other option mankind can offer. He never tells us to seek a friend or a loved one when difficult circumstances arise, but rather to seek him first! Why? Because it's always in the middle of a problem that we seek out first those whom we trust the most. If we choose to live a life of faith, seeking God with humble hearts should be our first response when facing any adverse or unexpected circumstance.

Out of all I could teach you through my testimony, it would be precisely that God is the very pillar of my existence in every situation, always, in every moment. God has always been my first option! Believe me, he has never let me down. I have had to learn, think, feel, and act according to what his Word teaches, and that is how I became an ardent reader of the Bible. And my wholehearted desire is to share these simple but transformational truths that I've discovered.

If we go back to the beginning in the book of Genesis, we see that Adam and Eve were created to live in a wonderful system, the Garden of Eden, designed for them to enjoy and manage. However, they lost their focus and sinned by listening to the serpent's advice and eating the fruit of the tree of good and evil. As a result, they were forced into a system totally different from the one God had prepared for them. This world's system was designed for the Adam who was removed from paradise and took on the unredeemed, fallen nature of man. As of that moment, he had to start earning his keep with sweat and hard work, a shift that affected all of us. But then Jesus came! He offered us the possibility of partaking of His divine nature[1] and grant us access, once again, into God's original, perfect system!

This issue of disobedience made me think. If you look at it carefully, Adam focused on the one thing he wasn't allowed to do, not appreciating every other thing he could do and enjoy in the garden. Now, was that piece of fruit worth throwing all of God's system down the drain? Of course, not! But when we focus on what we don't have or can't have, we end up wasting all the other opportunities that we do have within reach.

When people decide to give their lives to the Lord, they sometimes lament those things they obviously would need to leave behind, such as drinking, smoking, partying, and lying, totally overlooking the fact that these things are designed to harm body and spirit. Therefore, God desires for us to seek after that which is good, pleasing, and perfect unto him. Have you ever noticed how in this world's system we only find pleasure in things that are harmful? Is that ironic or what? It's precisely because of these contradictions that God asks us to let him renew every area of our lives to see things from his perspective. So, we can start enjoying what he's made readily available to us by changing our lifestyles and aligning them with his system.

Of course, every change in life is challenging; but this is precisely when we need to be strong and allow our faith in him to prevail over all the other things this world presents to us as

---

1 2 Peter 1:4

attractive. As I've always said, true intelligence means letting yourself be led by someone smarter than you, and who better than our Creator? Another example is how the Lord asks us to be humble when someone offends us, as opposed to the world's solution of payback! So, what do we need to do if we want to live by faith?

To begin, we need to obey what God has defined as right and not let ourselves be controlled by our human nature and instinctive urges. When we truly start to live by faith, our Father begins the work of perfecting us, comforting us, and filling us with his peace. He strengthens our wills to the point that we can close our eyes and walk in trust, following his instructions alone.

The Best System

From my point of view, the first step to living by faith is to recognize that God's system is the best and to be willing to obey it. This opens the door to a life full of expectation, along with the ability to dream and imagine. It's like being born again. Born again, however, into a life in which we are direct heirs to the promises we find in his Word. If you take that step, I guarantee that he will have wonderful surprises in store for you.

Because God is our Creator, he knows exactly what to say regarding how everything works. He has the power and authority to tell us how to act and what's best for us. He loves us and desires for us to be fulfilled in every area of our lives! If you want an ally with influence, who better than God? It's like taking your vehicle in for service. Sure, you can take it to any mechanic, but nothing tops taking it directly to the dealership where they have all the original parts and systems needed to fix it. Don't try to fix your life with this world's flawed system. Follow the instructions from the manufacturer, our Creator, who knows us inside and out. He is the only one who can heal you, restore you, and prosper you. God's system and this world's system are always at odds with each other, which is why after giving your life to him, you will also need to change your manner of thinking. If you draw near to him, you'll be renewed to live by faith!

What are some of the foundational principles of his kingdom? Communicating with him and experiencing forgiveness are some of the basic ones, which is why he asks us to pray at all times, with the right attitude, putting aside all anger and bitterness, and forgiving other people's offenses.[2]

Jesus taught his disciples much about prayer because effective communication is vital in order to switch systems. After all, you can't really love and have faith in someone whom you don't

Don't try to fix your life with this world's flawed system. Follow the instructions from the manufacturer, our Creator, who knows us inside and out. He is the only one who can heal you, restore you, and prosper you.

know. On one occasion Jesus taught his disciples about the need to pray without ceasing by using the parable of a persistent widow who kept asking a judge to intervene on her behalf, even to the point of tiring him until he did. The widow didn't employ this world's system, but rather Jesus' kingdom system, which teaches us to persist in faith until we get an answer.[3]

The world says, "Use my system, find someone with influence or someone you can bribe to get things done." On the other hand, God says, "Use my system, I know what I'm saying. Show me your faith, call on me day and night, ask and act correctly."[4] No one has

---

2 1 Timothy 2:8
3 Luke 18:1–8
4 Luke 18:7–8

as much power to help you as the Lord, the Judge par excellence, who grants you direct access to his throne of grace for help in time of need. His Word says that he will not delay in answering, but above all he needs to see your faith. If you don't get what you desire, it's because you are taking too long in asking him for it! Remember that with God nothing is impossible, which means that everything is possible if you believe and ask him!

Our God is clear when he says that we'll receive everything we ask of him.[5] Of course, that does not include anything in the area of sin. If you're connected to him, you will know that you can't ask him for something that will bring you harm or that will separate you from him. But everything else is acceptable. So, what are you waiting for? Start asking! And if you want to, try asking him for something that's "not so good." You'll see, he will answer, but in this case it's obviously going to be a great big *no*! But there's no harm in trying.

Who cares what others might say. Let them pray their own way, but if you ask in faith it will be done. This is what our Father teaches us. I am convinced that it is true because I've asked him in faith and he has come through every time, especially when he knows that we will give him the glory and the praise. Jesus teaches us to ask for everything in his name. He has chosen us and wants us to bear fruit in which the Father is glorified,[6] and that occurs when your requests are answered, and every yoke of sickness, poverty, pride, separation, and disappointment is destroyed.

When you operate in Adam's system, you look for natural solutions. When faced with a sickness, the first thing you do is see if the medical insurance will cover the treatment. But if you operate in God's system, nothing will disturb or trouble you because you know that Jesus' sacrifice has made you whole. When it comes to your finances, no matter how many business deals might fall

5 Mark 11:24
6 John 15:16

through, he has promised to provide for you supernaturally. You'll receive calls from people who will want to bless you with work and opportunities for your provision. Pray for those open doors, and in the meantime, tell the Father, "I know that everything's going to work out, because I'm trusting in your system."

We must be guileless as children before the Lord, relying entirely on his power, grace, and lovingkindness. I have experienced this in my ministry. When I have been obedient, he takes control of things, provides the resources and prepares the way for every undertaking to benefit many in which he receives the glory and honor. Begin to access his kingdom system that operates supernaturally through faith and do not rely on this world's system.

Seek to walk righteously before him and there will be no obstacle to hold you back from your prayers. It's not about being perfect, but about having a heart according to what he asks. Choose to live by faith today! Dive in deep into his kingdom!

2 IMPERFECT

Our Father
loves us
and desires
for us to
come boldly
before him.

King George V, the father of shy and stuttering Prince Albert Frederick Arthur George, without even knowing it highlighted certain traits in his son that made it even more difficult for him to communicate. I can just imagine how relieved the king must have felt thinking to himself, "I'm so glad it's my firstborn Edward who'll succeed me on the throne and not George." He never imagined the possibility, but less than a year later Edward would in fact relinquish that privilege. Many blame his commoner girlfriend for the decision, but the path Edward embraced in life demonstrates that the relationship was perhaps merely an excuse, because he was not ready for the responsibility of kingship, nor did he want it.

Indeed, Prince George wasn't the ideal candidate for that position. In fact, his mood swings and speech impediments were some of the worst defects any leader could have. Despite that, he was humble and the way was paved for others to help him in his weakness. Against all odds, he achieved a level of success that granted him worldwide fame and a place in history.

We need to accept our human nature and recognize our flaws with humility. Humility is a vital element in our Father's kingdom. For example, God urges us to confess our faults and to pray for one another. An attitude devoid of arrogance is ideal to prepare us with willing hearts to draw near to him for effective conversations. The Bible says that the prayer of a righteous person is powerful and effective.[1]

People often ask me how much time I spend in prayer, because they tend to believe that the amount of time we pray is the key. However, the secret lies in the quality of the time we give to prayer. If I were to say that I spend just a little time in prayer, people would be shocked and say that it is inexcusable. If I were to say, however, that I spend my entire day praying, the same people might feel ashamed for not being able to do the same. The key is not a matter of how much time, but rather the faith I exercise when I come before my Father in prayer. It's that simple. Do not allow yourself to be distracted by this world's system that quite often only complicates things.

Subject to Like Passions

One day, while trying to solve a sensitive matter concerning the construction of our second sanctuary, which we dedicated in 2013,

---

1 James 5:16

I noticed how easy it was to fall prey to my old ways of complicating things. Still, right in the middle of all that worry, the Lord, ever so kindly spoke to me and said, "Elijah prayed. He was a man with similar passions, but he prayed." God repeated this many times until it finally sank in and I said, "You're right!" Why am I racking my brain with this aggravation? What I need to be doing is praying and taking authority in God's divine system. I shouldn't be focusing on my weaknesses and imperfections, but rather putting my faith in action, trusting in God.

Indeed, as we read the Bible, we find that the prophet Elijah was also a man subject to similar emotions. He, too, was rash and impulsive at times—or perhaps just feeling overwhelmed. Think about it. One day he confronts more than eight hundred false prophets and the following day he's fleeing and hiding from the threats of one woman. Nonetheless, those extreme and irregular emotions didn't keep him from praying fervently and effectively, shutting up the heavens from all rainfall, and further down the line opening them up again.[2] Whenever you pray, never look at how good you have been, because it's Jesus alone who validates you and opens the way for you to come before the Father.

Adam's system tells you it is impossible to be blessed with all your flaws and weaknesses, because it sets your focus on your own abilities, which can never begin to compare to God's. Then, you fall into a cycle of doubt and hopelessness when what you should be doing is humbly recognizing that you are weak and beginning to use your rock-solid faith! And here's another one: Never pray according to your reason, but according to God's love. Our sinful nature can never be greater than our Father's grace!

Peter was the disciple Jesus taught most about faith, humility, and obedience, perhaps because he was training him for what he

---

2 James 5:17–18

would soon face in his own life. We know that on one occasion Jesus asked him to push the boat out from the shore to be able to better teach the people. Then later, after finishing the message, he instructed Peter to go out deeper into the lake and go fishing. Peter's initial reaction was based on Adam's system, and it is clearly seen in his reply about having spent all night fishing and not catching anything. But then he seems to shift into God's system by saying that he'll gladly obey.

The way Peter jumped into action is important to receive a blessing in God's divine system, and he experienced firsthand a supernatural catch.[3] Believe as Peter did, and you'll have to ask others to help you receive the vast blessing God will pour out! You will receive it to share with those around you, which is another vital principle in the system of God's kingdom.

A Love That Forgives

After the miracle, Peter felt quite unworthy, and though it was in his earthly nature, we have seen that this is not a hindrance in God's divine system. He knows that we aren't perfect, and still he wants to bless us! This is not to say that we are free to sin and then pray to receive, because living in God's kingdom system requires an effort on our part to live according to his commandments. We must not draw away from our Father and think that he will punish us for being weak.

God will always love us, forgive us, and receive us with open arms. This is something we need to understand. Draw near to him, recognize that you are a human being with weaknesses, make every effort to improve, humbly ask for forgiveness, and do not be afraid

---

3 Luke 5:1–8

to express your needs in faith. Listen and believe, and stop looking for excuses. There are only two paths: either continue living in Adam's world's system or start engaging in God's kingdom system, allowing it to function the way it should. Don't seek the world's influence, but rather the Lord's influence for your life and family!

On another occasion, we see Peter challenging Jesus to let him walk on water. And Jesus simply says, "Come!" Peter immediately obeys, but then fear sets in. Once again he switches systems and starts to sink.[4] It is not easy to start living according to a system that is contrary to the one you live day in and day out. It is quite normal to have doubts and fears, but I can assure you that God's system works. Stop flip-flopping between systems and choose to be radical, not double-minded. If you doubt, you will weaken and your mind will default to the system that is not in your best interest.

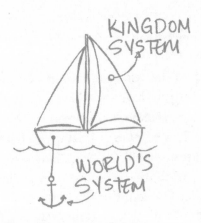

No matter what others might think, if you sow you will reap! If you humble yourself, you will be exalted; and if you ask, you will receive! Set your sights on the Lord, because you are born again and he is right there before you. Don't ask him to bless your system;

---

4 Matthew 14:22–32

rather, live according to his. Your life would have changed dramatically a long time ago if you had just prayed with the same persistence with which you have been calling that company for a job.

A third example of Peter learning to operate in God's system was when Jesus told him to go fish and the first one he caught had a coin in its mouth to cover both their taxes.[5] Would you consider that extreme? It certainly had to be a challenge to obey! However, after seeing the multiplication of the five loaves and the two fishes, and witnessing the sick being healed, Peter undoubtedly was opening his understanding, little by little, and allowing his faith to be strengthened.

On this occasion, the situation was even more sensitive because it was not about a miraculous catch, but about learning to remain within God's system and following his Word at every point. It was almost like Jesus telling him, "There's a wonderful adventure waiting for you, and I'm going to teach you to live it with joy and faith!" The same thing applies to us today. Without trusting in him unconditionally, it will be difficult to face the challenges that come with serving the Lord.

Now we see another interesting situation take place. We know that Jesus' ministry was constantly being provided for and that Judas oversaw administrating everything that came in. The Bible tells us this disciple controlled the money bag and would periodically dip into it for himself.[6] Despite having all these available resources, Jesus still challenged Judas to operate in the kingdom system, because even with the funds they had, it was still going to be impossible to feed a multitude or prepare everything that was necessary for the Passover. Jesus wanted them to understand his divine economy, and with Judas as a treasurer, miracles would be more necessary than ever.

5 Matthew 17:24–27
6 John 12:6

So then why didn't Jesus tell Peter to ask Judas for the money to pay the taxes? I would like to think that he was also teaching Judas that he didn't have to steal to have abundance. Indeed, if we would just trust and embrace our Father's kingdom system, corruption would be done away with.

I would like to believe that Jesus wanted to save Judas's life, since finances should be the least of our worries when we learn to depend on God. If what you need is money, he can provide it for you! Convince yourself to stop depending on bribes, kickbacks, or tampered invoices to lower your taxes. That would be living in Adam's system, stubbornly insisting on operating in this world's system. Your financial worries will come to an end when you choose to operate once and for all in God's kingdom principles.

In your work, trust that your Father can provide everything that you ask for in faith. Don't try to understand it all; just believe and be steadfast! Follow his instructions no matter how ridiculous or far-fetched they may seem. Learn to live within his system. If he tells you to look for a coin in the mouth of a fish, then do it. Remember, it is HIS BLESSING that will provide you with more than enough, until you are overflowing. He is the one who saved you, and only he can sustain and lead you in his kingdom. Tell him right now, "Father, I want to live my whole life according to your system and your Word. I promise to live, grow, and serve others in love."

3 HEIRS

We are his children by choice, not by force.

When my cousin Yuri Cristina was killed in a car accident, her daughter Andreita was left in her grandmother's care, who is also my Aunt Yuri. This was obviously a traumatizing event for the young girl who years later once again had to face the bitter pain of losing a second mother. In a curious way, my wife began to have dreams in which she saw herself becoming pregnant again. Were we to have another daughter?

We always enjoyed a close relationship with my Aunt Yuri, so when our children Cashito, Juan Diego, and Anita said, "Let's have Andreita come and live with us," we did not give it a second thought.

21

In fact, God had already planned everything out. Cashito was getting married so we had another room available, along with all the love in the world to receive her. A process of adjustment started that would involve our entire family, from shifting our schedules to learning the love language that Andreita was most suited for. The moment she set foot in our house, she was like another daughter to us. Little by little she settled into her new environment. Our desire was for her to feel that she was a part of a family that loved her and treasured her. We continually prayed for the day she would officially ask us to become a Luna. That day would arrive, but I'll save that story for later.

Andreita became our daughter because we had chosen to love and accept her. In like manner, God planned our adoption through his Son as a wonderful act of love. That is the most incredible revelation of all! The Scriptures assure us that we are children of God, heirs of his kingdom, and coheirs with Christ.[1] We know that the Holy Spirit engendered Jesus in Mary's womb[2] and that God has adopted us. He has given us the authority to be called his children. In other words, he signed the legal documents that grant us the power to feel proud of our identity.[3] How many times have we heard siblings teasing each other or trying to make them feel bad by saying, "You know you're adopted, right?" In God's kingdom system, adoption is one of the greatest privileges a person can have because he literally handpicks us for adoption as sons and daughters.

I grew up without a father, but that void disappeared the day I accepted God as my Father. I remember telling him back then, "I don't know what it means to obey a father, or honor and respect one, but now you are my Father and I want to serve you and love

---

1 Romans 8:15–18
2 Luke 1:34–35
3 John 1:11–13

you with all my heart." Sometime later, God told me, "I've accepted your love son. I've let myself be loved by you, and now I want you to let me love you back. I want to give you everything a father gives a son." So, I asked him for the Holy Spirit and for all those good things I knew he wanted to give me. Because he loves us, he wants to give us his anointing and provision.

As heirs, Jesus persistently teaches us to ask the Father for everything because that is how we prove that we are living by faith. In fact, as we read the Bible, we see that before highlighting our obedience to his commandments, he urges us to ask in order to receive![4] The joy of the Lord is for us to receive what we ask for. Remember, you are the one who needs him, and coming before his presence without asking him for anything is like saying that you don't need him.

The Lord is glorified when you ask of him and receive, because then you can tell others about what he has done.[5] He wants to answer your requests so you can bear witness to his love. Remember that because of sin we lost everything, coming short of the glory of God. And once we accept Jesus as our Lord and Savior, we are born again and receive eternal life, but not that splendor. We do not recover that glorious inheritance we were designed to receive until we ask for it. For example, Jesus never assumed he would get that glory after his resurrection; on the contrary, we see him explicitly asking for it back: "And now, Father, glorify me in your presence with the glory I had with you before the world began."[6] Contrary to what we may have learned, asking things of God is not what carnal or immature people do, but rather acts of children confident in their Father's loving care.

---

4 John 14:13–15
5 John 15:7–8
6 John 17:5–7

A Righteous Exchange

Life is an unending request for something. We always expect something in exchange for our actions. A worker expects some form of compensation in exchange for his effort, and a supervisor expects results in exchange for wages paid. You sow in order to reap. It is not true that our love is unconditional. In marriage, you love and are faithful because you expect the same thing in return. Deception leads to great disappointment. Children should love their parents with obedience and material gifts. As a parent, you never turn down what they give you because you expect it in exchange for what you give to them. We approach the Lord expecting to receive life and salvation. Thus, asking the Father for things means humbly accepting our human need of receiving to the measure that we give. You need to be humble and honest in this respect. Recognize that you need your Father and ask of him with boldness. He wants you to recover what you have lost as a result of living according to this world's system.

Psalm 2 is a Messianic Psalm that prophesies about the Lord's return. Verses 7 and 8 declare, *"The king proclaims the Lord's decree. The Lord said to me, 'You are my son. Today I have become your Father. Only ask, and I will give you the nations as your inheritance, the whole earth as your possession.'"* Do not forget that even while you were still an embryo, you were blessed by God. This issue of faith is a matter between God as Father and his children. It is not a religious matter. It is not an option. It is a mandate to recover every glorious possession we lost because of the fall. How then can it be unimportant to ask of him if it was one of the first things he said to us from the moment we were conceived?

This psalm speaks about asking for the nations, which is also a powerful revelation. The term *nations* here is a reference to races, which in the original Hebrew meant "gentiles" or "peoples." Thus, the Father is telling the Son that the plan was to save the Jews, but also the other "peoples," if he is just asked. Had Jesus not asked for it specifically, we would not be saved today!

Now that I think of it, the connection here is curious. Jesus is the Son of God, yet he became the adoptive son of a mortal couple so that we, as children of mortals, might be adopted by a heavenly God. Notice how priceless his sacrifice was! If you think about it, no son ever calls his father by his first name, but rather "Dad." If he really wants something from him, he will say "Daddy." Abba Father means exactly this: "Daddy God." God wants us to recognize him as our Father and to develop a loving, intimate relationship with him.[7] The relationship depicted here is that of a Father with his children asking for their inheritance. And if the Heir asked for his, then we as coheirs must also do the same. Be free to exercise your faith and ask for every good and holy thing that you dream and need!

If you are born again, then you need to operate in the Lord's system. It is the only one guaranteed to work, even though some may not understand it. The

Be free to exercise your faith and ask for every good and holy thing that you dream and need!

things of the Spirit are spiritually discerned, because the natural mind cannot understand them. We can't explain how miracles happen, but they do. All we can do is simply ask, receive, and be thankful for them. Access the kingdom of God today! Live by faith, convinced that you are a child of your Father and your eyes will see his wonders.

Understanding that God is our Father answers many doctrinal and religious questions that can hinder us from engaging in an intimate relationship with him. If the fact that he is our Father

---

7 Romans 8:15–17

means that we belong to him, then everything he possesses belongs to us as well. Don't you think our children know that everything we have is theirs? Of course, they want what we have. They try to wear our shoes and want to be like us. I remember one day looking for my contact lenses and asking my son if he had seen them. "Yes, Dad, I borrowed them because I was pretending to be you."

I keep going back to the Lord's Prayer because there is so much to learn from it. Once while I was in prayer, I asked the Lord why he first tells us to ask for our daily bread before asking for forgiveness. I had always thought it should be the other way around. But then he answered, "Because I am first a father, then a judge." That truth filled me with so much confidence and helped me realize that sometimes when facing financial difficulties, we tend to think that God sent us those trials, but nothing can be further from the truth. God never punishes his children by stripping them of their daily sustenance, just as we would never do it to our own children. Have you ever told them, "You flunked two classes, so no food for a month!" By expecting our daily bread first, it is almost as if the Lord wants to sit at the table with us and spend a good time together, then later telling us, in love, what areas we need to improve.

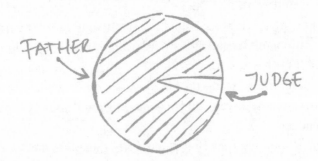

Jesus had a special and unique teaching style; he communicated deep truths through simple, everyday stories. On one occasion while he was teaching about asking God for our needs, he shared the parable of a man who showed up at a friend's house at midnight asking for some food for his guests. After complaining a bit, the friend finally gave him the food. Jesus then went on to describe God as our loving Father, who longs to give us his Holy Spirit, and how he will do it without any complaint or feeling of imposition.[8]

The comparison is an interesting one, because there is a vast difference between a father and a friend. We might have any number of friends, but we have only one father. It is important for young people to understand the deep love their parents feel for them, and who, contrary to their friends who only want to have a good time, desire to prepare them for a better life. Parents need to tell their children, "I'm not just another one of your buddies. I am your parent."

It is also important to notice in this same passage from the Scriptures the metaphor Jesus uses of the Holy Spirit regarding how a parent would provide his children bread, fish, and eggs. Jesus relates the Holy Spirit to the daily sustenance required to nourish our body: proteins, carbohydrates, and fats. He does so to highlight that being filled with the Holy Spirit is just as important as the daily food we need. And we must seek him and ask for him always. He is not a luxury, but rather a necessity that our loving Father wishes to satisfy. Just as we love to eat every day, so should we long for the fullness of the Lord's presence!

We find a parallel passage in Matthew 7:11, yet with a slightly different ending. He doesn't refer to the Holy Spirit directly, but to all the good things our Father has in store for us. So why is there this difference? Both Gospel writers wrote the same truth, but from different viewpoints, each one emphasizing something unique. It happens throughout the writings of Matthew, Mark, Luke (the Synoptic Gospels), and John and it provides us with a great amount of wealth. In this example, the teaching is about the Father giving

---

8 Luke 11:5–13

us his greatest gift—the Holy Spirit—in addition to every good gift we ask him for. What a wonderful promise!

What is more, Jesus foresaw some of the contradictions that we might come across in his Word, because it isn't one bit blasphemous to ask of our Father and envision the best things from him for our lives. Any theological or religious conflict comes to an end when we understand that God is our Father. He is the one who can provide for every type of need we have, be it spiritual or material. He looks after his children in every area: body, soul, and spirit. It is the reason why he gives us his Holy Spirit and everything else we need for life. Believe him and ask of him with confidence!

When we receive Jesus in our hearts, we are born again and his Word becomes the eternal promise that guides us. It is forever firmly established.[9] Just receive his love and give yourself to him as a legitimate son through the adoption of the Holy Spirit. Then exercise your rights as a son and an heir! Love him, honor him, believe in him, ask of him, and accept his faithful and unlimited protection and provision.

---

9 1 Peter 1:23

STAR
WARS

"May the Force be with you!" were the words uttered by Master Yoda to Luke Skywalker after training him for battle, just as Master Yoda had done with his father many years back. I believe this to be one of the most famous phrases in the history of motion pictures.

Probably 85 percent of human beings between the ages of seven and ninety have an idea of the meaning of that phrase, which in space jargon is the equivalent of a "God bless you." Of course, it's the number one touchstone in *Star Wars*, the epic saga that has influenced more than one generation in our lifetime. We have all heard many characters say it, including Obi-Wan Kenobi, Qui-Gon Jinn, Padmé Amidala, Princess Leia, Han Solo, the Knights of the Jedi Order, and even the Supreme Chancellor of the Galactic Republic.

In this science fiction thriller, the Force is a powerful, omnipresent energy field throughout the universe, which one can learn to control and use for justice and peace. However, it also has a sinister dark side used by evil that is driven by rage, fear, and hatred. Sound familiar? I think it is reasonable to say there is a faith that can move the world and that everyone, without exception, believes in something or in someone. The only difference is who we believe in and how we choose to use that faith.

In that first film (episode IV) released in 1977, Darth Vader—a classic villain who was a former Jedi with enormous power but who fell prey to the Dark Side—uttered another emblematic phrase when he said "I find your lack of faith disturbing." Yes! Those were his exact words to one of his lieutenants of the Galactic Empire who challenged him by saying that the power of the Force was no match to that of the Death Star, the most sophisticated battle station ever created and a symbol of the Empire's might.

Darth Vader was so enraged that he started to choke him with one of the Force's techniques—telekinesis—as was his custom. He had a blind faith in the Force, an invisible, yet very real power. Despite his dramatic transformation to evil because of devastating personal blows and losses (including the death of his beloved wife), he knew that nothing in the universe had the same devastating power to build or destroy as the Force.

Ironically, he shared the same faith as the Jedi. My personal theory is that he continued to be a Jedi despite the atrocities he had committed since joining the Dark Side. And I am sure there is a path of redemption for his beleaguered soul. Though the saga's outcome of good conquering over evil does not necessarily hinge on that phrase, Darth Vader became one of my heroes in the faith due to his total conviction that nothing created by man could ever compare to the supernatural power of the Force he had learned to master. But then, of course, my favorite character is Han Solo. Though his personal motivations were not entirely based on the struggle for the Republic, he is nonetheless a hero. And, in the end, he got to be with the princess. We, too, become heroes and can do mighty exploits when our faith in God becomes the force that drives us, sustains us, and compels us even in the midst of our own galactic battles.

4 MORE THAN CONQUERORS

Though we go through difficulties, faith and obedience will always secure the victory Jesus won for us on the cross.

There is much I don't know about a lot of things, but I'm an eager learner, hungry to know and discover more. One afternoon I received a text message from an excited art fan saying, "Can you believe it? Joaquin Sabina just published a book with all his drawings." Since I didn't know what he was talking about, I listened intently, appearing to be thrilled at the news.

As it turned out, 2016 was the year an unparalleled work of art known as *Garagatos* was published. It is a limited-edition book (only 4,998 copies) containing the drawings of Joaquin

Sabina, a famous Spanish troubadour and poet. During an interview, he admitted that he never considered himself an artist or painter and that his sketches were merely personal expressions that he had never intended to publish. He was surprised that a publisher would be interested in them and willing to produce such a grand and exquisite masterpiece. Still, the drawings leave no doubt as to Sabina's talent and artistic skills. Like my friend, those who love his poetry-laced songs would easily urge Sabina to develop skills as a painter as well.

Having faith in the artist means having faith also in his or her creation. Sounds logical, right? In other words, if we claim to believe in someone, then we also believe in what that person can do. So, if we claim to believe in God, then why not have faith in his creation as well? If everything that he has done is good, how much more so are we whom he has made in his image and likeness and adopted as sons. Consequently, our faith in God ought to be reflected in the trust we place in our own selves as well as in the abilities and skills he has entrusted to us. And all this, coupled with his grace, is the perfect combination to carry out mighty exploits.

Having faith in the artist means having faith also in his or her creation.

One day a boy brought a note home from school. He saw his mother open the sealed envelope, take it out, and read it as her eyes swelled with tears. After noticing the anxiety in her son's eyes, she read it out loud: "Your son is a genius and this school is too small. It doesn't have the right teachers to train him. Please, teach him yourself at home."

Many years later, after his mother had passed away, the son, all grown up, found the letter in a bunch of old family belongings. And it read: "Your son is mentally ill and we can't allow him in our school any more. You'll need to teach him at home." The man wept for hours upon realizing the truth that could have left a negative impact on his entire life. But it didn't, thanks to a faith-filled mother while he was still a child. And he wrote in his diary, "Thomas Alva Edison was a mentally challenged child, but thanks to his heroic mother, he became the genius of the century."

God has that same kind of faith in us! There is no reason to put yourself down or to pay attention to the voices of those who try to hold you back. He knows you, he formed you, and he knows the potential he has placed within you. You have no right to doubt yourself. Just trust in your Creator because his works are always good, and they always have a specific purpose in mind. Living by faith means aligning yourself with what God thinks of you and accepting the challenge of being equipped beforehand to reach great and mighty goals in life. It's that simple. Just believe in him, and believe in yourself!

In life we are going to face many battles that require full confidence in our own abilities. To a certain extent, I like to think that our battles are already won because Jesus has given us the ultimate victory. You see, he conquered death and sin, and according to his promise, he has made us more than conquerors as well. He fought the battle and won so that we can receive the benefits without having to die on the cross. It's like a boxer who takes a pounding in the ring but wins the title by knockout and goes home to hand the prize check to his wife. Sure, the boxer beat his competitor, but his wife ended up more than a conqueror because she received the purse without having to step one foot in the ring.

This is what happened in the movie *Cinderella Man*, where Jim Braddock endured painful beatings in the ring, so that his wife could stay at home and raise the kids. Braddock would fight and win to support his family, but they would share in the victory thanks to their loving father. In real life, the same thing happens with our children when we empower them to be more than conquerors by allowing them to go to school without having to get a job. We work hard to provide better opportunities for them. We fight the battle so they can receive the benefits, and our Lord Jesus is just as kind and generous with us. He believes in us because we are his children.

How do we identify someone who is more than a conqueror? It is someone who takes the Lord's hand no matter what they face in life, be it good or bad. There are some people who only draw close to God when they are in a predicament—such as on the verge of divorce or bankruptcy—but they pull away when everything is going well. Some young singles stop serving in church once they find a husband or wife. It's easy to know if a relationship is of the Lord by how close they desire to remain to him. Everything or everyone who causes you to draw away from God's love will lead to failure. Moreover, there are those who are close to God, but who pull away when things don't go well, when nothing should ever separate us from the love of God.[1]

The Lord assures us that we have already defeated the enemy.[2] So why do we sometimes allow Satan to win over us? Because deep down we struggle with accepting the victory we already have. When we truly learn to accept it, we'll begin to manifest that victory in every area of our lives. However, if we only trust in our own strength, we will never be able to overcome.

We have already seen that God created Adam and gave him dominion, authority, and victory.[3] Notwithstanding, it was his disobedience that caused him to lose it all. We now have been redeemed by the blood of Christ, and, thanks to that, we have recovered our original authority. The problem is that when we sin, we suffer the collateral damage of losing faith in our identity and in our capacity to overcome our mistakes. As if that were not bad enough, we still

---

1 Romans 8:23
2 1 John 2:13–14
3 Genesis 1:28

have to tackle our family and financial issues, because every time we fall prey to temptation, we squander our resources and fall away from those who love and care for us.

For example, let's say you have a vice and you spend your money on it, but as a result you have to face difficulties with your wife and kids. That's what I mean by collateral damage. When you are sick, that collateral damage manifests itself as poor performance at work, not to mention the costs of medicine and treatments. If we view this from a different standpoint, giving our lives to Jesus also carries with it many collateral benefits, because by leaving our vices behind we can offer a better life for our families and our relationships take a turn for the better. If you dedicate yourself fully to your wife, you will have more than enough time, resources, and peace in life.

When you turn away from God and make mistakes, you start losing confidence in your work, your performance, and your relationships. So trust in the Lord and accept his redemption in your life which will restore your victory over the enemy that would like to take you down. It may seem strange to speak about the devil as our enemy, but that is who he is. Forgive me if addressing this subject makes you feel a little uncomfortable because you're not familiar with it, but if we desire to walk by faith, we need to open our spiritual eyes.

Jesus, the second Adam, came to save us and provide a spiritual birth. We have seen that through this new life we can recover the authority we lost, because God alone has all power over heaven and earth.[4] You, too, can overcome with the authority that now dwells within you. See yourself as a conqueror, restore your confidence in Jesus and his victory will be yours. To have faith in God means trusting in your ability to achieve great things, since he has already provided you with everything you need to reach your highest potential.

---

4 Matthew 28:18–20

Your Fight Is Fixed

In the Bible we read about how the people of Israel conquered the Promised Land after wandering in the wilderness for forty years. One of the first cities they conquered was Jericho, known for its high, impenetrable walls. Yet, God told Joshua, Moses's successor, that he had already given them the city, and he gave specific instructions to follow.[5] Perhaps there have been doors in your life that have been shut up until now, but the Lord says to get ready because those walls are about to crumble and you are going to enter into things that seemed to be impossible. Just trust and obey God's instructions because he has already fixed the fight for your victory, just as he did with Israel and Jericho.

The instructions Joshua received weren't to sharpen their swords for a fight, but simply to march around the city seven times. That might have seemed odd for an experienced warrior, since marching around it for seven days and sounding trumpets wasn't exactly the ideal battle plan. But by simply obeying they proved that nothing was going to separate them from their trust in God. And the same thing applies to us today. If you obey your heavenly Father in everything, what used to take you seven days to complete, you'll complete in one. However, the first step consists of reinforcing your faith.

Sometimes you might feel that all your effort isn't producing anything. You grow tired. You feel that loving, forgiving, and blessing others simply isn't paying off, but do not stop! Sometimes you might have to do something seven more times than usual to see the results God wants you to have. With God your victory is as good as won, but you also need to be convinced of this. In the thick of battle, there is no point in a general knowing what he needs to do and giving out orders if the soldiers don't believe in their own ability to

---

5 Joshua 6:1–4

obey them. Each time the people of Israel marched around Jericho, God was probably saying, "They're almost totally convinced, but I've got to be sure." On that seventh day, as they marched around seven times, he must have said, "This is it! This is the moment. Nothing's going to separate them from the faith and confidence they have in me. It's time to bring down those walls!"

What overcomes this world is our faith. If circumstances have kept you down, rise up in victory because nothing can defeat you when you are in the Lord. Only faith can fill you with the boldness to fulfill what God is telling you. It is God's power that brought those walls down, and not the people marching around them. Do what his Word says and let him handle the rest.

Never Destroyed

When we go through adversity we need to learn to distinguish the external from the internal. We might feel perplexed, struck down, and persecuted, but these are simply external signs. Because it is not the same to feel knocked down as it is to be defeated. And the faith we place in the victory he has already provided for us will keep us from feeling agitated, desperate, hopeless, and destroyed, despite everything negative that takes place around us.[6]

In the first *Rocky* movie, actor Silvester Stallone portrays a passionate, inexperienced boxer on the road to success. By the end of the film, he ends up battling it out with the undisputed heavyweight champion Apollo Creed. During a highly emotional, combative bout, we see both boxers knocked down time and time again, yet never giving up and getting right back up again. In the end, Apollo wins by a split decision, but it also represented a major victory for

---

6 Joshua 6:1–4

Rocky, who throughout the film seemed to be struck down, beaten as the total underdog. Although all these external signs were painful and negative, he never was defeated nor knocked out; quite the opposite was true. Although he was in physical pain, he was victorious. He overcame his fear of failure, won the respect of those who didn't believe in him, and opened up a path for an unprecedented career. The same thing applies to us: we might be knocked down, but we are never defeated. We might feel persecuted, but we are never in despair. Our trainer, the heavenly Father, has equipped us to withstand any enemy. All that is left is for us to jump into the ring and fight.

Anxiety and a lack of inner peace, hopelessness in thinking there is no way out of your dire situation, and the despair of feeling neglected or abandoned by others should never become a reality in our hearts if we reaffirm, time and time again, that nothing is going to knock us out, even if at times we do stumble and fall.

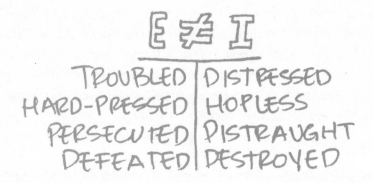

Begin to utilize your faith to counter the negative things that rise up against you so that you may receive the good things God has promised you. God has given us this gift of faith and we can be confident in his help for all that we can achieve. He has made us strong and we can be effective in everything we set our hearts and minds to do.[7] You will achieve what you set your mind to do if you believe in what God has given you. Everything starts with that step of faith designed to sustain your life. Your dreams will become a reality once you start acting like that child of God who trusts wholeheartedly in his Father and in the skills and abilities that have been given.

---

7 2 Corinthians 4:7–9

5 THE BEST WEAPON

To put faith into action one needs decisiveness, character, and courage.

It is said that in war weapons are useless if one does not know how to use them. The same thing applies in the spiritual dimension. There is no point in claiming to believe in the promises of God if one is not going to have the courage to face difficult situations and see his plans fulfilled. Why haven't you launched that business you have been thinking about? If you believe that God will support you, then you need to take that leap of faith and build the future he has promised you. I say this respectfully, but we often tend to disguise our cowardice with spirituality, seeking countless confirmations from God before stepping out and doing anything. How much more confirmation do you expect to receive before getting married after years of dating? The Bible says that the "violent" take their promises by force; in other words, it is only by being decisive and taking action that you will get the victory that has eluded you for so long.

We have read what Hebrews chapter 11 teaches many times, but it is still necessary to review several key elements concerning our faith. First, we read that God is a rewarder of those who diligently seek him, so one way of showing that we seek him is by attaining those prizes. When it comes to our relationship with God, there are only two testimonies that really count: ours, which speaks about what he has done for us; and his, which speaks about what he has seen in us and is pleasing to him. In the case of Abel's offering, we see that God gives a good report because it was acceptable. The same is true of the men and women of faith spoken about in Hebrews chapter 11. It is God's testimony about the courage of these people who through their faith received their reward.[1]

Our faith must be reflected in every area of life: work, family, ministry, marriage, new businesses, health, friends, everything! Our faith must be demonstrated holistically, in the sense that God's grace has been designed for every area of our being, and not just our spirit. Let me give you an example. When you give your life to serve and honor the Lord, you will also find favor with others. They will say things like, "I don't know why, but I just want to do business with you." The blessing of God consists of his testimony on top of ours, a direct result of the courage and boldness to live by the faith that he has placed in us.

It is amazing how many times the Bible mentions that "the just shall live by faith."[2] Faith not only guarantees us eternal life, but also provides the key to living a full life here on Earth. It is easy to say after accepting Jesus Christ as our Lord and Savior that you will

1 Romans 12:3
2 Hebrews 11:1-11

have your spot reserved by his side after you die. It is much more challenging to speak faith into those things God has promised you to fulfill here on Earth, because for that you will have to demonstrate corresponding attitude and works. Yet, that is the confidence you need to have, since it is the only way to please God. Faith needs to be displayed every day of our lives, and not only to get that raise you wanted. That faith needs to be evident even on those cloudy days when you don't even feel like getting out of bed.

Hebrews 11 speaks to us about Noah, who attained righteousness by building an ark in faith. Many in our time would claim that they would have participated in such an endeavor, but it is difficult to accept that when they have trouble just facing their day-to-day challenges. Before claiming to have believed a mad builder of a giant boat during a time when no one even knew what the word *rain* meant, prove that you can believe God for your joy and success today. These are the feats you are called to carry out now.

If you want to talk about faith, look at Abraham who took his wife and left his homeland to follow God, not knowing where his love for God would take him. Compare that to the feelings of depression after being unemployed for a month, all the while crying out, "Why have you forsaken me, Lord?" Where is that faith that causes you to rise up and knock on doors, nonstop, until one opens? The issue isn't claiming to have faith, but rather using it when we face trials and difficulties in our everyday lives. It is in these moments that we can test and activate our beliefs to see mighty wonders.

Faith Is a Lifestyle

What happens if you come to the end of your life without ever receiving what God has promised you? Just like Abraham, Isaac, Jacob, and Joseph, you must proclaim to your offspring that they will see the promises of God fulfilled because he is a faithful God who cannot lie.[3] Faith is the best heritage you can leave your children, because it leads to lives full of expectation and purpose. Not having expectations in life is pretty much like being dead. Living by faith means enjoying the present as well as the future framed with optimism.

Those of us with real faith always think and speak of what we expect to receive in exchange for our effort and trust in God. Abraham, for example, could offer his only son Isaac as a sacrifice because he knew that God would fulfill his promise of provision.[4] The heroes of the faith teach us to not waste time

> *Living by faith means enjoying the present as well as the future framed with optimism.*

focusing on the past, but rather to project ourselves into the future. Fight for your future, because the best is yet to come!

Another vital element to live by faith is courage! Think of how many times God tells us not to be afraid. It is mentioned more than 365 times in the Bible. You could say that God mentions it each day for an entire year, so we can remember every morning when we wake up to cast all fear aside as part of our daily confession.

What does God mean when he talks about rewards? It is not just about material things, because people always tend to think in terms of houses or other material possessions. But God wants us to look beyond all that. His provision is designed for every area of our lives: spiritual, physical, emotional, and material.

There is no point in having all the money in the world if it is the result of sin and of a lack of faith. Moreover, faith sets us apart from those who try to achieve those same acts without it. In the end, they will drown just like the Egyptians when they tried to cross the Red Sea while pursuing the Israelites. We are the children of God and his

3   Habakkuk 2:4
4   Hebrews 11:12–13

power will always sustain us when we choose to live by faith, and he has promised that we will never be put to shame for it. Don't doubt for a second that you will be able to part the waters of your problems and walk on dry ground, or even on water itself, if need be!

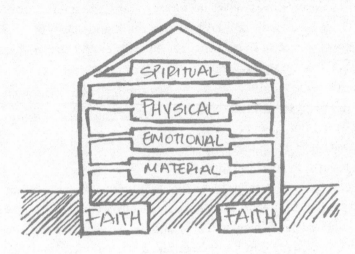

It Takes Guts

Even Rahab, whom the Bible states was a prostitute,[5] received a reward for her faith, God himself bearing witness of her in Hebrews chapter 11. She believed in the God of the Israelites and helped them conquer Jericho. I recall wondering about this part of the Bible that refers to her as a harlot, because by then she had already been justified by faith. That is until the Lord told me, "It is an example so everyone might see that it is within anyone's reach. There are no excuses. It is their faith that justifies them with me, and not their works." I got the message loud and clear.

Rahab believed and helped the spies who went on to survey

---

5 Hebrews 11:30–40

the land, because living by faith requires courage and boldness. As we like to say sometimes, "It takes guts," because it does not come easy. To leave everything behind, as Abraham and Moses did, requires determination. For example, you haven't started that business you've wanted because of a problem with courage and pride. You simply have not believed in your own abilities and in God's support. You are always in doubt, questioning yourself, *What if I fail? What are people going to say? What are they going to think of me?* Using your faith means you depend on the Father, because he has the last word! And he is always going to back you up, because he wants the best for you.

When the people of Israel were slaves in Egypt, everyone knew that God would deliver them, but only one person, Moses, had the guts to face up to the pharaoh. That courage obviously came from God because, if you recall, Moses had to flee the country after slaying an Egyptian. Nonetheless, even in that dire situation with no chance whatsoever for a happy ending, everything still worked out for good. There was no way this man could have done anything in his own strength, but with the grace and power of God operating in his life, he could conquer his fears and take on that formidable assignment.

We also read how Noah had the faith to obey God's command, but it was courage that led him to build the ark despite all the people's mocking. David not only had faith, he also had the guts to confront Goliath. In none of these cases was the task ever easy, but it was attainable.

When the Bible says that the kingdom of God suffers violence and that the violent take it by force, it is referring to those with the boldness and courage to fight for what they believe in and take it. Jacob, Isaac's son and Abraham's grandson, had the faith and the grit to wrestle with the angel of the Lord all night for the blessing.[6]

---

6 Genesis 32:26–29

6 ALL POWER

The Lord has given us the power to bless others and conquer every enemy.

At Casa de Dios we built two sanctuaries for our church, both on the outskirts of Guatemala City, in the specific sector God instructed. Both have been colossal challenges, not just investment-wise, but also because of the criticism we have had to endure. This has been particularly true because we have endeavored to do things with excellence, always seeking the best design, the best materials, and the best equipment. Why build this way in a poor country with so many needs? Where do we find the finances for such undertakings? Doesn't God want us to be humble? These are some of the questions and there is a specific answer for each one. The overall answer is that both daunting feats are a direct result of believing and obeying God's instructions.

These projects have never been based on the finances we have available but on our faith in what God has instructed us to do. For some people, it is logical to believe God for a house for their family, and for us it is just as logical to believe God for a house for him. Some questioned why it needed to be built? Our answer was, why not? Someone must believe God that excellence is possible in a country such as Guatemala. And we must all have the faith to believe that we, too, can be heroes when those challenges arise.

If God has given us such a beautiful and perfect property, it is logically our responsibility to use it wisely and build works that dignify and honor his creation. Our God made everything with excellence, and we as his children should do no less than to imitate him. But what gets me excited is that in a still developing nation, projects such as these aren't just sources of employment and social development; they are also testimonies of God's continual provision and care. If God could raise this ministry from a vision he gave me—just an average Guatemalan—there is no doubt that he can do it with you if you just believe him, follow his instructions, and develop your potential. Indeed, God has given each one of us the ability and the measure of faith to carry out mighty undertakings.

When talking about faith, however, it is common to believe that this only refers to spiritual matters, when, in reality, faith is designed to impact every area of our lives. Or are we a spirit without a body? Of course not! We are mortal beings made of flesh and bone, who live in a corporal and material world. Although we might dwell in the natural realm, we tend to lean toward supernatural laws. That is not to mean that we are disconnected from the physical realm our heavenly Father has designed for us; after all, he is the God of all of heaven and of all the Earth.

Does this seem complicated? It really isn't. It's just a matter of diving into the Word and discovering the blessings that he longs for us to enjoy. We know that God has all power in heaven and on Earth; furthermore, we know that we are his children and ambassadors,[1] though sometimes we are led to believe that he is in some distant world, sitting on a cloud somewhere, observing everything he has created. But when you read God's Word, you see that this is not the case! He is always addressing earthly matters. In fact, Jesus came not only to give us the blessing of eternal life, but also life in abundance here on Earth. He wants us to be his witnesses. Our existence here on Earth isn't merely a step toward eternity; we also have a purpose here.

We have been entrusted with a span of time that we need to enjoy and to use responsibly. It is vital that we open our eyes to understand both the earthly and the spiritual dimensions, because our faith is designed to uphold us in both realms. There is a here and now, just as there is an eternal future, and both scenarios are impacted by our faith. Remember, he has promised to be with us until the very end.

It is by embracing our loving Father's power over all things—spiritual, physical, natural, or supernatural—that we will ensure our enjoyment in this earthly life, as well as in the eternal one. This is according to his will, which is always good, pleasing, and perfect. We have to envision our lives this way. Sometimes we believe that we were sent to Earth to suffer and to earn the right to live in paradise with God one day. This outlook alters our vision of faith and it keeps us from seeking God's utmost blessing in everything we do. And to make things worse, we start criticizing those who have this perspective in life, who do work hard, labeling them as "carnal" or as people just interested in "worldly possessions."

However, it is our heavenly Father who is good and who wants

---

1 Matthew 28:18–20

us to prosper in everything. That prosperity is holistic in nature, and does not refer just to our finances. As long as we follow the teaching of the Word, our Lord wants us to reap good fruit in every area of our life, be it spiritual, relational, emotional, professional, ministerial, or financial. God wants the best for us, and he expects us to work toward achieving everything he longs to give us.

This is the reason why it is important to think carefully on this whole matter of the natural and supernatural realms around us. In the Scriptures we see Jesus walk on water,[2] but we are actually seeing two miracles take place. The first one was to walk on a liquid surface, and the second one was the water itself, since it's a natural element that was created supernaturally. When we read the Bible we see Jesus moving in power, because he himself knew his power in both Heaven and on Earth. Moreover, he even told his disciples that if they didn't glorify God, the very rocks would cry out.[3] Jesus cursed the fig tree and it dried up. He replaced a man's ear that had been cut off, raised the dead, turned water into wine, and the list goes on. All this because he had authority here on Earth. But he also cast out demons, because he had authority in heaven as well. Didn't he say that everything we bind on Earth would be bound in heaven?[4] Do not minimize your privileged position, nor yield any power to the enemy. He is already defeated, but we must exercise with power the authority we have been given, here on Earth and in heaven as well.

At what point will we enter that dimension of faith that empowers our abilities and grants us the liberty that God desires for us? Do not focus on your fears. True, the devil is our enemy, but you need to focus on the fact that you have more power than he. Remember that the best defense is a strong offense. We should be like Jesus

---

2 Matthew 8:23
3 Luke 19:40
4 Matthew 16:19

whom demons would cry out and beg him not to torment them.[5] We are called to be a blessing on this Earth, and we need to release and deliver God's promises to every person.

Isn't it ironic that demons, those dwellers of the spiritual realm, would recognize the greatness of Jesus more than many foolish humans. They would commonly say, "We know who you are."[6] And why would they say that? Because Jesus had to reveal himself to mankind, and it is necessary for us to have faith in order for him to manifest himself in power. Furthermore, it is only by knowing him and recognizing his nature that you can love him, honor him, worship him, and serve him.

Our faith is based on the Word of God and his power. Jesus' teachings are not just empty words; they are also deeds, exercising dominion over everything. He didn't just say that he was the Son of God; he also demonstrated it so there wouldn't be the slightest doubt. So how can man's wisdom now be used to deny God's power? It is a grave mistake! How long shall we continue to deny the obvious? When the Holy Spirit descends and fills people, the scientific-minded, in their quest to provide a logical answer to the supernatural, write it off as collective hysteria. Why not just simply give thanks and receive that wonderful gift of God? We wouldn't be disciples without the manifestation of the power of God. Moreover, the apostle Paul said that his preaching was not with persuasive words of man's wisdom, but in the demonstration of the Spirit and the power of God.[7]

This glorious gospel and his power shall be made visible to all! When we choose to work in Jesus' mighty name, we'll be amazed at the results, just like Jesus' disciples.[8] We have the power to destroy

---

5 Matthew 8:28–34
6 Mark 1:23–27
7 1 Corinthians 2:1–5
8 Luke 1:17–29

the enemy. We have the power over every principality of darkness and over every spirit of sickness, disease, and oppression through the power of God that lies within us through the anointing of his Holy Spirit. Therefore the laying on hands for the sick and liberating those who are bound by the enemy should be something totally natural for us.

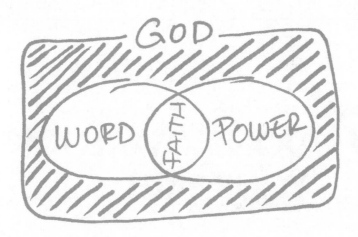

Signs and wonders will follow once we are fully convinced of the power we have in Jesus' name. Our faith will be visibly evident, but first we need to accept that we do not believe by sight, but only through the love of him who never lies and whose Word is always faithful and true. If you are feeling weak or burdened, only believe in Christ and you will be set free. Declare that you are filled with his Holy Spirit, that every yoke is removed, and that you have the power to do mighty wonders, and it will be so.

7 DON'T OVERLOOK YOUR PATH

Show the right attitude in the face of adversity, for though your process might be difficult, your final destination will be wonderful!

Much has been said about the life of David, a young shepherd boy who defeated a giant and was called by God to become a mighty king. Although he had a heart after God's own heart, there was a moment in time, during his stay in a cave known as Adullam, that he was the leader of a band of men who were in trouble, in debt, or just plain bitter.[1] Just imagine this strange scenario for a man who had been prophesied to rule an entire kingdom!

---

1 1 Samuel 22:1–2

Facing these quite depressing circumstances, David could have been discouraged, complaining and saying "This is no castle and these people certainly are not the entourage I expected!" Yet he didn't. Now what would we have done in his place? We probably would have started doubting the prophet's words, or perhaps have become depressed, complaining that everything that had been said about us was a lie because there was no sign of it coming to pass. The promise to David was that he would be a king, but in that cold, dark, dingy cave, surrounded by society's wretched and stinky outcasts, he probably did not feel much like a future monarch. Despite what all his senses were telling him, he still placed his sights on God's objective for his life. As impossible as it seemed, that is exactly what happened.

Often we find ourselves in similar circumstances, in our own kind of dark cave, or as they say in Guatemala, "with no father, no mother, nor dog to call your own." Whether it's having been diagnosed with an incurable disease, a rebellious child leaving home and not knowing know where he or she went, your marriage going down the drain and seeing your dreams of a happy family dissolve before your eyes, your business going under or being laid off from work, it can be easy to think that there is no way out. Unless our faith in God during these hard times is rock solid, we will feel that it's over, that we have been tossed into an abyss from which there is no way out or that we are sinking because the ground below us feels like quicksand. But if you believe in his promises of good for your life, you will fight through your battle, and retake what the enemy attempts to steal from you.

The seeds of faith have been planted, the promises have been given and they are found in his Word. We have heard this countless times, but many times we do not begin to gauge their impact on our lives until we go through difficult times. We need to be the good soil for that seed of faith. We need to care for it and nurture it by continual seeking after God. Otherwise the birds will eat those seeds and leave us fruitless.

During that time in the cave, David could have thought that he would never be king. As a matter of fact, he wasn't even a part of the royal lineage. It was Jonathan, Saul's son, who was the successor to the throne. However, God's Word is always true and it can supersede any circumstance, even to the extent of having a legal heir move aside to let David be the king. This did not turn out to be easy, but it revealed Jonathan's pure and loyal heart. Though he was one of David's most intimate friends and the king's son, Jonathan never sought prominence, but took a backseat for God's will to be fulfilled and to allow his friend to reach his ultimate destiny. It is also worth mentioning that true friends have a similar attitude to that of Jonathan's, rejoicing in the success of others, and if need be, sacrificing whatever is necessary for them.

We should be willing to fight for what is ours, even when circumstances might be difficult, and it appears that nothing good will come out of it.

When you stop to think about it, that is a similar attitude to the one Jesus showed us. He humbled himself completely to give us life. He knew perfectly well what the plan was and he obeyed it, despite the extreme suffering it entailed. Nonetheless, he endured it because he had set his eyes on the final goal, the reward, the prize. We, as well, need to embrace this attitude in life, since God has set aside a privileged position for each and every one of us. We are destined to be the head and not the tail, to assume roles that no else can ever supplant. We should be willing to fight for what is ours, even when circumstances might be difficult, and it appears that nothing good will come out of it.

From a Manger to the Throne

The birth of Jesus also shows us a very adverse circumstance that did not become an obstacle, since the promise was much greater than the reality they were experiencing at that moment.[2] We are no longer talking about an earthly king such as David, but about a heavenly one who had to overcome adverse circumstances right from the time of his birth. Many people say that Jesus was born in a manger to teach us humility, but that was not the case, since neither Mary nor Joseph had planned it that way. According to the story, Mary, the mother of Jesus, laid him in a manger because there was no room for them in the inn. However, it was never intended to be a lesson on humility. Just think about it. If we being humans would never willingly place our newborn child in a situation like that, how much less Mary and Joseph who knew the divinity of the newly born child. If it was intended to be a lesson on humility, it would then be a sin for us today if we were to find the best hospitals we can afford for our children to be born in. Don't you think?

God did not create any overbearing imposition by making all the guests leave the inn for the birth of his Son. Nor did he send an earthquake to cause them to run out. He simply let his plan play out, because that is just the way he is. He is a God of process, and patient to see his plans fulfilled. Of course, sometimes there are instant miracles, but they are always the culmination of a series of events. Jesus healed the blind and the lepers, and their healing was immediate. Nonetheless, they had suffered their ailments for a long time. Sure, the Israelites conquered the Promised Land, but there were other variables to consider before that, such as centuries spent in bondage in Egypt, and the years of Moses's preparation in the wilderness. God's power will act according to the measure that we believe and activate it.

---

2 Luke 2:7

It is not a matter of our being patient, but rather of the patience he has had with us up to the moment when we finally activate that faith about which he has spoken to us time and time again. If we consider the manger where Jesus was born, we can see those were difficult circumstances. Even though it was not his destiny, it still had to be confronted. And if he could do so, then why do we complain so much when it is our turn to face adversity and challenging circumstances in life? Why are we always wanting everything to be instantaneous, when not even our salvation came about overnight?

There was no golden crib waiting for Jesus, nor was there a throne awaiting David, but both were convinced that trying circumstances in their lives were temporary because their final destinations would be so much more glorious. Don't allow your beginning to become your destination. Don't be a fatalist, but rather learn to identify the path to your destination and appreciate the fact that it will help you to develop the character of an overcomer.

If you have your degree in marketing but can only find a position as a salesman, take it and work hard at it, even if you think you are above that and are ready for a management position. Everything in life implies a process and you need to prove that you have the character to take on the necessary challenges.

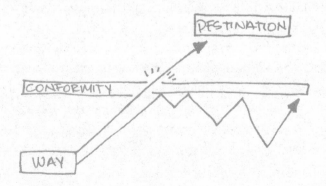

Adversity is unavoidable and we need to overcome it. Trust in yourself, in what you have learned and in your capacity to show that you deserve so much more! Now just think if Mary had been arrogant and said, "Let's expect that there will be room in that inn for our baby's birth. He is, after all, the Son of God. He needs to have a decent place!" But that was not the case, because the time had arrived and they had to overcome those challenges so the promise of salvation could be fulfilled. Given the circumstances, Mary had a wonderful and practical faith. We can be like her and face every obstacle without complaining, searching for solutions and thanking God in advance for the victory we are sure to achieve.

God's plan for his Son was never a manger, but a throne. Still, in addition to other painful and challenging circumstances, the manger was necessary for the throne to become a reality. Jesus was born in a manger, but he did not stay there. You need to say with conviction, "I am not going to stay in this difficult situation. I am going to have the right attitude, and God is going to bring me out." Mary may not have been too happy with laying her newborn in a manger, but she was not angry, nor did she blame Joseph about that situation. Perhaps another mother might have said, "You see, I told you. You should have made reservations in advance!" My wife would have killed me, or at least stopped talking to me for some time, if I hadn't made all the arrangements for our children's births. But Mary, being the obedient woman that she was, accepted her situation and sought to make the most of it, confident that this was part of a greater purpose.

Don't get caught up in the negative aspects of difficult circumstances. Look ahead to the broader landscape that is greater than any current circumstance in which you may find yourself. Tackle every difficulty with the right attitude, with optimism, and with faith. Embracing that attitude will mold the right character in you so that you may enjoy the blessing when it arrives. You can also learn from the Wise Men of the East who never stopped to judge or evaluate the situation. They simply pressed on toward the goal of honoring the child with their gifts, despite finding him lying in a manger. Your goals and God's promises for your life should always rise above any negative trial you may be experiencing.

Where you were born is not what matters, rather, it's what you do with your life and what you achieve before death. Some may say, "I didn't ask to be born. Why am I here?" Stop whining already! You're alive now and you must make the most of that precious gift God has given you. There is a purpose for your life in which both the natural and supernatural aspects of our heavenly Father are brought together in you. I am not just saying this as a trite motivational mantra, because to believe in your value and your divine purpose is a matter of faith in God. It is time to transcend what you have lost in the past and move on in faith.

At another moment in Jesus' life, after his baptism, he was led into the wilderness for forty days and forty nights. However, he did not stay there, because he knew that it was just one more step in the process of blessing others and fulfilling his ultimate purpose. We see how he willingly fasted and rejected every temptation. He was strengthened in faith to do miracles and he endured the pain of the cross. What is your character like when you are going through your wilderness? May you be filled with patience and wisdom to overcome!

If you want God's grace to be with you, and you want to come out of the wilderness as an overcomer, then you have to believe and grow, strengthening both your body and your spirit. In fact, Jesus prepared his body for the cross because he knew it would be how he would save mankind. Someone else with the wrong attitude might have said, "Why bother taking care of my body, if I am going to die anyway?" You need to prepare yourself for both good times and bad, because your wilderness might be right around the corner. At all times you need to bask in the Father's faithfulness.

Overcoming Pain and Rejection

Jesus also had to face another difficult ordeal when the people chose Barabbas over him. There is no doubt that the feeling of rejection must have been painful after having done so much good for the people, and still they preferred a murderer over him. Where were those ten lepers, the woman he saved from being stoned, the demon-possessed Gadarene, the young lad he raised from the dead, and so many others? They may have been fearful to come forward, but nothing or no one was going to divert from God's divine plan.

Satan wanted Jesus' heart to be filled with bitterness, causing him to sin in order to derail the pathway of salvation and to keep him from ascending to the right hand of the Father. But Jesus didn't fall for that temptation. Even while nailed to the cross between two thieves, with his dying breath and a heart filled with compassion he said to his Father, "Forgive them for they know not what they do." That is our supreme leader speaking, and we need to imitate him! Satan is going to try to stunt your growth and fill your heart with resentment because of rejection, possibly from mother or father, a spouse, a sibling, or a friend. But do not fall victim to that, because it is designed to keep you from fulfilling your purpose. No matter what, ask God to fill you with the strength to overcome all pain and rejection. Ask him to heal your heart, to cleanse you and to become a healing and soothing balm on your wounds.

Don't complain about your problems. When you go through hard times, say in faith, "This is not my destination. It is only the path and I will endure it because my loving Father has excellent plans for me." Sometimes bad things happen to good people. Jesus never did anything wrong to deserve the suffering he had to endure, yet he went through it because the promise was so much greater than any difficulty he was facing. Whether it is a manger, the pit into which Joseph was thrown, or the desert cave of Adullam, wherever you find yourself, seek God and place your circumstances in his hands. He will help you to overcome. Remember that you are his son or daughter and he will never leave you nor forsake you. Your faith will uphold you throughout any adversity. Trust in God and trust in yourself, because you are also one of his wonders.

When you go through hard times, say in faith, "This is not my destination. It is only the path and I will endure it because my loving Father has excellent plans for me."

If you are currently going through a difficult process, I may not be able explain to you why you are experiencing it. What I can tell you is that with the right attitude you will achieve the victory. Thank God for his good plans for your life and strive hard to reach them. Trust in the strength he gives you. Make the most of the path that he has laid out for you to reach your destination.

STROKE OF GENIUS

Ahhh, Bobby! The incredible Bobby Jones, one of my favorite heroes and sportsmen and the only golfer to achieve the unbelievable feat of winning the Golden Grand Slam—US Open, US Amateur, British Open, and British Amateur—all in the same year. The year of that incredible feat was 1930, and though still a young man, this genius golfer had already mastered unbelievable skills. Moreover, he wasn't just a prominent golfer but an excellent student academically as well.

The film *Stroke of Genius* that masterfully depicts the story of Bobby Jones's life isn't a moving story in which he emerges from obscurity, nor is it a story of overcoming adversity, family conflicts, or social transitions. Bobby's story is one of the progress of a man with a gift; one which he developed through listening, hard work, and focus.

To Jones, golf was an inherent gift that he learned to master over many years of great dedication. He discovered his passion at a young age, and from that moment on, he set clear goals on which he focused and worked hard to reach. That was not an easy task, with outside voices attempting to influence him. Little by little, however, he made room for everything in his life: his family's dreams for him to earn his law degree, his wife's dream of having a loving and devoted husband, and his own dream of making history in golf.

Throughout the process he had to wrestle with physical limitations, including a painful spinal cord disorder known as syringomyelia and a sanguine temperament that caused him to manage his stress levels in unconventional ways. This led him to a temporary golf suspension because of his fits of rage on the field. Every time he would miss a shot, he would curse, kick, smash his clubs, and even throw them in the air. Although apologies would follow, many times it was too late, for he had already injured someone or placed others at risk of being injured.

Bobby had to learn to change how he listened and spoke. Don't get me wrong. He wasn't a madman on the prowl, nor was he a violent or irrational person. But just as it can happen to any of us, sometimes he would let his frustrations get the better of him and he would end up saying things he would later regret. Did this limit his results? Of course! He was banished from the sport and it was not until he apologized and promised to change his attitude that they allowed him back on the playing field.

Forced to control his words, he had to learn to channel his reactions, which helped him develop a high level of concentration that ultimately led him to win the Grand Slam. That touch of genius had to be forged, little by little, by exercising control over his every thought and word. He clearly understood this and memorialized it with the following saying: "Competitive golf is played mainly on a five-and-a-half-inch course . . . the space between your ears."

Bobby Jones referred to the game as competitive golf and not as professional golf, refusing to turn his passion into a business. In fact, he always played as an amateur and was known to say, "I play for love, not money. Golf is a pleasure, not a job." He chose to retire when he was twenty-eight, devoting himself to his family and helping to design and build the Augusta National Golf Club, the most beautiful and prestigious golf course in the United States.

To achieve success, Bobby settled not only for what he knew, which was necessary, but also exercised his faith, listened to advice, received correction, and learned to speak appropriately to mold his character. Our graciousness as well is comprised of so much more than just knowledge. It includes our willing attitude to listen, to speak, and to act in faith.

8 POWERFUL WORDS

Listen to the Lord to release the bountiful blessing he has prepared for you. Your words must be one with his.

When the young wife learned just a few months after her wedding that she was expecting her first child, her heart was filled with joy. She knew that baby was a gift from heaven. After that initial burst of emotion, doubts started to cloud her thinking, but she sought to answer each one with optimism. How would she break the news to her soldier husband, serving his country thousands of miles away? What would happen in her body? Would she be able to carry her pregnancy to term with the incurable sickness from which she was not expected to survive? Despite all these anxiety-provoking thoughts, she decided to be optimistic and enjoy her pregnancy.

One of her first steps was to write a diary for the baby. Each day she would jot down every thought and message of love that came to mind, everything she felt as that life started developing within her. When she found out it was a girl, immediately she started calling her by the name both she and her husband had selected. She spoke words of hope and trust, fully aware of the possibility that she would never get to know her child. Oddly, her words seemed to strengthen them both. She could feel her precious child move and react to her voice, her reading, and her singing, quickly leading to her discovery of how powerful that communication was. Months later, while holding little Sofia in her arms, she could affirm with tearful joy that the intimate connection with her daughter from the very start was responsible for sparing both of their lives.

It is a fact that our words can prepare us for good or for bad. This is why when we talk about faith, we have to address how we speak and how we hear. It is crucial that we learn to speak about our future, leaving the past behind, and to stop talking so much about the trials we may currently be experiencing.

We all know that David, the young shepherd who defeated Goliath and later became the king of Israel, was also a wonderful poet. In addition, he is well-known for his songwriting abilities to the Lord. He was the author of many of the psalms in the Bible, including one of his most famous ones, Psalm 23:

> The LORD is my shepherd;
>> I have all that I need.
> He lets me rest in green meadows;
>> he leads me beside peaceful streams.
>> He renews my strength.
> He guides me along right paths,
>> bringing honor to his name.

Even when I walk
through the darkest valley,
I will not be afraid,
for you are close beside me.
Your rod and your staff
protect and comfort me.
You prepare a feast for me
in the presence of my enemies.
You honor me by anointing my head with oil.
My cup overflows with blessings.
Surely your goodness and unfailing love will pursue me
all the days of my life,
and I will live in the house of the LORD
forever.

This psalm represents a powerful declaration of faith in which David addresses his future. Although he is afflicted, he still feels anointed because the Lord takes the time to prepare a table in the presence of his enemies. One of the verses, "when I walk through the darkest valley" is in the present tense, which denotes that David was obviously going through a difficult time, yet his attitude remained hopeful. He continually spoke about his future in terms of blessing and optimism as in the phrase, "I will not be afraid, for you are with me." The same should be true in our lives; our cup should continue to run over in any tribulation, because we continue to trust that God is going to give us a better future. We must declare what we hope to one day enjoy, not our present life experience. We must look ahead, not remaining stuck in the past that is impossible to change.

If you are a Christian, then you know that going to church will not fix your problems at the snap of your fingers, nor will it serve to numb the pain. At church, we present the Word and the direction we need to take. We cheer each other on, although no one can walk in another person's shoes. Each one has to advance in the promises of God with faith, overcoming the past, living in holiness in the present, and trusting in a better future. Change how you speak, leaving out every pessimistic word. After many years, I have learned that every bad thought can be eliminated with the right confession from the Word of God. You need to look in the mirror and say, "My trust is in the Lord and his words alone will be my guide and show me my destiny."

We need to understand that our words are powerful and they can produce effects in our lives. The prophet Elijah demonstrated many times that his words were filled with power, to such an extent that both the rain and the dew would obey his every word. His story speaks to us about a process of obedience and the first step was to go to a brook just as God commanded to be fed by ravens whom God had ordered to take him meat every day, despite the fact those birds were carnivorous and would be giving him what was perhaps their own food.

That alone was a mega-miracle, just as it was asking a widow to feed him, since widows normally needed to be provided for, not them providing for others. Both deeds were incredible, just like expecting a child to give you a delicious piece of chocolate cake untouched. That's exactly how bold God is! We don't know exactly when the ravens and the widow received the command, but God had already planted that seed of blessing within them, to bear fruit at the precise moment of Elijah's need.[1]

Today's world is filled with words from different sources: yours, the world's, God's, and from those around you wanting the best for you. In the story of the widow and the prophet Elijah, there are many words exchanged: from Elijah, the widow, and from God himself. And every one of those words was fulfilled. *God's word*, because a little bit of oil and flour the widow had was multiplied;

---

1   1 Kings 17:1–16

Elijah's word, because it stopped and started raining just as he said; and *the widow's words* when she said, "We are going to eat and then die." Later in the chapter, her son did fall sick and dies,[2] although Elijah later raised him up again.

The widow's experience teaches us that our words are powerful and they do come to pass. Consequently, we need to make sure that our words are intended to bless and not to curse. The widow thought they were going to die. She was worried, despite having seen the wonders of God, who had miraculously caused her food to increase. There are many things around you that die because of your words, and you need to change that. Nurture yourself with God's words and cancel out every negative thing you say such as: "I'm never going to get out of this problem," "I'd rather die," "I'm just useless," "I can't do anything right," "This is probably going to turn out bad too."

Allow the Lord to lead you and stop sitting at the scorner's table. That is, stop sitting with friends who lead you to say what you shouldn't. Instead, prophesy a future of success because you will not lack any good thing if God is with you! Stop idly speaking foolishly about your crisis or your debt, and start talking about abundance to position yourself to receive it. Remember, it is God's words aligned with yours that will ultimately release the blessing!

When Elijah obeyed God and told the widow to find containers to fill them with oil, that was when the blessing was released. If he had not done that, everyone would have missed out on the blessing of obeying and serving God. Heaven, the widow, even the oil and the flour had already received their specific commands from God. Have you seen the film *Inception*? The storyline is about individuals with the ability to intervene in other people's dreams and steal their ideas. However, they are discovered and threatened into carrying out an opposite mission: that of planting an idea instead of stealing one.

---

2 1 Kings 17:17–20

The moment I saw the movie I immediately associated it with God, whom I see as a master planter of blessings in our lives. He plants instructions in each of us to bless others as that chain of obedience is activated. When you choose to obey, you release obedience into others as well. The original meaning of the word *command*, to give instructions, is to "load," as with preparing a pistol to fire. Obedience is a detonator that releases the blessing through those who have orders from God to help you.

And so the chain operates in the following way: you hear the Word and you declare it with your mouth, you obey the Lord and cause a response in those who are ready to give you a harvest from what you have already sown. If you are sick, fill yourself with healing promises from God's Word. Declare them day and night over your life. Surround yourself with people who believe with you, who encourage you and urge you to believe for your healing. And yes, you might have to seek medical attention in the process, but in that faith-charged atmosphere, God is going to place the right people designed to bless you with a complete recovery. Dare to take that step of faith to witness every wonderful thing that will happen in your life, in your family, at your workplace, and in everything you do.

Obedience is a detonator that releases the blessing through those who have orders from God to help you.

Obey and Everything Else Will Be Added unto You

God gave us this story of Elijah so we could know that with faith everything is possible. Elijah's first request of the widow was, "Give me to eat first, and that oil and flour will never run out." This brings to mind scriptures such as: "Seek the kingdom of God above all else, and live righteously, and he will give you everything you need" and "Do not to worry about everyday life—whether you have enough food and drink." Change your confession and obey his instructions to activate that chain of blessing for many. No one is blessed by oneself, but rather through others: ravens, widows, prophets, or those who surround you.

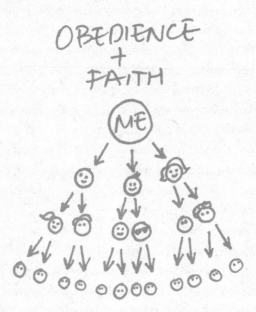

You will be surprised by the unexpected people and places that will seek to bless you once that chain starts! When you visit a dealer to look for a new car, the sales agent is going to say, "You know we have a special discount right now." He might not even understand and think, "Why did I tell this customer and not the previous one?" It is because God himself is opening the doors of heaven for you. Throughout all my years of service, I've seen countless testimonies of people who have been blessed by others around them because our heavenly Father always acts on our behalf.

Every good thing is multiplied in your life when you choose

to obey and be generous with others. You have the power to activate that blessing. When I purchased the land for our church, many people came to me saying that I had made the greatest mistake of my life because no one would ever travel so far to attend church. But thanks to God's lovingkindness, his plan has come to pass. We are a thriving congregation that welcomes everyone who comes seeking after God, and everything was activated by our obedience, which had an impact on those who were "charged" to follow that path of blessing.

Tell the Lord that you will obey him, that you will take steps of faith and release every blessing he has prepared for you. Thank God for his Word and choose to make it an intricate part of your confession every day, declaring your future with optimism and faith.

Serving the Lord for more than thirty-five years has shown me many things. I have seen people accept the Lord and others abandon him, and people who know much about the Bible but never practice it. However, I have also seen thousands strengthened and moving forward thanks to the trust they have placed in their heavenly Father's love. Not long ago, I was talking with a friend who was unemployed and going through a difficult financial situation. He was desperate. He had always been close to God, studied the Scriptures, and he knew much about theology. But the moment arrived when he needed to place all that knowledge into practice. The problem is not in knowing the Word, but in believing and applying it with a positive attitude, even when we do not know what is happening. In life, it is not what you know that makes the difference in the results you get, but what you believe and the attitude you embrace as you stand on that conviction.

The problem is not in knowing the Word, but in believing and applying it with a positive attitude, even when we do not know what is happening.

77

9 THE MARTHA SCHOOL

There is no point in knowing the Scriptures if you don't move forward in faith.

In the Bible we can learn much about the difference between *knowing* and *believing*. When Jesus arrived at the home of Lazarus, who had been his close friend, Lazarus's sister Martha demonstrated great revelation and knowledge.[1] Indeed, she engaged in a doctrinal conversation with Jesus and showed that she knew about prayer and the resurrection of the dead, because she had learned it from the Master himself. How could they *not* have known much about the kingdom of God!

---

1 John 11:20–27

However, Martha was about to receive more than her share, because she was about to learn that faith is so much more important than knowledge. The key question Jesus asked her was, "Do you believe in me?" If you are a Christian, I want to ask you, "How many Bible verses do you know, even if you believe they do not always work?" Truth be told, every verse in the Bible is a great revelation, but they are pointless unless you willingly choose to move forward in faith.

After his exchange with Martha, Jesus headed for the tomb and asked them to remove the stone. Before removing it, however, Martha expressed to Jesus that the corpse probably smelled bad by then. What was happening to Martha? Why so much reasoning, yet so little faith in what Jesus could do? Her grief over her brother's death had limited her ability to believe in the Lord's power. How long is your list of excuses that has kept God from doing something in your life? The effectiveness of his Word in your circumstance depends on your faith! If you want to see the glory of God, you must believe! This is exactly what Jesus told Martha so she could finally understand the miracle that was about to take place.[2]

While we were in the process of purchasing the land for our second sanctuary—one that would fill the need of accommodating more people—we were offered a property right in the area we wanted. The size was ideal, though the dimensions were not ideal because its length was much greater than its width. The property was owned by several family members and all assured us that they were willing to sell. We had a few meetings to negotiate the price and the terms of the sale. At the first meeting, before stepping

The effectiveness of his Word in your circumstance depends on your faith! If you want to see the glory of God, you must believe!

---

2 John 11:38–40

out of the car, I prayed and God gave me the details on what to offer and request.

To my surprise, the owners agreed to everything without major difficulties. "This is it! There's no doubt that God is behind this negotiation," I optimistically said to myself. After all, I know when he is in control of something, and when we work according to his plans, everything will always come together and flow smoothly. Overflowing with confidence and joy, I presented the plans to the church board and everyone agreed. *Great, they're behind it! Thank you, Lord. Everything is going super well,* I thought to myself. During those days I was scheduled to minister in Mexico, but I did not want to leave without closing the deal, because the trip was right after the date we had agreed to sign over the deed. I called the owners and they told me not to worry, that everything was in order, and the paperwork was going to take a little longer than expected.

So I traveled with a friend, but not before sharing the wonderful news with the congregation and making preparations for the initial payment. While in Mexico, I received a call from a staff member who broke the news: "Cash, I just got a call from the family's lawyer and the news is not good. They apologize, but they have changed their minds and are not going to sell." I said, *"Whaaat?"* How could they go back on the deal when everything was set, and the church was ecstatic with joy? I am not going to deny that I took it quite badly, to such an extent that I even joked with my friend saying, "I feel like I did years ago, when you are really disappointed and just felt like going out for some drinks to get over the pain."

My buddy tried to console me with every verse he could recall: "Remember that the righteous fall seven times but they get right back up; you can do all things in Christ who strengthens you; God is your shepherd and you shall not want; think on all these things that are just and holy; God's thoughts for you are of abundance and blessing, and not of evil to give you an expected end." He gave me his entire battery of Scripture verses to counter my depression, but the fact is that it was not about that. My confusion was that I was sure I had heard God speak to me and had given me specific instructions about the matter. Something was certainly off: either I had misheard God, or the property really was ours and everything was going to work itself out.

Anyway, I thanked my friend for his support, but vented, "I feel totally discouraged right now. I sure hope God isn't hearing me. I mean, it's not every day that someone believes him for so much, and puts everything on the line like I did. I sure would like to see God try to do what we're doing without being omnipotent and omniscient. This is totally confusing, but I'm just going to place it all in his hands, and allow him to work it out." Returning to Guatemala, I gathered the leadership team and broke the news, urging them to not stop trusting in God, because he had something better for us; although right there and then, we just couldn't see it.

Days went by and nothing changed. I would pray, asking God for instructions, but I just could not hear him. One night my wife was fast asleep in bed, and as I was stroking her hair, I heard God say, "Son, there are things that you simply do not know. I am going to give you a better property and you will build on it so that the ministry can expand. You challenged me to try and do what you are doing without being omnipotent and omniscient, but how about you trying to do what I do, being omnipotent and omniscient, yet still trusting in you!" That was it! It was all I needed. The faith God has in us has always exceeded the faith we have in him. Those words literally breathed life back into me and I wept uncontrollably in gratitude. God was behind us, and he wanted us to believe and trust in him, beyond every possible circumstance or scenario that might seem opposite to his will. Basically, he was asking me to move forward in faith and not by sight!

Indeed, a few months later, the miracle did happen, and we met with the owners of a property that was much better, with better access points, in a better location and with much better topographical features for construction. Real estate agents had approached me asking if I was interested in a piece of property for my house, but I said, "No, I don't want land for my house. I want one for the Lord's house." When we met with the owners of this new property they said it was not for sale, that they would only lease the land. One of the clauses, however, was to never lease it to a church. But God specializes in the impossible, so there was no shadow of a doubt that it was him who was working behind the scenes on our behalf. After a few follow-up meetings, the owner agreed to lease it to us. The negotiations went in our favor, because by greatly reducing the initial investment, there were many more funds left over for construction.

When we visited the parcel of land with my pastoral team, the Holy Spirit came over us and we became drunk in his presence. Then I heard him say, "You said before that you felt like drinking, so here you have it." I could not help but yield once again to his everlasting love, manifested in the simplest of details. After all, those were the exact words I had told my friend months earlier when I had suffered that major letdown. When faced with uncertainty, I acted like Martha, with arguments and reasoning based on the knowledge I had and in what I could see; but then I learned the lesson. He is also telling you today to remove that stone if you know that Jesus is the Resurrection and the Life! God is telling us like he did Martha, "I assure you that if you just believe, you will see my Glory!" Let's not be stubborn. Sure, we can know a lot of things, but we will only be able to see the fulfillment of those promises for which we believe in our hearts. Don't ever let your knowledge stand in the way of your faith!

Jesus is our intercessor, standing before the Father on our behalf. There is no point in taking classes, receiving prophecies, and going to conferences if you do not make a willing choice to strengthen your faith in power and intercession before the Lord. Learning is well and good, but it should be focused on helping you believe more in God and in his ability in your life. Don't be like Martha who knew much, but only with her back against the wall could Jesus revive her faith. Remember, you are saved by what you believe, not by what you know. You are healed by what you believe, and not by what you know. Your family is blessed by what you understand that God has promised you and because you believe it!

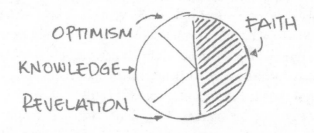

Jesus also thanked the Father because he knew that this family he loved was going through a process designed to revive them. The death and resurrection of his close friend would mean a new beginning for them. It also meant the renewal and strengthening of their faith, and that of many others who would also witness that miracle. Martha, Mary, and Lazarus were very close to Jesus; they knew exactly who he was, but they had somehow lost their way. Their faith had vanished and they began seeing him more as a friend than as their Lord. You can experience a renewal today, your dreams can come back to life, your life can change, and a new path can open up before your very eyes if you choose to believe in Jesus with all your heart. And if you are already a believer, then renew your first love for him. I promise you, he will not let you down!

Our Foundation

As we read the Bible we see and accept many works that were out of the ordinary. We are convinced that our faith is based on unusual situations such as fathering a child with a barren wife, parting a sea for a people to walk to their freedom, walking on water, or seeing loaves of bread multiply exponentially. The apostle Paul, who took our Christian faith to the ends of the earth, urges us to never be ashamed of the gospel of Christ for it is the power of God. Another type of shame is knowing much about the gospel, but never believing in it. Faith is for superior minds because it can take us beyond the place where reason drops us off. What we need is not a deeper revelation of God, but a greater level of trust in him. I have heard many revelations and prophecies in my day, but only faith has lifted me up. Why do we need so many confirmations about what we can achieve? Dare to believe and act on that faith!

Of course, we want God to allow us to know him better. That knowledge, however, will be of no avail if it does not help us believe him wholeheartedly. What does a child do to receive a healing miracle? A child does not fast, does not search deeply in the Scriptures; he just believes and receives. Therefore I always ask the Lord to instill in us an innocent, yet mighty childlike faith. Learn to see problems as opportunities to get to know the Lord and his mighty works.

Had the Israelites never been in bondage in Egypt, Moses would have never known the Lord the way he did and have led the people to their freedom and blessing! If there is an abundance of food, then you are not going to need a miracle of bread and fish. If you are wanting to see miracles, then prepare for problems and challenges in your life, otherwise there would be no need for God's supernatural intervention. Martha's experience is the best school of faith and theology because it teaches us to believe by making proper use of the knowledge that we have. I have decided that nothing is going to hold me back from seeing the fulfillment of his Word in my life! Honor God and recognize him as the only one capable of turning your circumstance into a blessing!

I've never been good at fixing things. Electricity and plumbing have not been my strong suits, but as the man of the house I have had to hold my own whenever I can. So I always make sure to have tools on hand in case I have to tighten a screw, including those that are sometimes in my kids'

Honor God and recognize him as the only one capable of turning your circumstance into a blessing!

heads! On more than one occasion, I have had to make a minor repair, and everything goes well when you have the right tools, because it makes the job a whole lot easier. After all, there is no point in having a screwdriver when what you need is a wrench. The same thing happens in life; the best tool in our arsenal is the Word of God, and though it is easily within our reach, we do not always apply it. Sometimes this is because of a lack of knowledge.

How are we ever going to believe in promises of which we are not aware? How can we claim an inheritance that we have no idea belongs to us? How can we apply principles that we do not know? The right tool is within our reach. We just must learn to use it. It is like having all the pieces to a jigsaw puzzle, but never taking the time to put it together. We all go through difficult circumstances in life. We have all had a broken pipe and needed to use a pipe wrench before the whole house became flooded.

I can share many challenging situations we have had to face as a family. For example, the day one of my children was diagnosed with leukemia, or when both my wife and daughter's lives were in danger during the birth. During those critical moments, I have cried out, interceded, and prayed with every ounce of faith I could gather. And I have had to apply everything I have learned from the Bible, fully convinced that God is the miracle worker, and he has always delivered.

It is during those moments that you might fall prey to saying, "Nothing is going to change. It has always been this way in my family. I am what I am and there is nothing I can do about it." Stop giving excuses or believing the enemy's lies instead of believing and claiming your heavenly Father's truths. Jesus is by your side, willing to work a miracle in your life, just as he did with Martha. And if you know that God wants the best for you, then prepare to receive it, thank him for everything he is doing in your life, seek to please him with your faith, and bask in the blessing he is going to pour out.

Don't get lost in ignorance, but neither in too much knowledge of the Bible. You cannot see miracles with what you know about God, but rather by what you are convinced that he can do. Don't let your resources and knowledge become stumbling blocks for your faith, but make the most of them by putting them into practice. Don't engage in the religious irony of knowing much, believing little, and getting nothing!

10 A MUSTARD SEED

Small seeds can become great trees.

Jesus was unable to do miracles in his home town of Nazareth because the people there only saw him as a carpenter, and not as the son of God.[1] He found no faith there, only distrust and unbelief. We know that the Word of God is alive and powerful, that it is good seed and does not return void. Still, the worries of life and the deceitfulness of riches have the power to choke it and make it ineffective. We need to learn the correct application concerning riches, according to biblical principles, so they do not exert more power over you than his Word.

---

1   Mark 6:1–6

When we speak about miracles, it is important to bear in mind the honor we are to give the Lord, for he can do mighty wonders if we believe in his ability to do so.

Unbelief and the cares of this world can neutralize God's almighty and limitless power![2] When I first read this in the Scriptures, I was left with my mouth open. In Jesus' own home-town, his power had been neutralized with disdain, disrepute, dishonor, and envy. It was like exposing him to kryptonite. When you start seeing Jesus as the one true Lord of lords, that is when miracles happen. Embrace the power of God, just as you would human science. If you see your pastor just as another good buddy, without due respect, how can you expect God to use him to bless you? Boldly proclaim your faith, and defend your beliefs, for your blessing depends on it. Honor Jesus as your Lord, and he will work in your life. Be consistent in your walk. If you claim that he is your Lord, prove it. Appreciate him, and yourself, for he has delegated authority to you.

We are all able to work miracles if we believe and honor each other. We are the children of God and he can choose through whom to bless others. Spouses can be used by God to bless each other, but they need to honor each other. Despite each other's flaws, God's power will not be hindered if he can find faith in the couple. You may view Jesus as your best friend, but do not stop seeing him as your Lord, honoring and believing him with all your heart.

I believe Jesus at his word, even with my thousand flaws, but I still believe him. When I was first invited to attend church, I showed up in a pair of torn jeans and a pack of cigarettes in my pocket. When I heard everything that Jesus had done for me, I got up without hesitation and accepted him as my Lord. I did not come

---

2 Mark 4:19

to him washed up, disappointed, crushed, or frustrated. I was in the prime of my youth, attending college, and running a small business. I did not accept him out of desperation, but out of gratitude, because despite the life I was living, he still loved me and blessed me. At that moment, I made the radical decision to believe him with all my heart.

In the same way I used to pay top dollar for the best liquor at nightclubs, I made up my mind to spare no expense when it came to buying the best Bible and investing in as many books and materials as possible to learn and share with others. I focused on growing my faith and I have never been let down. I responded to the calling I had felt as a child, and the Lord prepared me because I did not have the slightest idea about how to preach, how to pastor, or how to give my life to the ministry. It was not an easy road. Anyone else preaching on a sidewalk outside the city zoo with not a soul in sight would have given up. Anyone handing out gospel tracks outside movie theaters or writing messages on the back of bus ticket stubs for distrusting passengers would have easily doubted the future that lay in store, but I chose to believe him! I embraced my calling, and I thank God for his unwavering support, despite my many mistakes.

If he did it with me, he can do it with you also. But do not take Jesus back to the carpenter's shop. Do not see him as the carpenter's son, but as the Son of God, sitting on his throne at the right hand of the Father, making intercession for you and for me. If you have not appreciated him, or yourself, ask him for forgiveness. Learn to view your neighbors as brothers and sisters in Christ, worthy of honor as well, whom God can also greatly use to bless you. Ask him to open your eyes to see him as he really is—the King of kings and the Lord of lords– and to see others as his children, his disciples, and his representatives. Ask him to teach you about honor and faith and to help you do away with every bit of unbelief.

Pay Close Attention to How You Listen

So how do you do away with unbelief? Well, for starters, by listening only to words that build you up. For example, when the disciples were unsuccessfully trying to cast out a demon, they asked Jesus what the problem was. He then explained that it was their lack of faith and used the example of the grain of mustard seed.[3] The analogy, however, was not about having a faith as small as a grain of mustard seed, but rather about having the same power, with the same properties and potential as the seed. You see, although it is so tiny, it has the potential to become the greatest crop in the garden, to transform into a large tree and provide an abundance of fruit.

Jesus also taught his disciples how to increase their faith through prayer and fasting. When we want to heal someone, we should not pray and fast for the sick person, but for ourselves, that our faith be strengthened and used as an instrument in the Lord's hands. This genre of unbelief can only be eliminated by seeking God wholeheartedly! Good things happen when you strip all unbelief from your life. No one with their eyes set on this earthly kingdom will ever accomplish great things. It is only when we set our eyes on God's mighty wonders that we will begin to see miracles.

This genre of unbelief can only be eliminated by seeking God wholeheartedly!

On another occasion, Jesus compared the kingdom of heaven to a grain of mustard seed extending itself mightily.[4] The best part is that the birds of the air can make their nests on those strong, fruitful branches. The blessings of the Lord will likewise "nest" on those who strive for their dreams and grow like the mustard seed. God will always do more if you use your

---

3 Matthew 17:19–21
4 Matthew 13:32–32

faith to believe him to reach your goals. In other words, we should not focus on who we are right now but on who we are called to be. You may be feeling small right now, but like that grain of mustard seed you are on your way to becoming a large tree that will provide shelter for many others in Jesus' name. Listen and believe that you have been called to greatness!

Never despise humble beginnings. Even the smallest of seeds is convinced of its great potential for growth. Can you picture a grain of mustard seed next to an orange seed, or a peach seed or an avocado seed? It wouldn't allow itself to be humiliated, but would probably say, "You might think I'm little now, but just wait to see just how big I get once I'm planted, fertilized, and watered." Don't ever forget that God's Word can make you great! That grain of mustard seed believes that it will become a tree instead of a vegetable plant. If you have faith, you, too, can be like that seed, because we all have within us an enormous potential to grow and bear fruit.

Do not see yourself as you are now, rather see yourself through the eyes of faith as the successful and happy person you already are. If you believe like that grain of mustard seed, everything in your life will be possible: wholeness, restoration, and salvation. Many people limit themselves by believing they do not deserve to be blessed. However, God's kingdom operates by faith and not by works. Do not look for a price tag, because Christ has already paid it in full. Just pray and believe! If a demon does not leave when you cast it out in the name of Jesus, you can fast and pray, not because the demon is more powerful than his name, but to strengthen your faith. An empty stomach in the middle of a fast is not stronger than Jesus. Prayer and fasting are effective tools to build your faith, not magic "formulas" to obtain desired results.

Faith comes by hearing and is released by our words. As men and women of faith, we take great care regarding what we hear and how we speak. The apostle Paul preached words of faith to help new believers overcome difficulties and persecution. Let us not forget that the Bible says the "just shall live by faith." In other words, faith helps you live a better life and get ahead day-by-day. And we need to feed off that word of faith to help us live, grow, and move forward.

11 ASK AND DECLARE

As you allow
God to work in
you, your words
will change
and you will
see the good
days you have
proclaimed!

Toward the end of 2014, members of our church organized many visits to Guatemala City's General Hospital, taking food and supplies to help in a crisis it was facing. In addition to the donations, we were allowed to pray and lay hands on the sick. There, in one of the pediatric wings, a tired, grief-stricken lady shyly walked up to me, her frazzled gaze contrasted with her friendly smile. She hugged me and asked if I would please pray for her daughter. As I approached the bed with her sleeping daughter—well, not really sleeping, but with her eyes closed—my heart was torn because of the pain she was in. It is hard to keep an uplifted spirit when you see a child in agony. It is in those moments, however, that our faith needs to not only sustain us, but also be transmitted to those around us. There in the hospital room, however, it was the mother, on her knees by her very sick daughter's bedside, who was filled with such an enormous level of faith and such a positive attitude that it seemed as if it was her faith that was rubbing off on me. As we prayed in that dank room filled with the stench of death, the cute young girl opened her eyes and smiled.

I will never forget that moment. They did not own much, but their faith was so great that they pretty much had it all. And I am absolutely sure they got their miracle. But beyond that, they received joy, peace, and every possible blessing God had for them. Their faith was not of the sensory kind, based on the conditions around them; they believed what their hearts said that God had in store for them. They truly were living by faith and not by sight!

The contrast is so clear when I compare it to other visits I have made to sick people in other circumstances. People that, God bless them, have every financial resource available to place their children in the best hospitals. Some, at the slightest sign of any symptom, are even able to take them to see specialists abroad. Nonetheless, their attitudes aren't always the best they could be. They are arrogant, irritable, even defiant at times, and their possessions seem to control their lives. It seems they have faith in their resources rather than in God, leaving him as plan "b" or even "c."

Your faith is nurtured by the object of your focus, and it is only when you set your focus on the Lord that your faith is built up and your senses open up to the good things he has for you. Everything you go through, even adverse situations, adds to your life. Only then does it make sense that God's power is perfected in our weakness and that we have it all. Even though we might still have nothing, we can do all things if he is with us.[1]

When you have faith, everything is added unto you; but when you don't, even what little you have can seem to slip right through your hands. I can bear witness to this, because even in my most difficult and trying moments, when I draw close to God and truly seek to hear him, my spirit is quickened, because his Word fills me with hope and confidence. On the other hand, I have seen friends who get wrong advice and fill their minds with bad, fatalistic advice. They lose their sense of peace, even if not actually facing any problem at that moment. That is what I understand by the Lord saying that they seem to lose even what little they do have.

There is a future full of blessing waiting for those who choose to hear in faith. Of course, there will be challenges, since it is the only way to demonstrate that you believe in the good things lying ahead. When I speak about nurturing our lives with his Word, you need to have the right interpretation. To illustrate, let's go back to the Lord's Prayer. It is so deep and complete that simply reflecting on one of its statements has the power to change your life: "Give us today our daily bread."[2] You might ask what could be so special about those words? A whole lot, I tell you! So much that they have been a pillar of faith for everything I ask of the Father. The key is found in reading it more carefully, for it does not say to give us this day our bread we need for today, but to give us today the bread we need, including what we need for other days as well. In other words, we need to ask him for abundance, and not just to fill a need. By praying this way, we show God that our faith is not just for today's provision, but also for the one he has ensured for our future.

This principle can also apply to sales. Ask God to give you today the sales for the entire month; the contract of the entire season,

---

1   2 Corinthians 12:9
2   Matthew 6:11

today; as well as every good thing you expect for an entire period of time. It all comes down to your faith. You can receive today the daily blessing allotted for your days in the future, if you ask him for new ideas, because once you believe that something is possible, you will find a way to make it happen. But if you start entertaining thoughts that something is impossible, you will never find a way to make it happen. Believe first for "what" you want and the "how" will always follow.

If we learn to embrace the Word of God as a promise of blessing, we will undoubtedly receive it. However, if we do not ask for discernment, even what we think we own will be taken away. God knows your thoughts and desires, but he will only grant them to you if you listen to him and ask in faith. Thank him right now for this wonderful revelation! Ask him to cleanse your ears to only hear words of faith!

Good and Evil Look for a Mouth

So what else is necessary? Is only listening important? Of course not. What you learn must also be set in motion by what you say and do in your life. Jesus said that whoever has faith in God will see the manifestation of what they confess with their mouth.[3] I love it when God says "whoever" because everyone can see the full manifestation of his power in their lives if they just believe and confess it with their mouths. This is why Jesus urges us to pray in faith to receive whatever we ask. Prayer is a matter of learning to hear and speak correctly, because in order to receive, we need to believe and declare it as well.

If we do not know how to express ourselves correctly with words, it will be all that much harder to pray since our desire is

3 Mark 11:21–24

for him to hear what we say. He longs to hear you and develop an intimate relationship with you, but that is only possible if you start by speaking to him. Is it possible to have a healthy relationship with someone who does not want to talk with you? Of course not! It is true that God already knows our thoughts, but to seek him and talk with him clearly expresses our desire to enter into a relationship with him. So, if you want to pray, strengthen your faith and learn to express your desire correctly with your words.

Sometimes we believe that praying is just about coming before God and pouring out our souls. We are led to believe that weeping before him is enough to get what we desire. But, what about the faith we need to exhibit by declaring our assurance that he hears us and claiming the blessing that we will receive? It is one thing to let off some steam, but another to believe and confess his Word, confident that he will perform it. To be fully convinced of his love we need to take the time to study his Word and learn about his promises and laws for our life. Otherwise, how will we ever be fully convinced that he really does want to bless us?

Open your eyes and your heart to realize that praying is so much more than just seeking God when you are going through a hard time. What we need to do is proclaim faith, based on the knowledge of his Word. That faith will uphold us and allow us to confidently press on, even in the middle of pain and problems. God responds when we declare our faith, but not to our whining and complaining. It was through faith that men and women in the Bible obtained a good testimony. Believing the Lord and expressing that belief with our words and actions is pleasing in his eyes.

In the Bible we read the story of Gideon, a young man chosen by the Lord to defeat the Midianites who continually attacked the people of Israel to steal their harvest. When the angel of the Lord found Gideon and gave him instructions, Gideon felt sorry for himself and offered excuses for not carrying out the assignment.

So God said, "You are right. You are weak, poor, and the smallest and most insignificant member of your tribe." No, that is not what he said at all! God did totally the opposite; he empowered Gideon by stripping away the pity party he was having and said, "Go now in this your strength and you shall defeat the Midianites." You see, God does not know, nor can he speak, the language of pity and defeat. Have you ever tried to talk with a person who doesn't speak your language? If they say, "What up homey? Love your threads, bro," it might be difficult for some to understand that they are actually complimenting you. The same thing happens with the Lord when you try to talk with him in the language of doubt. He simply doesn't understand it, because with God, nothing is impossible. But if you say, "God, I know the situation is bad, but I believe in you. I know that you are watching over me and you are going to bring me through," it catches his attention, because that is the language he knows, hears, and understands.

I Believed, so I Spoke

We can have a full heart, but nothing will ever spring to life until we declare it. Of course, when you speak, you need to be careful to not be boastful or arrogant. Show that you trust in God and that you have the right attitude to proclaim what you want and receive it. For example, a doctor might say, "Sorry, we diagnosed cancer and you are going to die." But you can counter it by saying, "I don't believe it, and I cancel every infirmity." Then the doctor is going to think you are crazy, but you are going to think, "He can run every test he wants, but I am going to set my eyes on God's promises." When we confess something, we reveal what is in our hearts. There is no way to be sure of the faith you have on the inside until you declare it. A couple in my church, whom thanks to their persistent and creative faith overcame a dire financial situation, shared that their process was also in that specific order of visualizing, planning, and declaring in faith.

The couple accepted an invitation to a meeting from some friends because they heard that there would be food. However, they almost walked out of the meeting when they heard the conversation turn to offerings. The husband told his wife that they were leaving, and she replied, "Just stay. What are they going to do? We don't have anything to give anyway!" Their situation was so dire, that just to go to church, she had to buy some crazy-glue to patch the soles of her shoes! That is how bad their situation was. As they began to open their hearts and their minds, God convinced them of his promises. They started going to meetings organized by leaders in the church, which we normally refer to as "Friendship Groups."

The day finally came when it was their turn to bring snacks for the group. They didn't know what to do, since they only had $2.50. So they bought a pound cake that cost them about two dollars and placed the other fifty cents in the offering. In other words, they acted against all logic, in faith. That same day their daughter surprised them at home with some wonderful news: A friend of the family had dropped by and bought them some groceries for the entire week. Their needs were not only met, everything started improving to such a degree that they ended up starting their own business and hiring a number of employees. Every chance they have, they now share their testimony knowing that it will bring hope to many.

Faith is like a river with a force so strong that no dam can contain it. It will always overflow. Release those torrents of faith that are locked in your mind and in your spirit. Through your lips and your confession, you can either activate that blessing, or open the door to bitterness, deceit, and negativity. It's not just saying, "I have faith and God is going to bless me," but a total change in how you speak, because it conditions how you think and what you do. We should not be hypocritical, having two minds and two mouths. Only speak words of blessing over your life. Yes, there are times when you are going to want to give your situation a piece of your mind like when someone hits your car, you get mugged, receive some bad news, or are insulted. The last thing you think of saying in those moments is, "God bless you." However, it is best to stay silent and ask God to fill you with patience, because it is in exactly those moments when we need to be temperate and self-controlled,[4] something the Lord strongly recommends. We should be known by a faith that is reflected in our words.[5]

We must be like babies just learning to talk. We first pick up concepts and then learn the words to refer to them. Following this same analogy, words can contain a myriad of meanings, depending on the context and how they are spoken. After all, it is not the same to say, "Mother!" in front of your mom as it is to say it in front of your friends or your children.

> *It's not just saying, "I have faith and God is going to bless me," but a total change in how you speak, because it conditions how you think and what you do.*

The magic of communication consists of what you say and how you say it. This is why, in the current world of chats and text messages, emoticons are valuable tools to convey tone and emotion in everything we write. Experts affirm that the true meaning of a message is comprised of 10 percent content and 90 percent how it is said; in other words, body language, voice tone, gestures, and attitude. Our faith, therefore, must become a lifestyle that reflects what we think, do, and say.

---

4   2 Timothy 1:7
5   2 Corinthians 4:13

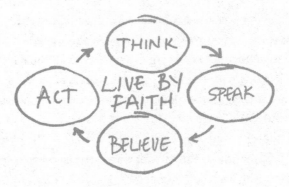

In the Thick of Affliction

The Lord often asks us to believe him and speak words of faith, even in the thick of trials and hardships.[6] We need to speak what God says, and not what our afflicted soul wants us to say.

If we do not willingly choose to speak words of confidence, our faith will be in vain and we will end up as empty containers. Faith produces something when we believe and confess it, not when it is tucked away in our hearts. Furthermore, words of faith are only received when you have a willing heart, otherwise it will fall on barren land. In the thick of affliction, you should not talk about how sad you are, but express the joy of the Lord, the strength he gives you, and the blessing he has promised, despite your situation. After all, what can we possibly gain by whining and feeling sorry for ourselves? The only result is to sink lower in our misery. Our words have a direct influence on our thoughts and our feelings, so learn to say the right things! If you have a low self-esteem, it will sink even lower if you start confessing it. Instead, speak about the security that you have in God and let it grow and strip away your feelings of insecurity.

Your quality of life is a direct result of what you speak. Long

---

6 Psalm 116:10

for truth and peace, and express it in order to receive it.[7] Show me how you speak, and I will show you who you are. Show me what you declare with your words, and I will show you the days that are to come. No one with negative speech can expect good days ahead. Declare what is good, the blessing you are going to have, and what your family will achieve.

Our speech is but a means, not the source. In the past I could be very foul-mouthed. But fifteen days after accepting the Lord, as I was reading Matthew chapter 12, I noticed that indeed it had been fifteen days since I had last spoken a curse word. My mouth was now speaking out of the abundance of my new heart.[8] Steer away from words that pollute, since it is impossible to bless God and curse your brothers with the same mouth. How could you call someone "you son of a . . . ." and then come before the Lord and tell him "You are my Lord and my Savior." Change the way you speak because it can be a great witness to others, as well as your best tool in talking with the Lord.

Renew the source, and the bitter waters will disappear. Strip away all envy, bitterness, and pain from your heart and you will see how those negative and offensive words will also fade away. If you still have hurtful and negative words coming out of your mouth, it is because your heart has not been renewed by faith. Change what is on the

Change the way you speak because it can be a great witness to others, as well as your best tool in talking with the Lord.

inside, and the outside will follow. One of the Lord's promises is to remove hearts of stone and replace them with hearts of flesh,[9]

---

7 1 Peter 3:10–11
8 Matthew 12:34
9 Ezekiel 36:26

meaning that he will give us new hearts from which only good things will spring forth. But this is only possible if we believe him.

What You Speak Shall Be Done

Jesus clearly said that whatever we say will be done. If we tell a mountain to move aside, it shall be done;[10] therefore, if you really believe, then you have to confess it for it to happen. When we speak about the future as if it were already done, we reveal our true convictions. And yes, sometimes our words might sound like bragging, but do not let that deter you. On the other hand, guard yourself from the pride of believing something that you are not, but also from the false humility of not recognizing what God has made you to be. Never be ashamed or embarrassed to proclaim every blessing that you will receive by faith.

Seek to build up others and extend grace through your words. Always express good things that will help those around you to develop and grow spiritually,[11] bringing joy to their hearts and their spirits as well to the Holy Spirit. Our tongue is a member with vast power and needs to be governed and used properly to bless others. Keep your tongue from defiling yourself and others as well. Jesus said that by our words we would be justified and by our words we would be condemned. Let us reach that justification and avoid all condemnation by always choosing our words carefully. The enemy needs your words to harm, and God needs your words to bless! The question is to whom will you yield? In faith, relinquish your words to God's divine will!

May God forgive us for every wrongful thing that we may have

---

10 Mark 11:20-24
11 Ephesians 4:29-30

permitted to enter our hearts. Let us tell God that we want to confess what we believe, that we are ready to receive his renewal and that we need him to help cast all envy, self-centeredness, bitterness, and rejection out of our lives. And may he fill us with his peace, goodness, love, and good words.

IV

TEMPLE

To be identified with autistic traits is many times seen as a disorder, the same as being diagnosed with a bipolar disorder, Down syndrome, or wrestling with ADD or any other psychological, neurological, or behavioral symptoms. While these are often considered to be limitations, many have overcome those prejudices and view those conditions as opportunities for greatness!

Temple Grandin is one of these individuals, and in the movie bearing her name we have a chance to explore a greatness that transcends what others might consider a hindrance. It is all about a different perception of reality that also carries its own challenges. As she states in the film, "I'm different, but not less. I have a gift: I see the world in a different way, perceiving all details that others overlook. I think on images and I connect them."

Temple's mother thought it odd that her small baby felt uncomfortable when held in someone's arms. For her, a gesture of affection that would normally instill security and comfort in most children was the equivalent of a cold shower. Little by little more autistic traits began to emerge, forcing the family to adapt and seek other options to develop their daughter's potential. Thank God they never labeled her handicapped, or the world may have missed out on a woman with extraordinary gifts and talents!

The life of this great zoologist, ethologist, and scientist has been a constant struggle to overcome areas that others consider natural and take for granted. Learning how to speak, conquering the fear of a noisy fan, or automatic doors, overcoming the fear of contact with other people, and breaking the socialization barrier were all doors that Temple had to open one by one. Indeed, they were steps on a difficult stairway to climb, yet she not only did so, but went even much further.

Her brilliant mind, which transformed everything into figures and pictures, did not allow her what would be considered an average level to live a normal life. However, she was able to open a way in which to make incredible contributions. She went from survival mode to a level of explosive creativity, with the help of people whose faith also transcended to new levels of great achievements. Her mother, her aunt, and her teacher, Dr. Carlock, were all instrumental in the process that made her bloom.

What can you say about a hugging machine now used in therapy for people with autistic traits? How about a new process in the management of livestock to greatly decrease unnecessary suffering? After all, it has been proven that animals also have emotions. Temple remarks that "nature is cruel, but we don't have to be. We owe them our respect."

Through Temple's exceptional eyes, we can view the world through a new and exciting perspective of faith that continually matures, step by step, through every challenge in life. None of us is "average," and there is a level of brilliance in each of us. It is a matter of opening our minds and hearts to every possibility, just as Temple did. I was challenged and did it, growing step by step, level by level, and God has really surprised me!

12 LEVELS OF FAITH

Faith in God must be the foundation for every area of your life.

In ancient times, whenever anyone wanted to leave a last will and testament, or establish laws and statues, they would write them on parchments or papyrus scrolls. Whoever wanted to enjoy the benefits would have to unroll the scroll and execute its instructions. This is actually the origin of the word *develop*. In a sense, then, we develop and reach new levels of greatness as we unroll, or unfurl, everything that has been written for us. This also applies to the will of God written in his Word. God's will is good, pleasing, and perfect for our lives, transcending anything we can imagine or desire,[1] because his plans and thoughts for us are always better than ours. This should be the conviction we embrace to develop the character, the abilities, and the faith we need to fulfill his vision. We know that everyone has received a "papyrus," so to speak, a measure of faith containing the promises and blessings of the Lord. It is up to us, however, to unroll it and fulfill it.

My wife and I have always loved sports. From an early age, we both played volleyball. In fact, this was something we had in common when we first met and Sonia recalled having seen me play. So I always joke and tell her, "You never could get over me the day you saw me play, until the Lord granted your request and we met again." But the truth of the matter is that God did fulfill my request and brought us together. So what I am trying to get at is that we both love sports and during these last few years we developed a passion for skiing, right after a friend first introduced us to it in Colorado. It is a fascinating sport and from the first time I fastened on my skis and felt that adrenaline rush, I simply could not let go. Now I have passed it on to my wife, daughter, two children, and their spouses. Now even my grandchildren are into it as well!

Little by little, at their own personal pace, each one has conquered new levels. After six seasons of practice, I have gone from a beginner to an expert level, though I still have much to learn. In the spring of 2017, along with my wife and daughter Anita, we experienced an adventure that I could say made me jump several levels right up to an expert instructor. I am exaggerating, of course! Still, it was an experience that caused me to apply every single lesson I had learned up to that point.

It was a fierce day on those Utah slopes. Our instructor apologized at the last minute for not making it due to a health issue. So just as we had learned in previous lessons, each of us charted the

---

1   Jeremiah 29:11

route we were going to take on our maps, trying to stay near cafeterias, which could also serve as shelters in case of an emergency. The plan was to use a new system of chair lifts that connected the two mountains. We spent an awesome day skiing, but on our way back, the summit became a bit challenging. The snow was somewhat slushy, and we could feel the chill in our bones. We also had to keep a close eye on the schedule. The last chair lift run was at 4:00 p.m., so we decided to head back around 3:00. Visibility was low and we ran into another group of skiers who were also making their way back. Without realizing, however, we each had taken a different route back, although figuring the other two were together. When it dawned on me that I was totally alone, I experienced one of the worst moments ever in my skiing experience. Time was ticking and the odds of not making it back to the gondolas increased by the minute. I didn't know whether I should head out and look for them or head back to the chair lift.

Every time I saw a new group I would ask, "Have you seen two women come by here, one with a red jacket and another with a white one?" The answer was always, "No." I finally made it to the chair lift just in time, hoping that they had already gone ahead. At the same time, I knew it would be easier to help them from the base station than up there on the mountain. That realization helped me press on, all the while praying for their safety.

Thank God I made that decision, because when I finally made it back to our rendezvous point, my daughter Anita was waiting right there for me. That is when we discovered that each of us had been alone! Anita thought that my wife and I were together. Sonia thought that Anita and I were together. And I thought that the two of them were together. It was total confusion, but it revealed how vital it was for each one to chart our route and mark it in our maps.

A few minutes later, Sonia showed up drenched, with her map in shreds. There is no doubt that all three of us reached a new level of trust and skill during that adventure. I am fully convinced that the same thing happens in our walk of faith. We go through different levels and overcome them, just as with any other learning process.

Born Again

If we view faith as a process of growth, the first level is being born again. The Word of God says that with the heart one believes unto righteousness and with the mouth confession is made unto salvation. Therefore, we are born again when we confess with our mouth that Jesus Christ is our Savior.

We are born again when we willingly accept him. In other words, we become new creations, ready to grow in faith.[2] On the same day I received him and said, "Jesus, you are my Lord and Savior, and from this day forward I choose to live for you," something happened on the inside. The more I read the Word of God, the more uncomfortable I felt with my life, and the more I wanted to go forward on the path he was showing me. The change was gradual, though, because reprogramming is not an easy task.

Faith and grace in Jesus Christ grants us a new birth,[3] and it is the first step on the road to our promises. Never forget that you are a new creation by faith![4] When we give our lives to the Lord, we are born of the Spirit who makes us partakers of God's divine nature. Can you picture it? If faith can cause the new birth of a totally new Carlos, a new Mary, and a new Steven, it can also restore your entire family, heal your body, and help you move toward everything you set your heart to receive. If you focus on developing an intimate

---

2 John 3:3
3 Ephesians 2:8–9
4 2 Corinthians 5:17

communication with God, and you learn from the Scriptures and apply it, you will literally have a new being within you. If you can believe that you are renewed and you see a new person emerge in you, there will be no sickness, sorrow, or poverty that can ever triumph over you. Your faith is powerful, giving you the ability to walk in newness of life and to hear God. It can change your circumstances and help you overcome every difficulty. The hardest part, which is being born again and seeing your name written in the Book of Life, is already done, so overcoming that financial or physical difficulty will be easy with the faith you have received.

Living by Faith

After accepting our new identity, the next step is to learn to live by faith, humbly yielding every area of our life to the Lord. This is often the greatest challenge, because we are so used to being in control and trusting in our own strength. We seek immediate results, but life in the faith is about reaching new levels designed to prepare and strengthen us. If everything was instantaneous, then what would be the purpose of forming us and training our will?

The hardest part, which is being born again and seeing your name written in the Book of Life, is already done, so overcoming that financial or physical difficulty will be easy with the faith you have received.

It's true, God can work miracles in an instant; I have seen tumors disappear, feet snap back into place, and sight restored to eyes. However, I still firmly believe that when Jesus said that we could move mountains with our faith, he was referring to a process, rather than to an event.

Some of the healings we have witnessed when we pray for the sick have been perfected with the passing of time. By faith, you are now a righteous individual who can live in full confidence[5] because we follow laws and commandments that enable us to believe in a joyful, stable, and peaceful future. Now that you know you are a new creation in the Father's love, you also need to live according to that faith that gave you a new birth.[6]

Those who are born in faith have no need to worry. The Word of God is clear when it says that we are more valuable than the lilies and the birds. So we should not spend our time worrying.[7] This does not mean that we are to cross our arms and wait for clothes and food to fall from heaven, but rather that our faith in God's faithful provision should prevail over every bit of worry or stress in our jobs. The person who works with faith in God, will always receive his blessing. Always work hard and give your best, because it is the best way to demonstrate your convictions. You must apply your faith in the little things as well as the big ones, in the simple things such as your clothes as well as in the complicated ones such as your nation coming to the feet of Christ. An economic crisis should never dominate your spirit nor your ability to press forward. If not even stray dogs starve to death, how much less you who is blessed by the almighty God.

I have never had to minister to lions, bears, whales, or fish that were worried about their future. However, I have had to minister to Christians who claim to live by faith! God's power is very palpable, and it is quite probable that you have been invited to a meal many times when you were right at the critical time in your finances. You have been taken to restaurants you probably could not afford even when you were doing well. This is God's way of telling you, "You are

---

5 Habakkuk 2:4
6 Romans 6:4
7 Matthew 6:25–30

important to me. Don't fear." So live confidently and work according to your faith. Always strive for the best, never settling for mediocrity!

Walking by Faith

On November 28, 2016, the world mourned a horrible aviation accident. The soccer team from a small Brazilian city, Chapeco, suffered a plane crash in Colombia as they were traveling for the final match of the South American Cup against Medellin's Atletico Nacional. There were several versions cited as the cause of the tragedy, but in the end, it turned out to be an electrical glitch, and as surprising as it may seem, also due to a lack of fuel! Cockpit audio revealed that the pilot maintained contact with the tower and had requested an emergency landing. Instructions to proceed were received, but the plane never made it.

We all know that a pilot does not fly a plane by sight, as we do a car, a motorcycle, a bicycle, or any other land vehicle. Due to the altitude, air traffic is managed by special technicians with an overall, panoramic view of infinite flight patterns. Every pilot must trust in the instructions they receive, just like the pilot who was flying that soccer team. However, the tragedy was caused by two basic elements: a lack of fuel and a delay in allowing them to land. Fortunately, we do not have to face those issues because our heavenly guide provides us with up-to-date, precise instructions and we will be constantly informed to ensure that we do not run out of fuel, remaining by the Lord's side, our never-ending source.

If the first level in our spiritual life is being born by faith, then the second one is living by faith, and the third one is walking by faith and not by sight.[8] We must be like the blind and allow

---

8 2 Corinthians 5:7

ourselves to be led by someone else, just like the pilots who follow the instructions of others to reach their destination. We do not see the way, but we can hear the gentle voice of our loving Lord leading us toward it. He has the whole panoramic view of our life and knows exactly how to guide us to our destination. Do not fear the future, for the Holy Spirit will guide you by faith.

Every morning can be pretty typical, as we get up still half-drowsy, pick up the newspaper, turn on the TV, or check our phone to stay informed. Of course, we need to do this, but the news should never control us. We should only consider it as the sad situation in the rest of the world. It can be hard to not feel depressed, but we need to be strengthened in the faith, so that events around us never eclipse the divine truths of our solid foundation.

Do not fear the future, for the Holy Spirit will guide you by faith.

Keep your ears open to hear God's voice and your eyes set on him to receive his instructions. Abraham, Israel's first patriarch, received God's instruction to leave the land of the Chaldeans. It is almost certain that Sarah, his wife, would have asked him where they were headed. I can just picture Abraham saying, "I have no idea. I'm just listening to the Lord and obeying."

Moses, the man who delivered the people of Israel from bondage in Egypt, also allowed himself to be led by God's voice. When they were finally allowed to go and they had arrived at the Red Sea, Pharaoh had a change of mind and sent his army in pursuit of them. What did Moses do? He did not say, "That's it. It's the end. Let's just surrender and give up!" No, he expected new instructions, even in the thick of that hopeless situation. This may have undoubtedly been the worst situation Moses had faced up to that point in life, considering that he was born into crisis. Life isn't about always having every solution on hand, but about seeking God every moment.

Persecutions, such as Moses experienced from the Egyptians at the Red Sea, present opportunities to believe, ask, obey, and walk in faith.

"All right, I understand," said one friend to another who was trying to explain the vast mystery of trusting in our heavenly Father for provision. Both Mario and Roberto were Christians who believed in God and salvation through Jesus Christ. But they were debating about how to apply faith to such simple matters as our daily needs. Mario argued that our provision was a product of our works, of our effort. And he continued explaining, "Look, even the apostle Paul told the Thessalonians that those who don't work, shouldn't eat." And Roberto responded, "That's true, but you also have to remember that Jesus said that we are much more important than the lilies of the field that don't work, yet they're always wonderfully clothed. Our blessing is already guaranteed if we just trust in the Father's love." So, who was right? Both of them. Jesus and Paul complement each other, never contradict. This teaching is about not setting our trust in our jobs but in the Lord, who will cause every effort we make to be fruitful. Our hope should not be based on the job we perform, but on the Word of God. Follow the examples of Abraham and Moses who walked by faith, trusting wholeheartedly in God's eternal love for them.

Fighting in Faith

Our heavenly Father is clear about his command that we fight the good battle of faith, remaining steadfast in righteousness, godliness, love, patience, and meekness. Fighting in faith is the fourth level. Abraham's life is an example of walking by faith and of fighting in faith, just like Joshua at Jericho, Elijah and the prophets of Baal, and David facing Goliath and the enemies of Israel. At the "living

by faith" level, you don't battle others, but you battle your own distrust and weaknesses when facing difficult situations. The battle
of faith, however, is a completely different scenario and involves
enemies visiting your home and trying to take your children away,
stealing your blessing and testing your fortitude. Temple Grandin
is a great example of someone who truly fought and accomplished
great victories.

It is only the battles we have with our enemies that make us
more than conquerors. If we want to experience victories, then we
will have battles. The levels of living and walking by faith are not
about battling, but about surviving. Just like going out to work and
training is not the same as staying at home and cooking a meal.
Sure, in both circumstances you are living and breathing, but one
is definitely more challenging than the other. Let us live our lives,
confident in the victory he has given us, and learn to conquer every
fear knowing that God is on our side and gives us the confidence
we need in life. We have been called to fight the good fight and
obtain the victory![9]

Dying with Faith

What happens when it is our time to come before the presence of
God? By faith we must tell our children what to expect when we are
no longer with them. As we read the story of the people of Israel,
we see a generational chain of faith. Abraham received the promise
of a great nation, and on his deathbed, he transferred it to Isaac,
who then transferred it to his son Jacob. Before his death, Jacob
worshipped the Lord and blessed his offspring as well, declaring
that God's promise would be fulfilled no matter what! After a life

---

9 2 Timothy 4:6–7

filled with challenges, death was gain, and the remaining step was to declare that his children would be well.

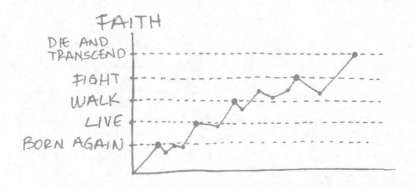

The security for future generations is the highest level of faith we can achieve. We are born in faith, we learn to live, walk, and fight in faith, but we must also die with a generational faith that can transcend our existence today. There are promises that your eyes will never see that you need to pass on to your children and grand-children, fully convinced that God does not lie. He is the one who helps you believe and expect what lies beyond the grave, because he wants your children and grandchildren to also live in fullness.

13 CHANGING YOUR LEVEL

Dare to change and grow by faith.

I can picture Peter as the most temperamental of Jesus' twelve disciples. Of course, each of them had their own unique character traits, but Peter was really a diamond in the rough. And Jesus, well, he was an extraordinary teacher, perhaps like Shifu for Kung Fu Panda in DreamWorks's animated film. Peter was a straight shooter, always saying what he felt. He was a bit rash, never applying any filters to what he said. In fact, we can see his transformation from being someone who wrestled with his character and emotions—at one point chopping a soldier's ear off and later denying Jesus—to the point of becoming the key-bearer for the kingdom, emerging as one of the spiritual guides of the church that was about to be born.

Despite his flaws, Peter teaches us many great lessons of faith. For example, he was the only one who dared to walk on water when Jesus called to him on that stormy night. He did sink, but he had the courage to try. If he had remained in the boat with the other disciples, he would have never been on the verge of drowning, but he also would not have experienced his faith in action and the love of Jesus rescuing him. What a privilege!

The root of it all was his faith, much like what happens when you embark on an endeavor, trusting more in God's promises than in what you see around you. Of course, there is the possibility of sinking, but take courage, because even if you fail, Jesus will lift you up just as he did Peter. We have seen the different levels of faith, and now we need to renew our thinking in order to take our faith to the level where God can manifest himself in power.

Never avoid doing something good for fear of what might happen. We do need to learn from past experiences, but it is our faith in God that must prevail above all else. He has promised to always uphold us, especially when we think we are sinking because we are weakening.

While thinking about Peter taking his first steps on water, I realized another way to look at the various levels of faith. We can go through them as we would in climbing a ladder or going up a hill. The first rung is drawing close to God, expecting to receive something we need such as health, restoration, provision, or comfort. When Jesus performed the miracle of the multiplication of the loaves of bread and the fishes, many people were blessed and their faith grew. Believing in Jesus leads to a new birth and everything changes for good, but you cannot afford to remain stuck at that initial level of faith.[1] You need to press on to the second level, which becomes evident as we start to obey him and our relationship grows in God, much like the disciples did when Jesus told them to go on ahead in the boat while he dismissed the multitude and prayed.

At this new level, we have already received God's blessing, we have witnessed his power and we serve him out of love. In fact, we could say that we are "getting in the boat with him." At this stage, we go through storms and face greater challenges than those who have not chosen to commit, who remain by the shore and settle for the material nourishment they have received. At this second level, we are able to witness and experience much greater miracles.

The third level of faith allows us to be used as Jesus was, just as we have seen Peter being used. He saw Jesus walk on water and wanted to be like him by taking a few steps, but when faced with the battle of faith, he began to sink. When you choose to walk down the path of trusting in the supernatural, in what you do not see, it will not be long before new battles emerge. You have to trust that he has already paid the price for your victory. We might ask ourselves, "Am I really doing the right thing?" Walking on water might make us doubt like Peter, whose faith weakened while he was actually doing it. Even when you enjoy a deep and intimate relationship with Jesus, you might fall into a trap and blink for a moment. You might believe that a bank loan is better than trusting in your heavenly Father's provision, or that discouraging words are stronger than the powerful promises

Don't trust in the safety of the boat, but continue to seek Jesus, taking steps of faith toward him!

---

1 Matthew 14:20–33

we have received from God. Don't trust in the safety of the boat, but continue to seek Jesus, taking steps of faith toward him!

Even If I Sink Again

The fourth level of faith allows us to believe that God will raise us up again. When Peter started to sink, his first reaction was to cry out to Jesus, who took him by the hand and raised him up. The Bible does not say that Jesus carried Peter back to the boat, but I picture them both walking back to the boat. Peter had taken a few steps that now had to be retraced, except this time it was hand in hand with the Lord.

Why did Peter sink? The first level of discernment will tell you, "Because he doubted when he tried to walk on the water." Notwithstanding, a second level of discernment will tell you, "Because he dared to challenge his faith." Had Peter remained in the safety of the boat, he would have never sunk; yet he was the only one who dared to be like Jesus. It is possible that back in the boat the other disciples might have started making wagers on what would happen. One might have said, "I'll bet you he's not going to make it back"; and another might have said, "I'll bet you he drowns." In the end, however, Peter made it back with Jesus. He was not left with an uncertainty of what would be possible through obedience. Isn't faith wonderful?

Jesus must have felt flattered by Peter's faith. Even though Peter had to be held up, Jesus saw the potential in him to do great things. It is like a child who is just learning to walk and will certainly fall more than once. But through persistence and getting up each time, he not only learns to walk, but one day will also be able to run.

Renew Yourself

Once again we see that renewing our understanding is the key. In Peter's case, his discernment was subject to the word of the Lord who had called him to walk on water like him. Time and time again, the advice is to leave all worldly limitations and excuses behind and begin walking by faith. Do not let your own resources limit you from striving for your desires. Do not use a lack of resources, opportunities, or relationships as an excuse for not doing mighty exploits. History shows us that individuals who never went to college have become very wealthy and prosperous. Of course, training and education is important, but nothing should stand in the way of achieving something great in life. All you need is to deposit your faith in the Lord, not in those things that will limit or hinder you.

Bask in the Peter-like faith of attempting to walk on water. He did not have to do it, since he had a boat to transport him. Still, it was a personal desire that he wanted to see fulfilled in his life. Indeed, Peter wanted to experience a new sensation of just how far he could go in faith, and thanks to Jesus, he found that it was limitless. Exercise your faith, set high goals in life, imagine and visualize them even if you think that it is something you no longer need to do. Remember, with God there are no limits! Exercise your faith not only in times of need, but also for the simple joy of witnessing supernatural miracles firsthand. Seeing beyond what is necessary means growing in faith and taking it to another level.

We should learn to see beyond our own judgment and logical reasoning. Getting laid off from work might seem like a great tragedy, or it could be seen as an opportunity to renew yourself and seek better opportunities. Do not attempt to understand why things happen to you. Rather, reaffirm that no matter what happens your unwavering trust in the Lord will always prevail, because he is in control. The question is not why you are facing that situation, but for what purpose? Don't complain or feel sorry for yourself. Fill your understanding with faith and reach the following level by saying, "God has a plan and something great is going to manifest itself through me. He is with me. He has never left me nor forsaken me, and he will always be with me, even when I fall." God longs to change your level of faith, but you first need to transform your understanding and be more positive.

Move Forward

To grow in your level of faith, you must first grow in maturity and allow God to transform you in order to discern his will. To do this, you must renew your mind, which is the birthplace of every thought pattern.[2] We must start thinking differently to reach the good things we expect to receive. For example, we know that God wants to restore our families, but many times we insist on making decisions and in doing things with our own understanding. What we should be doing is asking the Holy Spirit for wisdom and steps to take. If you have been acting and thinking the same way for a long time now without getting the results you want, don't you think

2 Romans 12:2–3

it is time to allow yourself to be renewed and search for other alternatives? Learn to be wise and allow yourself to be led by faith. It is important to find new ways to understand what is taking place.

A friend who was going through the difficult experience of adultery and divorce spent too much time trying to get his wife to forgive him. She had become his god, his idol, and his obsession because he lived and died on how she responded to him. Although he did the right thing by trying to restore his relationship, showing that he was willing to radically change for both her and their children's sake, by acting in his own understanding it seemed as if his wife's heart was just getting harder and harder due to the pain, the deception, and the arrogance that started to settle in. What advice could I possibly offer my friend if he had already tried it all? Moreover, what could I tell him if everything he had tried was right?

He had faith, and each morning he waited for a miracle of restoration that was taking longer and longer. He was lonely and frustrated, on the verge of giving up, convinced that condemnation would be with him for the rest of his life. Yet we know that is not God's plan for our lives and there is always hope. Even though we do not deserve it, our sins have been forgiven by God's grace and love. What my friend was lacking was setting his focus on God and not on his wife, to be patient and keep from acting in his own wisdom, even if the whole world was telling him that it was the right thing to do. He needed to seek a deeper, more intimate relationship with his heavenly Father, giving him glory and honor, and thanking him, knowing well that he would work wonders in his shattered family.

God needed to restore both him and his wife. They both needed to die to their old manner of living and be born again. His level of faith needed to grow and be strengthened in the middle of that terrible storm, perhaps the most dreadful one a man could ever face. That is exactly what it means to renew our understanding through faith. I know what some might be thinking, "Sure, writing about it is easier than doing it," but it is in these moments that you need to believe that you can do all things through Christ who strengthens you.[3]

As we wait for a miracle, we often seize the promise that everything is possible for those who believe and that through faith we can move mountains. We need to understand, however, that the first mountain we need to move lies within us, the one that causes us to doubt when we face a disappointment. The first miracle my friend needed was within him. He needed to change his mind-set and focus, yielding fully to God, releasing that burden and shame, and embracing the fact that he was indeed worthy of the forgiveness God had already provided for him.

To get on the right road to restoration, he needed to finally be able to say, "Father, I know that your will for me and my family is good. I have faith. I give you full control and I trust in your work more than my own." At that moment he would be filled with the peace and patience that surpasses all understanding, especially considering that a process such as this could take years. It is not a matter of God wanting to punish us, but a recognition that each one is responsible for the healing of his or her own heart.

So we are talking about renewing our understanding! Let us allow the Word of God to reprogram our ability to truthfully assess our situation, coming to reasoned conclusions without exaggeration of misunderstanding. Let us take the time to analyze because it is important to understand before judging; misunderstandings can lead to incorrect judgments. We often make the mistake of judging people without really knowing them, just as some misunderstand Jesus without first allowing a reading of the Gospels to influence their understanding.

Some have claimed that Jesus was a gentleman, but in reading

---

3 Philippians 4:13

about the miracles he performed, I notice that he would do things that today would seem very unrefined, like spitting on dirt to make mud for healing a blind man. Let's face it, if I were to do that now, there would be no way I would ever be considered a gentleman. When we allow God to renew our understanding, our perspective on everything shifts, and rather than judging the method, we would celebrate the miracle.

Do not allow room for negative thoughts. This includes learning to process information we receive in a positive light, trusting always in his infinite love for us. In contrast to what the world says, the Lord says, "Think on whatever is good, pure, kind, and honest."[4] To whom will you surrender your will? Repeat the following statement until it really impacts your mind, "God's will for me is always good, pleasing, and perfect. That is why I need to seek him with all my heart!"

Perceive in Faith

Throughout the Bible we find many examples of the renewal of the mind that God wants for us. One of the miracles Jesus performed was healing a young man who was blind since birth. In that case, Jesus evoked a change in the disciples' understanding, by urging them to stop looking for someone to blame, and instead to focus on the will of God, which here was the opportunity to heal and save that young man.[5] Do you see how one situation can be seen from different views with different results? In this case, God's work manifested itself as a miracle. In other situations, however, it may simply be the ability to overcome an impairment, as in the story about a

---

4 Philippians 4:8
5 John 9:1–3

young blind child who enjoys mountain hiking with his father. Both stories are wonderful. What we should realize is that no matter what happens, God's glory will be manifest in my life, because his will is perfect for me, and I will praise him in every situation.

The situation is like a friend facing a terrible diagnosis for which he was expecting a miracle. However, time went by without seeing the miracle, causing his faith to waver. That is, until God helped him renew his understanding by telling him, "You are waiting on a healing miracle, but while you wait you are also experiencing the miracle of my love and strength in the trial. I am and will always be with you, son." That revelation restored his joy and strengthened his faith again! It helped him recall that there is no such thing as a lack of purpose with God. No matter what our situation is, he has a plan for us. We simply need to be willing to align our thinking with his. By doing so, all frustration will disappear, and we will no longer struggle for our will to be done, but instead we will be looking for his will in our life.

There is no doubt whatsoever that the works of God will be manifest if we simply change our way of thinking, which in turn will shift the way we judge and perceive every ordeal we face. That renewal will raise our faith to a new level. If we go through a difficult financial situation, we must direct our thoughts toward prosperity, which will change how we perceive and evaluate those things around us. We will start enthusiastically seeking new options, sowing in faith in order to reap a harvest. God will manifest himself and raise us up. Learn to see opportunities for miracles where others see sin and defeat. We need a different perspective to good results. I have experienced this firsthand in our Nights of Glory, the healing crusades we organize throughout Latin America in which many people are healed, despite having no understanding of what the Bible teaches. They simply believe with all their hearts and God manifests himself as a direct result of that unwavering, limitless faith.

If we long to reach new levels, we need to renew our minds, to start thinking as God and acting according to his will. The story of the woman with the issue of blood who was healed when she touched Jesus is another example of how he sees things from a totally different perspective, beyond what others may normally see.

Learn to see opportunities for miracles where others see sin and defeat. We need a different perspective to good results.

Jesus noticed that someone had touched him in faith and that healing power had flowed out, whereas others only focused on the throngs of people and the woman's audacity.[6]

We know that faith pleases God, and that he is a rewarder of those who diligently seek his intimacy.[7] We do not have to feel free of sin to come before his presence. In fact, when Jesus healed, he would first perform the miracle and then urge them to stop sinning to avoid worse effects. Do not think that you need to do a thousand penances for God to help. All you need to be heard by God is to have faith and be thankful to him with a humble heart. If you have made mistakes you need to ask forgiveness, but to feel unworthy concerning receiving what he is already wanting to give you will strip you of that blessing. Do you expect for your children to be perfect before loving and providing for them? Well, neither does God. Draw near to your heavenly Father so he can renew you. Show him your faith by acknowledging that you need him in every area of your life. Don't pretend to be perfect to receive his love and mercy, because perfection is a tall order to fill. This would mean spending a good part of our lives, if not all of it, in search of perfection far from the Father. In reality, it is only God who can help us reach that level of excellence.

Many times circumstances may try to discourage us and say,

6 Luke 8:43–48
7 Hebrews 11:6

"Just give up, you will never receive what God has promised you." So we need to be extremely careful what we set our eyes on. Avoid any signs that might steal your momentum from pressing on and reaching every good thing you have asked for. We know that faith is the substance of things hoped for and the evidence of things not seen.[8] If you are working on a project and you stop because of a difficult situation, it would mean that your faith is based on what you perceive and not on the results you expect to happen through your effort and the Lord's help. If you are praying and still do not see what you expect, do not give up!

---

8 Hebrews 11:1

14 FAITH WITH AUTHORITY

We must believe and strive in the authority that makes us the Lord's children and his heirs.

The Bible does not present perfect men and women, but rather individuals with flaws, mistakes, and fears, who were nevertheless bold and courageous. We know that Abraham, Samson, David, Joshua, and even Rahab ended well, so we believe that God was with them because he supported them. The question is believing that he now wants to do a work with us, despite our inability to know what the future holds. Today we don't have to build an ark nor defeat a Goliath, but we do need to face challenges no less daunting, in areas such as work, marriage, family, friends. It is in these daily circumstances that we need to display our faith. What is the key for that conviction to operate and be manifest in our lives? For that to happen we need to take authority. To what do I refer? That we overcome the fear of seeing our faith in action.

It is not hard to believe that Jesus healed many who were sick. The challenge is believing that he also wants to heal us today. <u>All reason is left behind when faith takes our hand.</u> Show that your will is in perfect obedience to God, who commands us to be strong and courageous. This is the moment that your faith will be challenged to engage that task you thought was impossible.

An example of this striking level of faith is that of the Roman centurion who exhibits authority in his position. To better understand this case, we need to look at the background and context. We first see that Jesus was part of the Jewish people under Roman rule during that time. When they asked Jesus whether they should pay taxes to Caesar, they were seeking to put him between a rock and a hard place. However, he correctly responded to give to Caesar and to God what was due each one.[1]

Jesus offered another important example when he advised the Jewish people to exercise humility by going above and beyond the requirements of the Roman law, walking an extra mile with the burdens they were obliged to carry.[2] Just imagine how controversial those teachings must have been to a people who were longing to be free. But Jesus wanted to heal hearts and strengthen lives. If you are made to walk a mile carrying someone else's burden, your wounded heart is going to want to drop the load once the mile is over. But those who learn God's work ethic will continue down that second mile, focusing on humility, patience, and the right attitude. Perhaps the rage in their hearts toward those who forced the

---

1 Mark 12:15–17
2 Matthew 5:39–41

burden on them will begin to dwindle to the point that they end up saying, "Well, that wasn't so bad. God bless those who challenged me to work even harder!"

If you want Jesus as your mentor, if you want his support in your life with new ideas and authority, you need to learn to work by his rules and allow him to heal your hurts. We need to be a people with healthy hearts, free of all bitterness. As slaves, the Jewish people were bitter, but Jesus came to free them of all resentment. His doctrine of peace frees us also, because it teaches us that we are healed when we give more than what has been asked of us. <u>We all want an abundant life, to be built up, but first we need a heart that is willing to give, in addition to a humble attitude.</u>

True, the Roman emperor required the Jews to carry soldiers' loads for a mile, but Jesus said that they should make it two miles. If we want to be productive, we need to work harder than what the world requires. We need vision and passion, because someone without passion will never commit to a vision. This is also a matter of faith.

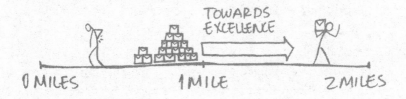

The Centurion

The passage about the Roman centurion reinforces the role of hearing in strengthening our faith. This man heard about Jesus and believed that he could heal his sick servant. If you want to be uplifted and not just receive help for specific problems, I strongly urge you to nourish yourself with the Word of God. Your faith needs to reflect that you really do believe God for great exploits. Remember that dreams are the only way to erase nightmares, so do not worry about asking for what you need beyond just help in your difficult times.

Do not ask God just to heal you. Ask him to also provide the resources to lead a healthy life once you are whole, such as being able to go to a gym or see a nutritionist. You have to use your faith to reach the top, not just to get out of a ditch.

The Bible clearly says that Jesus marveled at the Roman centurion's faith.[3] Do you know what it means for the almighty God to marvel at someone? The centurion was not even Jewish, meaning that we also can cause God to marvel at our faith. After all, he is always willing and available for anyone that is willing to take him at his word and ask of him. What we learn from the centurion's faith is that he dared to ask Jesus to meet his need.

As a soldier, the Roman centurion must have researched Jesus and known that he was the man who taught the multitudes about loving your neighbor. But Jesus also was the one who taught them about respecting authority, paying taxes and offering more than what was expected. The centurion must have been amazed by the teaching he had heard, so he asked some Jewish elders to bring Jesus, knowing well that he would not be turned down. After all, Jesus was also a part of the people who were under Roman rule.

As Jesus neared his home, the centurion sent out friends to give him a message. This is when the man's faith stood out. The Roman centurion exercised his power over Jesus and it is amazing to see how he used a parable describing a relationship of authority: "Lord, don't trouble yourself by coming to my home, for I am not worthy of such an honor. I am not even worthy to come and meet you. Just say the word from where you are, and my servant will be healed."

---

3 Luke 7:3–9

What he was essentially saying was, "I respect your authority, just as you respect the authority of the one I represent."

This man was basically commanding Jesus to perform a miracle! Seeing such a grand attitude, Jesus couldn't help but marvel at the centurion's powerful faith. It was that security and unwavering conviction that impressed Jesus. Allow your faith to come alive like this. Do not let it rest, but put it to work. Open your mind, because everything is possible if you believe with authority!

Be Bold

When the centurion told the elders to bring Jesus to him, he knew very well who he was summoning. As I read this story I cannot help but ask myself two questions: first, why did the elders urge Jesus to go to the centurion's home if they were wanting to kill him? Second, since when did a centurion build a synagogue to the God of the slaves? I am pretty sure that had the Caesar heard of it, the centurion would have been severely reprimanded.

These questions lead us to two possible answers: the centurion really did believe in the God of the Jews, or that he oversaw the area so well that he did things in order to gain favor with them. Whatever the case may be, his faith exceeded the faith of many of the Jews, and his influence helped save the life of his servant, whom he obviously cared for deeply.

The Roman centurion dared to do with Jesus what many times we do not. He practically commanded Jesus to work on his behalf. His faith in Jesus was so great that from his perspective he never doubted for a moment to present his situation to the Lord. The centurion was confident that Jesus' great power was in his authority. There is nothing greater than to have faith and authority over someone with power.

We all want to have influential friends. What greater influence than that of the Son of God? How was it possible that a Roman who deemed himself unworthy because of his sins would dare to exhibit so much faith in Jesus, while we, his true children and co-heirs with God do not? The Roman centurion felt a certain level of guilt because he stated that he was not worthy to receive Jesus under his roof, but that did not hold him back, and nothing should hold us back either! Especially since we know that we are saved thanks to his lovingkindness.

This man exercised his right "over" Jesus, but we today can exercise our right "under" him. <u>Our authority is based on the Lord himself and that is powerful indeed.</u> To a certain degree, the Roman soldier in that given moment felt he had a right over Jesus. In our case, however, Jesus is over us and we are established under a line of divine authority. He has the greatest influence in existence and he is on our side. Since we have the advantage, let us use it!

Why do we feel uncertain about asking "upward," toward the authority of God on which we rely, when the centurion did not hesitate at all with asking "downward" toward someone who presumably had to obey him in the condition of a slave? We have many more rights today to ask of Jesus than the centurion had back then, because we do not see him as our subject but as our mighty Lord and Savior.

Our Lord knew about authority. This is the reason why he did not get upset with the centurion's request. In the same way, Jesus will not be offended by you coming to him in your position as a son or daughter and saying, "I'm an heir of these promises and I want you to fulfill them." There is no doubt that Jesus is going to respond, "Wow! Now that is some kind of faith." You see, we do not have authority over Jesus, but we can recognize his authority, which is so much better. Within that chain of authority, we know that we have rights as heirs that were purchased at the cross of Calvary. It also makes me think that perhaps it was this same centurion that might have ordered Simon of Cyrene to help Jesus carry the cross. This Roman clearly demonstrates how we should use our authority as children of God to get the blessing we desire by employing the faith we have received. Follow his lead and you are bound to reach a new level of faith.

Faith and Leadership

The Roman centurion was a leader, a fact we cannot deny even if he was part of an oppressive regime. There are all types of leaders, but what makes someone a leader is a great idea set in motion with excellence and determination. All leaders throughout the history of mankind have had ideas that they have made a reality. For example, the Wright brothers envisioned that man could fly, and they did. They risked it all to make it a reality. Newton, Galileo, Christopher Columbus, and many others came up with ideas and became leaders in the process. We all want great ideas, but sometimes we don't keep an open mind to receive them. We stick to certain parameters and shut the door to the new thing God wants to tell us.

God only gives ideas to those willing to receive them. The mind is like a circuit board filled with on and off switches. Always remain connected to God so your circuits will remain in the "on" position. There are times when we want to do something, but we lack confidence and think that it would be impossible. Faith is the main ingredient to receive new ideas from the Lord and make them a reality. If you want good advice, you have to trust the advisor. Have you taken the time to hear a good idea from the Lord that will allow you to become a productive leader, without being overcome by anxiety?

In addition to asking God for new ideas, we also need to learn to adjust to change and avoid letting our profession and university studies limit us. In fact, that motivation to graduate could turn into your greatest obstacle if you do not place everything in the proper perspective. Everything you have learned until now should serve to broaden your horizon, not to condition you on a rational level that could close doors to the supernatural.

Once again we see faith playing a vital role because it keeps us open to new possibilities. When we activate our faith in the Lord, we go from natural limitations to infinite possibilities in the kingdom of heaven. With our faith set on God, we cease being of this world and our results become truly extraordinary. I can bear witness to this. You see, the more skills and abilities we develop, the more prone we are to remove faith from the equation, and this would be a serious mistake. As leaders who have renewed our understanding and who trust in the Lord's power, we need to not only train and equip ourselves, but also keep an open mind so that faith can support us.

Finally, do not forget to face every challenge without fear. I recall a person calling me for advice. He shared how production in his business wasn't enough to cover the expenses, and to meet his financial obligations, he was offered some invoices that would reduce the amount due on his taxes. Obviously, I told him that he should avoid that route and to consider if that situation in his company could be a red flag from God to set his focus elsewhere. Sometimes God's message might be to change direction and you need to dare to believe the new ideas he sends you! Faith is not about rules and religious boundaries, but rather about overcoming every limitation that would hold us back from trusting in the One who has no limitation whatsoever.

When we activate our faith in the Lord, we go from natural limitations to infinite possibilities in the kingdom of heaven.

I find it hard to believe that throughout the ages we have taken the Word of God and built religions around it, when what we should be doing is taking his teachings and rebuilding lives with them. We know the Bible is God's Word, and that it speaks to us through the relationships God had with others. The Bible gives us the stories of his relationships with men and women who believed him, and to whom God also revealed himself to take them to another level.

I hope you have depleted your own strength in order to once again take hold of faith to see your life grow and emerge like never before. Tell the Lord that you are going to believe in him and that no Roman centurion will ever supersede your faith! Be a leader who will raise his or her level of faith and be willing to face all challenges with authority.

V

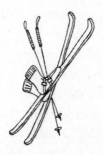

THE EAGLE

A five-year-old child bade farewell one evening as he put on his backpack saying, "Bye, Mom. I'm off to compete in the Olympic Games." Quite sure of himself and with a serious look on his face that eclipsed his mischievous eyes, Eddie opened the door and walked out to the bus station of that small English town where he lived. It was not the first time he had done this, because three minutes later his dad drove up in a small station wagon with a look of "You did it again, Eddie." He drove the child back, but as the years went by, the child never lost a drop of excitement and continued to search for the sport that would shroud him in glory.

Eddie was obstinate, but his resilient spirit allowed him to overcome the taunting and discouragement of others throughout his entire life. To be honest, I have never seen anyone quite like him, so determined, with a kind of holy stubbornness. Yet that determination helped him achieve the dream of one day representing his country in an Olympic competition. This is the amazing and humorous story of the film *Eddie, The Eagle*.

Nothing and no one could hold him back. Not even his physical limitations. His knees were weak, causing him to have to use leg braces throughout his childhood. This caused him to walk like a rusty old robot. He was not one bit athletic! He was no Rocky Balboa getting up at 3:00 a.m. to run countless miles and develop his ironclad muscles. Nor was he a Michael Jordan, born with the height and agility to dunk basketballs. Eddie was myopic, with an average height and a bone structure that was incompatible with physical exertion.

In fact, it was totally illogical for him to want to devote himself to any Olympic sport, but his faith was just as illogical, far-fetched, and visionary. Growing up, he tried it all: long jump, obstacle course, shot put, pole vaulting, but nothing worked out. And the box his mom had given him to store all his medals only served to place all the pairs of glasses he had broken. However, either providence or luck, whichever way you want to see it, played in his favor one day while accompanying his father, a professional painter and plasterer, to a construction site. Upon seeing the white landscape filled with skiers, Eddie had a revelation. It was there, while watching everyone speed down the ski slope, that he decided to practice downhill skiing and try out for the national winter team. However, this, too, ended in failure. Time and time again he could not qualify, ultimately hearing those fateful words, "You will never be an Olympic athlete." Did that hold him back? Absolutely not!

His new option was ski jumping, an extreme sport practiced by only 0.001 percent of all Englishmen. However, in those statistics, where others only saw a limitation and a warning, Eddie saw an opportunity. So he did what any passionate young person with faith in more than just surviving would do—he searched for experts from whom to learn. He risked it all, overcoming all odds, including facing death and surviving the "hands-on" training of leaping off the ramp time and time again.

Eddie tells that he never knew how he would cover the expenses for his next trip and had to sleep wherever he could. He even slept in a mental institution in exchange for some painting jobs. Of course, he could not afford to buy equipment, so he was always borrowing boots and other gear. He would wear up to six pairs of socks, also loaned to him, in order to use the boots of skiers whose feet were much larger than his. In fact, he was so persistent that he continued training even while recovering from an injury. He once trained with a brace on his neck to hold his dislocated mandible in place. Among professional ski jumpers, he looked like a penguin between graceful gazelles.

He continued this way until he was finally able to convince, or rather, blackmail former athlete Brandon Peary to help him reach a score that would allow him to qualify for the 1988 Calgary Winter Olympics. It was a miracle, but he made it.

It was in those Olympics where he got the nickname "The Eagle" and he won over the hearts of fans. Was it through unbelievable performances on the ramps? No! He became the most famous athlete in those Olympics because of his charisma, a direct result of the faith that would not relent, telling him, "It's your destiny. It's logical to reach your dream." When he made the 70-meter jump, landing on his feet, every single person leapt to their feet in applause, because many had believed that he would leave on a stretcher. After landing squarely on his feet, he raised his arms in celebration as if he were about to fly.

This achievement emboldened him even further, and he announced that he would attempt the 90-meter jump, a feat reserved for the experts and the daring. But nothing was going to deter Eddie, whose faith granted him the dream of not only representing his country, but also much more, as he set many national records.

The reason for setting those records was because he had no competition. No one else in England has dared to practice that acrobatic and suicidal sport! It practically doubled or tripled Eddie's accomplishments. You and I are the same. The Word of God says that we can defy what seems illogical to others, leaping and flying, if we just have faith.

15 LOGICAL AND ILLOGICAL

Life is a process and faith should accompany every step of the way. Trust in the Lord who is already at work for you.

"Mom, my head hurts," a little six-year-old girl cried before doctors discovered a tumor at the base of her brain. "Honey, bad news. I was laid off today," a father with two children tells his pregnant wife. "Today I start my master's degree," a young businessman with everything going for him tells his young girlfriend. What could these totally different lives, some facing terrible circumstances and others in the prime of their lives, possibly have in common? Faith! Because faith is the number one element you need in every situation and circumstance in life.

It should be the key ingredient in something as immediate as healing to survive a terminal cancer, as it is for the process of raising up a business you will one day hope to leave for your children. Faith is needed not only to have our sustenance for today, but also to get that job that will provide for our livelihood as of this moment. It is not the same thing to have faith for a thirty-minute sermon as it is to graduate from college. We do need faith for immediate and unforeseen things, but it is even more important to have it to see a process through to the end.

A businessman needs faith to make his company thrive every day, helping him sell, cover expenses, and earn a profit. We need faith to cope with processes. Miracles happen in a moment, but if your faith is not consistent, you can lose that miracle as quickly as you received it. For example, the Lord can bless you with a good business to start you on the road to financial prosperity, just as he can break a generational curse over your life. But you may not see the results immediately and your faith will have to sustain you until the process is complete, even if it is your children and grandchildren who will receive the benefit of your steadfastness. Faith operates in situations that seem logical and natural to us, just as it does in situations that seem illogical, supernatural, and extraordinary.

According to What You Believe

Jesus said, "Because of your faith, it will happen."[1] Although it might be hard to believe, the Lord also uses faith in the context of what you eat and what you wear, because every single thing, from the most mundane to the most supernatural, requires our trust in him. This is why I enjoy talking about logical and illogical faith. We

---

1 Matthew 9:29

could say that there is an illogical faith that works mighty miracles, such as parting a sea or multiplying the loaves of bread. However, there is also a logical type of faith designed to work in daily, commonplace things such as our daily food. Do you have enough faith to believe that God can give life, but not enough to believe that he can provide for everything necessary to maintain that life he has given you? How can we believe in miracles such as turning water into wine and the multiplication of the loaves of bread and the fishes, but we wrestle with God providing our daily food?

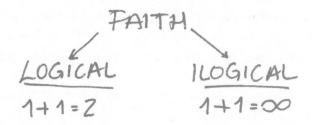

Our God who has given us such incredible bodies will also provide the clothes we need. By understanding this truth, which seems simple but is really quite powerful, we understand that as children of God we cannot be going through life dressed in rags. It might seem arrogant, but our personal presentation should always reflect how valuable we are to God. My mother always said, "mended, but clean," meaning that we do not need designer or high-priced clothes to look good, but we should always dress respectably to reflect our self-esteem.

In the past decade we have seen a number of new TV programs aimed at one's personal image. There is one in Spanish that I like called *Don't Put That On!* The idea is to submit a person to a total image change, much like the US hit show *Extreme Makeover*. I never cease to be amazed by the reasons people the world over give for dressing shabbily: "They should accept me the way I am."

"Fashion isn't my thing." "I'm not superficial." "What matters is the inside, not the outside."

In that TV program, the main job for the stylists is to change people's attitudes and mind-sets. They tape secret videos and do special activities to demonstrate that the proper care for our personal image and how we present ourselves to others is the only thing that is going to cause someone to take the time to get to know us. It is not about superficiality or appearance, but about dignity and respect toward ourselves. In fact, it has been proven that taking care of our appearance also makes great strides in our attitude. Why? Because a good appearance helps us feel good, and not the other way around. Finally, I share this thought with my case for faith because God takes great interest in even the smallest, most mundane details of our lives.

In 2010, a Casa de Dios member was greatly affected by Hurricane Agatha, and his factory was literally swallowed up by the earth. When I called to console him, I was greatly surprised by his optimism. I asked to meet with him and he showed up at my office, flawlessly dressed, well-kept, and talking about how he was starting over again because the Lord had shown him that with

> *It is not about superficiality or appearance, but about dignity and respect toward ourselves.*

faith everything is possible. He went on to say, "I first came to this church ten years ago. I went to a business seminar and God helped me to open my factory. Now I have sixty families depending on me, which is why I know for certain that he is going to raise me up. I just went to the sinkhole that swallowed my factory and said goodbye to the past. Then I called my wife and told her to not bother coming because there was absolutely nothing there. All I could recover were my business cards, but I know that it will be enough to start over again, because God will never leave me nor forsake me." And that is exactly what happened.

Little by little new doors began to open and a few months later God had supplied him with new equipment and a new location to restart his business. His "logical" faith could face the processes in life, and was evident from the moment I saw him standing at the door to my office. He did not come complaining, nor in apparent distress, though he had plenty of reasons to be.

What would your attitude have been? Would you have been all upset and depressed? Or would you have settled in saying, "Praise God, we're alive. I may have lost it all, but God is still in control and we will get through this"? Many of us have been mistakenly taught that God is interested in our lives but not in our material well-being, which is why we can believe for grand miracles such as healings, but not for simple or "small" ones such as our daily provision or his blessing to achieve a dream. Keep in mind that how we view things as great or small is not necessarily how God sees them. He longs to bless us in every area of our lives. How logical or illogical his love may seem will depend on how you choose see it.

Difficult or Impossible

I greatly enjoy the story in the Bible about a mighty general by the name of Naaman.[2] This man of steel was no more and no less than the leader of the mighty Assyrian army. Can you just imagine it? He was not just any old platoon leader, but a man of eminence, with a very important, highly-respected role, loved by the king and feared by nations. But unfortunately, he became gravely ill and his affliction was as great as his influence: leprosy! I can picture the agony he must have been going through, since his profession required physical stamina. No doubt that his illness must have taken a great toll on his life and performance.

---

2 2 Kings 5:1–7

So when they offered him the possibility of a cure, he immediately grabbed at the opportunity, not minding that he would have to seek help from a nation under his rule. Filled with hope and expectation, he made his way to the place where he could find wholeness, but it was not at all what he expected. The prophet Elijah, entrusted with the instructions to make him whole, did not even step out to personally receive him, but sent his messenger, ignoring protocol, to tell the general what he had to do: dip in a nearby river. Naaman was angry because his expectation was different from what he was presented.[3] Wrong expectations can easily turn into bitterness, resentment, and anger, and we should be careful when setting them. In Naaman's case, that expectation and perception concerning the prophet's instructions could have easily limited him to the point of missing his healing and remaining a leper all his life.

Obviously, the key was not in the Jordan River, for those waters have not been recognized for their healing properties, but rather in the words of the prophet. Naaman became angry, considering the request humiliating. His servants, however, started reasoning with him, "General, you are a brave man. If the prophet had asked you for some mighty feat, you would have done it. Why not then do this simple task? Please, just dip seven times in the river, because we hate seeing you suffer with leprosy under all that armor." Thank goodness they could convince him. And thank God for friends who bring us to our senses, despite our fits of rage. We should always have someone to help keep our emotions in check, or even to help keep us from missing out on miracles.

In the end, Naaman grudgingly obeyed. He dunked himself in the water once, twice, three times, but nothing happened. I can imagine everyone nervously waiting for the healing their master expected, but that required the illogical process of having to dip seven

---

3 2 Kings 5:9–14

times in a river. Perhaps to us that does not sound like much, but for him it certainly was, especially since he probably expected a miracle at the snap of his fingers. That is why everything hinges on our perspective, which all too often is not the correct one. What should be the perspective of our faith? "With God nothing is impossible and I'll do whatever he asks of me!"[4] I think that from the prophet Elijah's perspective, it was the most logical thing to do, because it was not too much to ask the general to dip a few times in a river to be whole. Right? We must learn to engage in faith processes, no matter how logical or illogical they may seem. Let us stop complicating ourselves by trying to reason in the face of the power of God.

It would seem to be illogical for our human minds to comprehend a supernatural healing without any type of medical treatment. That would mean that doubt is the obvious, logical way to go. The challenge, then, lies in believing in the Lord's power and in his relentless desire for our well-being. Why would God have created us as rational beings if he didn't expect us to use our minds? He loves it when we analyze things, reason and reach conclusions about them, but he overflows with joy when we break through any rational barrier in our minds to believe him. He wants us to choose him and to challenge everything if we tell him, "I know that it's logical to question, but it is illogical for me to even think that you won't watch over me; that you don't want to see me fulfilled with the life you have given me."

Bobby

During the first years of our marriage, in our neighborhood there was a stray dog that we called Bobby. Although he had no official

---

4 Jeremiah 32:27

owner, he had it pretty well. He had three square meals per day because we would feed him, as well as our next door neighbors and the ones in the house across the street from us. When Bobby was cold, he would simply slip under the last car to park in a driveway and enjoy instant heating. When it was vaccination time, Bobby would be vaccinated by us, our next-door neighbors, or the family across the street. The only thing he was lacking was a health insurance policy! One day as I left home I was a little concerned about provision for my family. But seeing Bobby lovingly wag his tail, the Lord spoke to me and said, "Look at Bobby the stray dog. He hasn't missed a single meal. Always sleeps comfortably and he's always cared for. Now don't you think I can take better care of you?" That brought tears to my eyes, thankful for that logical reasoning that cast aside every illogical doubt in light of God's infinite love!

It's typical for younger siblings in large families to get hand-me-downs from the older ones. That is why as parents we always try to buy the best quality clothes. And mothers always wash them with great care, so they will last a few generations. But then again, that is not always possible. It works with shirts, jackets, and sweaters, but is almost impossible with men's jeans or slacks that almost always end up with holes in the knee areas. If you are part of a large family, you know what I am talking about. However, this is never the case with our heavenly Father. He always has more than enough to give us without having to recycle. Jesus referred to those always worrying about their provision as people of "little faith."[5] Jesus is referring here to a logical type of faith; he is not talking about parting a sea, nor bringing down walls, but about our daily food and clothes. Think about it. When God makes flowers that are probably going to dry up and wither in less than a week, waste is the farthest thing from his mind because creating things of beauty is natural

---

5 Matthew 6:25–32

for him. He loves you and wishes to bless you with that same love, authority, and creative power.

A logical type of faith will always cause us to say, "My provision is guaranteed." Life is more than what we eat and the body is more than what we wear, so stop worrying about what you will eat or the brand of clothes you will wear. All that is superficial! Instead, worry about your body, your skin, which will stay with you right to the grave. Touch your skin right now, feel it, pinch it. It's perfect, right? There is no man-made fabric that can ever compare to it. You know it is "God's Brand" designer skin. Clothes rip, they get worn out and they are hard to repair, but our skin is such a wonderful creation of God's that every time we injure it, it miraculously heals itself without us even asking.

Leprosy taught Naaman to value his skin over his armor. Indeed, it is worth repeating, "If God has given me life, he will also provide the food I need. If God has given me this body, he will also give me the clothes I need. And if he gave me his only Son to save me, he will certainly provide everything I need to succeed."[6] There is a direct link between a life of faith and our perception of our value and worth. We see this in the question Jesus asks comparing us to the flowers of the field, "Aren't you far more valuable to him than they are?" What he is saying is, "Aren't you more worthy than all of them?" *Dignity, value,* and *esteem* are key words for us. Jesus poured out his blood to forgive us; it was the price he paid to save us. Consequently, we are so much more valuable and the ransom he paid was the perfect blood of the Son of God. In economics we say that a price reflects the value of something, and you need to convince yourself that you are more valuable than anything else, since the price that was paid for you was the most valuable life that has ever existed.

6 Romans 8:31–32

Do not think that God is offended when you face illogical challenges such as serious illnesses and a logical doubt begins to set in. However, I believe that doubting his faithful provision is an illogical doubt that breaks his heart. Stop worrying. After all, he is not asking you to part the waters of a sea or to cause the walls of a city to tumble down! All he asks of you is to believe him for your sustenance, for your life, for your projects and your dreams, because his promise is to never forsake you, regardless of the difficult moments or processes you may be going through.

Your life in Christ is not about waiting for everything to fall from heaven, but about getting up every day believing that God is ready to bless your work and provide for you in abundance, fully persuaded of his promises and willing to live according to his wisdom. As God started calling me to travel to share his Word and anointing, I began to worry about my family and he would say to me, "If I gave you your children, won't I also help you take care of them?" The day I told my family about this new endeavor of traveling to share God's Word, my eldest son was around eight years old. Every time I recall the moment I told them that God was calling me to take his message and organize healing crusades in other nations, my eyes tear up a little. My son walked up to me, gave me a great big hug and said, "Daddy, we're with you. If God told you, we're behind you, Daddy." There was no better confirmation I could have asked for! God was telling me to not be afraid because everything would be fine. He strengthened my faith through my young son's words. And now, many years later, I never stop thanking the Lord for being so faithful with my family. Of course, there were difficulties to face and challenges to overcome along the way. We are not a perfect family, but our faith has always sustained us. My three children grew up seeing us give our lives for God's service and one by one each also answered God's call to serve in the ministry.

We need to be a little more logical in order to believe in God!

Illogical unbelief, considering the logic of his love, is the worst type of unbelief. Our Father is saddened every time we doubt his love. The Bible says that Lazarus, whom Jesus loved, was sick and he died. So it is not right to think that God does not love you if you are sick or if something bad has happened to you. If you are faced with a moment of unbelief, and you start doubting God in the most basic things in life, I have a word of encouragement for you. Believe in his love! Do away with every illogical doubt, because it is so much more reasonable to believe in what is written in his Word. He never lies and his Word is eternal. Tell

Illogical unbelief, in light of the logic of his love, is the worst type of unbelief.

him today, "Lord, you and I together form a majority. You are by my side. You are my defender, my supplier, my provider, my healer, and my justice. Thank you so much for loving me!"

16 IN THE PROCESS

Faith
sustains
us at
all times.

I never tire of using the example of Peter walking on water because it is so clear that he used his faith, but it was for an immediate need and it was not enough. It was a logical level of faith that needed to turn into an illogical one. If you have more faith in the moments rather than in the processes, you might risk losing the miracle as fast as you received it. Many people are disappointed when they receive healing and then fall sick again. Where they really miss it, however, is in the failure to have faith to see beyond the moment. Doubt can sweep away everything the Lord has given you.

Stop agonizing over what you do not

have. Restore your trust in order to feel at peace. Even at a time of great need, you still have faith to see you through and encourage you to find better solutions for difficult times. Understand that faith is a lifestyle and not just a miracle moment. Peter needed faith to experience the miracle of walking on water, and he also needed it to continue walking, but he was not able to do so. You can take a step of faith and be surprised, but you can also lose it in the following twenty-four hours.

I know of a family that spent more than eighteen months without finances because both mother and father were laid off during one of the worst financial crises in the history of Guatemala. During the first month they remained optimistic, claiming that it would soon be over, but that was not what happened. Weeks and months went by with no job in sight. Do you think they drew away from God bitter and angry because "he would not answer their prayers"? No! Even when their electricity and water was cut off and they were unable to enroll their eldest daughter in school because they did not even have money for food, they still held on to the Lord's hand, harder than ever before, fully convinced that this time in their lives was just temporary.

So what happened? God took care of them. There was always a helping hand to lift them up. For example, the owner of their home waited eighteen months for them to catch up with their rent payments, and when they least expected it, there was a knock on the door with groceries from someone. They persevered in their faith. They searched for ways to make it to the services every Sunday, even if getting there meant sitting in the back of a pickup truck. Through rain, sun, heat, or cold, they never missed a single service. They fed off God's Word, searching the Scriptures more than ever. They joined a Life Group in church, strengthened their family relationships, and overcame the process.

It was not an instantaneous miracle, but it happened. The eldest daughter would keep her backpack clean for the moment her parents could afford to put her in school again. It was heart-wrenching to see her do this and her parents would ask her, "Honey, why do you wash it? We still don't have money for school . . ." And her answer would be, "Because I know that I will be using it soon." They did everything imaginable: sold food in front of their home and painted billboards, despite both having a university degree. They faced that time of adversity with the best possible attitude, and their faith payed off.

After two years, they each got a job. They got back on their feet, but it was not easy. Everything seemed to be against them. I have tears of happiness as I write this because it is not just one testimony, but many others that can attest to God's faithfulness. Casa de Dios, the ministry that God has allowed us to raise is for his glory and honor alone, is a church with people of faith brimming with countless stories of restoration, healing, and provision. I am not talking about abstract theories. My interest is not apologetic in nature, nor am I trying to convince you that it is reasonable to believe in God. What I long for is to transmit the passion that many have experienced by choosing to live by faith, fully persuaded that nothing nor no one can ever love us the way our Father does.

This testimony and many others remind me of the story of Joseph in the Bible. He was one of Jacob's twelve children and had a pretty rough time for some fifteen years. Just like you read it, it was year after year of frustration despite having received a promise of leadership and eminence. He was his father's favorite and had the gift of dreams, but that also stirred up envy in his brothers who devised a plot to kill him. In the end, they decided to sell him to slave traders. He crossed the desert with those merchants, suffered hunger and thirst, weariness

Nothing nor no one can ever love us the way our Father does.

and cold, not to mention the burning sting of his brothers' betrayal and rejection. He was sold to an important man in Egypt, who later noticed his talents and promoted him to administrator. Did his situation improve? More or less, because it also drew the attention of his boss's wife. You know! A young, handsome man with sculpted muscles through hard, physical work and educated. Wow! But after being rejected, she accused Joseph of attacking her sexually and he unjustly ended up in prison. Talk about things getting complicated! Many could easily fall prey to the enticing temptation of a beautiful woman. Right? Joseph, however, drew strength from potential weakness and resisted.

So the process went on. Potiphar, Joseph's boss and aggrieved husband sent him to prison. While there, Joseph interpreted the dream of another prisoner, which was his ticket to the Pharaoh. This is where his ascent began, to the point of becoming the most important man in the empire. However, the Bible says that this did not unfold until he was thirty years of age. When you do the numbers, Joseph's faith had to persevere for quite some time.

Do not live off instant, fleeting moments such as Peter's experience on water. That is not the faith that is required to go through the extensive processes of life. Sure, you can receive the miracle of your husband returning home, but without real, genuine change, those problems will persist. You need to show your faith with a different type of attitude, one that is patient, passionate, loving, and filled with esteem and value. A barren woman might receive the miracle of conceiving a child, but her faith must also be consistent for raising that child to lead a full life. Your faith should not be momentary; you must believe the Lord at all times!

Abraham, Israel's first patriarch, demonstrated his ability to have faith in that difficult process of fathering a son toward the end of his life. Despite everyone's doubts, he still believed. His miracle was very difficult to imagine, since there was no precedence and nothing or no one could assure him that it was possible. Nonetheless, his faith sustained him until the end.[1] Perhaps our challenge today is that we read the testimonies in the Bible and feel that we are not as worthy, but the Lord says that it is possible! Abraham did not have audio sermons nor Christian programming on TV. He was simply connected to God and he believed. Whatever you do, never lose hope!

Hope Against Every Obstacle

Abraham's case was unparalleled because God was asking him to believe for something that was totally and utterly impossible in the natural. He was called to exercise his faith for something completely illogical and that only worsened with time. To put it another way, his faith had to get stronger, because the situation was not going to get better. The challenge wasn't to win a war or conquer a city, a request that would have been easier. The Lord was asking him to blindly trust in his more than ninety-year-old body. Despite being an old man, he still believed that he could father a child in his wife Sarah's barren womb. This was not only an illogical faith, it was also a totally mad one, in an even more insane process! The result of that unwavering trust, however, was Isaac, and with him, the nation of Israel. I smile, because I can picture Sarah right now hearing the promise of God and gazing at Abraham with a loving look on her face. Elated with the idea of conceiving a child in her old age she says, "Will I once again have pleasure with my lord?"[2] These are my heroes, and it is no wonder God calls Abraham his friend!

Abraham's faith was strengthened to the extent of believing

---

1 Romans 4:17–22
2 Genesis 18:12

that even if he could procreate, he would not have the strength to raise the child and see him grow. No one, not even Abraham was ready for that miracle; nonetheless, he was faithful and believed. Your attitude should be the same. You need an unshakable faith even when others, circumstances, or even your own flesh tell you it is impossible.

Becoming a person of faith, beyond just instant miracles, requires engaging in a challenging process in which you might feel alone, with nothing more than hope with which to battle against an adverse hope. This has to do with being worthy of seeing God's dream fulfilled in our lives. Don't fall prey to discouragement or bitterness if you feel that you are all alone with no one to turn to. I went through the same. When the Lord first called me, I would preach wherever I could, even on city buses. No one seemed to listen, but I persisted. I wrestled against all hope foreign to mine, and came out victorious, a new person, ready to become a man of faith and able to witness God's mighty deeds. Don't settle for moments of faith, but face every process to become a man or woman of faith, ready to receive and keep the blessings!

Problems are designed to strengthen us, not to weaken us. They prove you are made of that raw material God has created. Tackle every obstacle in faith, because it all depends on you and the confidence you have in him. Don't give in to the first problem that comes your way, but strive to grow your business, to earn your university degree, to reach your dreams. This happens in sports and we can see what happens in World Cup competition when fear overpowers the will. Many teams struggle in handling the pressure of a tied game, or a less than favorable final

Don't settle for moments of faith, but face every process to become a man or woman of faith, ready to receive and keep the blessings!

score. They lose their focus and with it, every possibility of advancing toward the goal—to win the World Cup. Abraham focused on exactly what he had to do to receive his miracle. There were no drugs or pills like we have today. All he had was his faith in the Lord!

It is not wrong to look at your circumstances, just like Abraham considered his own body. But he did not stop believing. If you go to the doctor and are diagnosed with a malignant tumor, just say in faith, "It does not matter. Jesus assures me that by his stripes I have already been healed, and I believe him."[3] Look at each crisis without succumbing to it. If your boss calls you to his office with a high probability that you might be laid off because of economic cutbacks, look the problem in the face and say, "It does not matter. Every time God shuts one door, he always opens another. I will come out ahead!"

Abraham was not afraid because he knew that the nation the Lord had promised him would continue through his son. He understood the challenges of having a son at his age, but chose to focus on the possibilities, rather than the difficulties. Your conversations also need to be about solutions and not choke on the problems. <u>Add fuel to the fire of faith, not to the fire of despair!</u>

FAITH   DESPAIR

There are individuals who come to talk to me about the same problem over and over again, never offering a single solution. That

---

3 Isaiah 53:5

attitude is not much help, and worse still, it discourages those who want to press on. Do not fall prey to beliefs different from yours, but believe God wholeheartedly and face that problem. Like Abraham, we should be men and women with a wholesome, robust faith, willing to face every challenging process that is designed to help us grow and see many miracles. Our faith should be logical for what we consider small and mundane, such as our daily sustenance, and illogical to believe for great and powerful miracles, such as supernatural healing.

The Work Is Finished

When God spoke to Abraham about his promise, the first thing he did was change Abraham's name to one whose meaning is "father of multitudes,"[4] although it would be years before his child would be born. The verbs used in this passage of Scripture reveal something very powerful. God never said, "I will make you the father of many nations," but simply, "I have made you." The verb is in the indicative perfect tense because in God's eyes the promise was as good as done.

When God promises something, we need to have the assurance that he has already performed it, even if we do not yet see the visible manifestation. In other words, God speaks about the future in the past tense, because to him it is already done! To speak Abraham's future into his life, God spoke to him in the past tense. It is like having a *déjà vu* moment—the sensation of living something in the moment that has already taken place before. This is the reason why the prophet Isaiah was so convinced about what he was saying that he prophesied in the past tense, "By his stripes we *were* healed." He did not say, "We *will* be healed."

---

4 Genesis 17:5–6

The book of Revelation says, "The lamb that was slaughtered before the world was made." This means that when Jesus went to the cross, in God's eyes, the event had already occurred. Faith is the assurance that God has seen your future of good, and you will see it fulfilled. Long before the dedication of our new sanctuary, I could envision our congregation there, worshipping the Lord, serving in his work, and sharing his Word. That is what it means to speak in faith. What God is going to do in your life is already done, and it is marvelous. The Lord has already blessed you beyond anything you can feel or think. Thank him right now for what he has done in your life and believe him wholeheartedly that you will be able to reach that future of peace and prosperity that he has already given you. The Lord first executes the plan, then he reveals it to us. His perfect plan for your life has already been established and it will be revealed when you believe.

17 MOMENTS... AND MORE MOMENTS

Trust in the Lord and you'll overcome every difficult circumstance.

My friend and composer Danilo Montero wrote a song that says, "There are moments that should never end, and seconds that should last an eternity." We have all experienced wonderful moments in life that we wished would never end. Everyone can recall sweet and wonderful moments, such as falling in love and all the emotions that followed: butterflies in the stomach, that first kiss, the honeymoon. However, no one enjoys recalling difficult moments like separation or death. In life, there are moments of sorrow, sickness, and bad news that cannot be avoided. During those moments, you need to learn to live through them and overcome them with the strength and fortitude that God can give us. Again, life comes together in moments and processes of faith.

To everything there is a season. The Word of God clearly says there is a time to be born and a time to die, as well as for everything else that is done in life.[1] It is good to ask and pray for difficult moments to pass quickly in order to enjoy the more pleasant ones. However, learn to live in your moment, regardless of whether it is a joyful one or one filled with grief. We need to live it intensively. This happens with death. We avoid facing it, because we do not see it as part of life, yet it also has its time.

In the Bible we read about Naomi, a widow going through a terrible moment: the death of her husband and two sons. All she had left were her two daughters-in-law. One was Orpah, who took her mother-in-law's advice and left them to find a new husband; and the other was Ruth, who chose to stay by Naomi's side and help her through this difficult moment. Naomi declared her situation based how she was feeling. Her affliction was so great that she even wanted to change her name to one that meant "bitter," although the one she already had meant "pleasant."[2]

We can contrast Naomi's situation with that of Job, another famous person in the Bible. He also went through a terrible and somber time. He was left with nothing! And added to that was sickness and a couple of foolish friends. Yet he never spoke against the Lord.[3] Notice the difference. Naomi felt deprived and afflicted of God. Job, on the other hand, humbly recognized that he came into this world with nothing and blessed the Lord. Despite Job's good

---

1 Ecclesiastes 3:1–8
2 Ruth 1:20–21
3 Job 1:20–22

intentions, it was not God who stripped him of his possessions, but the devil. We need to be clear about the fact that in God's will there is always a purpose for good, never for evil. Situations happen as a result of decisions we and others make, or simply because their time has come. For example, we will all die eventually, but it is not God who takes our life; it is simply that the time has come to appear before his presence.

The fact of the matter was that Naomi let her feelings get the best of her. Ruth, on the other hand, was brave and remained with her despite the turmoil they were facing. Had she not done so, she would not have met Boaz and become part of the lineage of Jesus. We need to learn to see the big picture, beyond the current moment. Even if we do not understand it, our trust in the Lord must always be greater than our pain. Do not allow your feelings to betray you. If you are going through a sad, confusing, or infuriating moment, express your emotions, but keep from saying anything harmful. Only speak what will be a blessing.

Declare that you know "God causes everything to work together for the good of those who love God."[4] Declare your future with boldness. Give thanks to God for his care during your situation, because all things really do work for good for those who place their trust in him. On the other hand, if you stop loving and serving him, not persevering in your fellowship with him,

We should be willing to fight for what is ours, even when circumstances might be difficult, and it appears that nothing good will come out of it.

that promise is null and void, because only those who love the Lord will see how all things can turn around for their blessing!

---

4 Romans 8:28

Whenever I face a difficult circumstance, I first live the moment. I cry a little and vent, but only to myself. Then I look for some calm in order to make good decisions. Following that, I make the right declaration of faith, and finally, I talk with God to hear his counsel. Of course, it is never easy to forget or overcome the pain, but it is possible to recall it with a healthy heart, free of bitterness and sorrow. If you have lost a loved one, of course you are going to miss that person for the rest of your life, but as time goes by, and you declare the right things, your heart will begin to heal and you will be able to reach out to whatever lies ahead.[5] Keep in mind that to open a new chapter, you first have to close the previous one. Keep the events of your past behind you, and move forward toward what is yet to come.

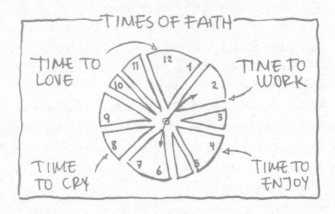

The prodigal son, that young man who demanded his inheritance and then squandered it, had to come to his senses before returning to his father in repentance.[6] In life, there are difficult moments we cannot avoid, and others that we ourselves cause. If you suffer from any type of addiction, or have problems in your marriage because of a disorderly life, you need to face the consequences of your choices and act in order to begin a process of restoration. Do not wait until

5 Philippians 3:12–13
6 Luke 15:17–18

you hit rock bottom; rather, open your eyes and come out of those bitter moments you caused. Our Father is rich in mercy and forgives us, but we need to make the right decision. Follow the prodigal son's attitude and declaration by standing up and returning to the Father. He is always going to reveal to you the path to blessing and righteousness. Everything you have been through is in the past. You now need to see this new chapter of your life with optimism, learning to live each moment in faith. God will help you live the moments and processes if you ask him. And he will raise you up so you can move forward confidently in his promises.

Manage Your Faith

Things will happen or keep from happening according to what you believe. Your ability to overcome a storm will depend on the confidence you have and demonstrate in each specific moment of the process. Jesus worked miracles in the moment, such as healing the leper, the blind, and the paralytic just by touching them. He also multiplied the loaves and the fishes, turned the water into wine, and calmed the storm in mere seconds. The Roman centurion knew about authority and not only received the miracle for his servant but also had the honor of being praised for his faith, all in the same moment. Sometimes we want to apply the same type of faith for something immediate as well as for a process, but that is not possible.

There is a difference between the faith required to reach something logical, like a job opportunity, and the faith to attain something illogical, such as the supernatural multiplication of our provision. The faith needed to get married is not the same as one required to stay married throughout an entire lifetime. There is a specific type of faith to enroll in college, and one totally different to complete a degree and graduate. The same thing is true when buying a home. The confidence required to make the initial down payment is not the same one needed throughout the process of paying for it. The difference is the character and the fortitude we develop as we deepen our relationship with God. We know that everything we can achieve with a person depends on our relationship with him. No matter how much a teacher might love her students, she will not give them the same things she gives her own children. A wife has more confidence to ask something of her husband than of her boss. The key to a mature faith is in intensely seeking our Father and enjoying our relationship with him.

I had the faith to begin my ministry, but to remain in the ministry and endure every difficult circumstance I need a deeper and more mature level of faith. Yes, I am visited by doubt from time to time, but I never welcome it with a cup of coffee. The opposite should be true. We need to cast out doubt as quickly as possible, and in my home and family we have chosen

The key to a mature faith is in intensely seeking our Father and enjoying our relationship with him.

to believe God and his promises. I married Sonia because I love her, but we have managed to have a stable marriage because of our faith to believe that we would come out ahead in this process of life together.

Believe God for instant miracles, but also exercise the faith to retain them in order to not lose what he has given you. Believe God also for the promises that take time. Abraham had to use his faith over many years, but the Syrophenician woman needed only a brief healing encounter with Jesus. Both cases were different, yet at the same time very powerful. When you have attained the level of faith required to transcend, you show that you have the character to see his promises fulfilled and keep them going.

VI

THE PERFECT GAME

Wouldn't it be great if our lives were like what in baseball is called the perfect game? In a game like this, the starting pitcher is the same one who completes all nine innings with such an outstanding performance that the opposing players are unable to get a single hit. Every team would like to be the only one to bat hits, even homeruns, and score runs.

That is exactly what a little league baseball team from Monterrey, Mexico, did in 1957 and the movie *The Perfect Game* recounts this touching tale. They won the Little League World Series in the United States, even though all the odds were against them, including racial discrimination and a lack of financing. Yet they had more than enough faith and passion to make up for it. In their small, hot, dusty town, a mining center of the nation, children dreamed of playing baseball, especially Angel, who was considered their best pitcher of all time.

Every afternoon, they would meet behind the church, gathered around Father Steven's radio to hear the games of famous teams such as the Yankees, Dodgers, Red Sox, or Cardinals. It was from this last team that a young player named Cesar was released, who then returned to his hometown, which was where these children lived.

Angel and Cesar ran into each other, or better said, Angel stumbled into Cesar's life when he started practicing his pitching with a baseball he found in some bushes. Upon finding it, Angel fondled it ever so gently, as if he had just found the most valuable treasure, and for him it was just that. What was a baseball in perfect condition doing in a small town in the middle of nowhere?

Without wasting any time, Angel looked for a place to practice, choosing a place he thought would not bother anyone, right in the alley where the factory workers lived. The ball bounced incessantly off the tin walls of the room where Cesar napped. That first encounter was a little abrupt, but it paved the way for the coach-student relationship they would one day enjoy. It was not easy to convince

Cesar to teach young Angel how to pitch, and his proposal of forming a team with his friends did not help. The children had to meet every condition Cesar gave them, because he was reluctant to train a group of inexperienced kids who had never held a baseball glove or bat in their entire lives.

The boys worked hard turning the cluttered yard behind the church into a baseball diamond and they brought together more friends to form a team. All right, "Let's do it," Cesar grudgingly agreed. The children's passion and drive, coupled with the support of the priest turned, finally convinced Cesar in this grand adventure. When Cesar would tell them to run around the field ten times, they did it. If he asked them to be there early each morning, they were there. The children looked up to him and followed his every command, even after finding out he had lied to them about being a coach for the Cardinals, not just a locker room assistant.

Through Cesar the team could get a sponsor, and they signed up for the tournament. But that was when the real challenge set in. Lacking finances, the team experienced cold weather and hunger, in addition to enduring the taunts and rejection of those who looked down on them for being Mexican. Despite all that, little by little, they made headway in the tournament, finding allies along the way who blessed them by feeding them and providing places to stay.

It was that kind of blind faith the children had that greased the wheels of the entire machine, because no one believed in them. However, during those training periods, each one began to discover their God-given potential. Especially Angel, who went on to pitch a perfect game in the last game of the championship, earning him not only his father's approval and respect but also the admiration of the people from two nations, the USA and Mexico.

It is only when we have faith and are obedient to the instructions of our heavenly coach, that we also can achieve a perfect game in life!

18 TOO EASY TO BE TRUE

Faith in God's ability to do the impossible should be the driving force behind obeying his simple instructions.

Both mother and son watched the door close and heard the steps walking away. It was time to turn the page and move on, but how? Sadly, the family had separated and she would have liked for someone to give her some advice. Her husband, the father of her child, would not be coming back. It seemed unreal, but it was all too true. How do you explain to a five-year-old child that his superhero, that man he looked up to as a strong and kind giant, would now have only half-custody and they would only see each other every other weekend? In moments like that it is difficult to say, "I have faith." Indeed, it is a challenge to believe that everything will be okay when there is so much pain, so many broken hearts, overturned lives, and uncertainty regarding the future.

What do you think that lonely mother would think in that moment if the only advice was, "Just trust in me and you will not be put to shame"? I think she would probably like to hear something more specific. Perhaps she would feel better if someone told her step by step how to emerge from the pit into which she had fallen and where all she could do was cry. The Lord knows how much we long for someone to take us by the hand and lead us when we do not know what to do. And this is exactly what the Lord does! All he needs is for us to be attentive to his instructions, to believe him, and to prepare ourselves to obey him, confident that whatever he asks us to do will not be the least bit complicated.

We already read about Naaman, a Syrian general who was disappointed by the prophet's instruction, considering it unworthy of his status as a noteworthy person. Perhaps he was under the notion that the prophet would call on the Lord and there would be fireworks, or some other notable manifestation. But Elisha simply sent him to dip in the Jordan River, one which the general implied was not as clean as the rivers in Damascus. In like manner, our way of thinking can limit whatever door God is wanting to open. His answer can bewilder us, for it is often far more simple than what we would have imagined or expected.

It can be all too common to believe that we have better options in life than obeying the Lord's instructions. We believe ourselves to be proficient and self-sufficient and are arrogant in thinking we can make it without God.

Test of Faith

Naaman was finally convinced by his servants to give it a try, since if he was willing to comply with a difficult task, there was nothing to lose by obeying this simple one. In the end he did follow through and was healed. It is hard to believe that sometimes we can be reluctant to obey certain instructions because they may seem too easy. On the other hand, when asked to do something difficult, we believe it and do it. We simply lack the faith to believe that something seemingly easy can resolve a difficult situation. We can carry out a difficult command, yet not believe in a simple one. When we are told that to be made whole we only need to have hands laid on us, we think it is charlatanism. Having faith implies a willingness to die to ourselves and to trust in the power of God. As the Israelites were about to enter the Promised Land, the Lord's instruction for bringing down the walls of Jericho—the first city to be conquered—was to march around it for seven days. The enemy army probably laughed at that, but by the end of the seventh time on the seventh day, the walls came tumbling down!

David defeated Goliath with a single stone because he had faith. A woman with an issue of blood was healed just by touching Jesus' garment. Gideon conquered the Midianites with trumpets and torches, singing and shouting, "For the Lord and for Gideon." The simplest instructions God gave were always the option for producing a miracle. Obedience to the Lord's instruction that we may believe to be too easy is the test of our faith.

Naaman wanted the prophet to exercise his authority over the leprosy, but not over him. To see mighty works in your life, you need to have the humility to obey the simplest instructions, even when they seem illogical. How do you do this? By becoming again like a child with a believing heart, choosing to live out your dreams with an intensive trust. It is easy to see miracles when we believe that they are possible. The Lord never offers difficult methods because he expects us to believe in what is simple and powerful. Our Father gave us minds with which to think and hearts with which to believe. The miracle will be near when you believe that it is simple to receive.

God specializes in the impossible, not in the difficult.[1] For anyone willing to believe, ask, and obey, anything is possible! Besides, why would anyone want to complicate what he has made easy? We receive salvation and eternal life by simply accepting Jesus as our Lord and Savior. However, it is hard for some of us to believe that and arrogantly think that it is through our works that we are saved. Believing in God's love and mercy is all it takes to change our manner of living and thinking.

> *The Lord never offers difficult methods because he expects us to believe in what is simple and powerful.*

Option Number Three

When Moses was finally able to convince Pharaoh to let the Israelites go, everything seemed well enough. Of course, we all know that it was not exactly Moses who caused this, but rather the dreadful plagues sent by God over Egypt that finally bent the Pharaoh's will. We also know that once he got over the loss of his firstborn, Pharaoh's heart was filled with anger and sent his army in pursuit of those he himself had released. This led to millions of people at a crossroads, the first of many they would need to overcome in their long journey.

Moses was at the front when they arrived at the Red Sea. It

---

1 Jeremiah 32:27

would have been a good opportunity to take a breather and make some decisions, but there was no time to sit down and take in the sea breeze. Word spread like wildfire that the Egyptian army was in hot pursuit, drawing closer by the minute, and it certainly was not to wish them a safe journey. They were coming with swords unsheathed, prepared to chop off heads. So there they were, trapped, minutes away from a bloodbath. Some of the Israelite men could have been armed, ready to give battle, but as former slaves against a professional army, the odds were certainly against them.

I can almost picture Moses facing the sea, then looking back at the approaching army with an expression of "Okay, Lord! Now what?" on his face. It seemed that he only had two options: one, ask more than two million people to swim to the other side; or two, look for whatever weapons were available to face off the enemy. But instead he cried out to God, who gave him option number three: raise his hand and command the sea to open so they could march across.[2] Either of the first two options would have led to certain death. The third one, which the Lord gave him, was the simplest to execute, but also the most challenging to believe.

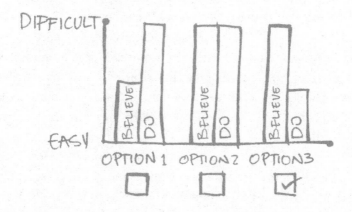

---

2 Exodus 14:15–16

If you think you have the strength for what is difficult, then show your faith to obey a simple instruction. The Lord says to you, "Give me that impossible situation in your life, for there is nothing too difficult for me." Sometimes you prefer the more difficult solution because you think that by choosing the simple one you will look foolish. Also, you may be wanting to receive acknowledgment of your own effort and abilities, when you should just allow God to work so that he gets the glory. When facing situations in life, you might have to resort to one of three options: two will probably be in your own strength and the third one will consist of believing and obeying God. It sounds easy because it is. However, it will require your faith to accomplish the impossible.

Believe, believe, believe! Don't ever grow tired of believing, because God is on our side. He can do anything and everything when we yield and obey what he asks of us. Have faith that he will prosper you, that he will heal you, and that he will restore your family. Take risks! Do not look at the circumstances that might seem difficult, but listen to his voice that says, "It's easy, because nothing is impossible for those who believe in me." Do not allow your feelings to lead you. Your Father has made you a partaker of his heavenly nature to use the power of your faith.

Allow yourself to be taken into a new level of obedience. Leave aside Naaman's mind-set that says it is unreasonable to think that something so simple as dipping in a river will heal that terrible illness. Always choose the better option, which is blind faith in the Lord, and obey his instructions, even when they may seem simple and effortless.

Before every situation we face, we must cry out like Moses and say, "Lord, I know there are other solutions I don't know about. But please, tell me what I should do, and I promise to obey." The Bible promises that if we call on the Lord, he will show us options we do not even think about.[3] If the answer is that it is no longer time for "calling out," but rather for action, then do not worry because you will know exactly what you need to do. Keep in mind that back then, there was no precedent for the parting of a sea. So, do not expect God to solve your situation by giving you the same instruction as before, since he can provide a brand-new formula to resolve any situation.

In Moses' case, which would have been easier? Swim across the sea, or lift his hands and trust? Of course, it was raising his hand, but which of the two options was more difficult to believe? Again, lifting his hands. We can see in this that God's solutions are often easy to carry out, but difficult to believe. We need faith to overcome our reasoning process and to start believing that everything really is possible, no matter how simple or ridiculous it might seem.

In life we all need to prepare ourselves, including in our formal education. Nevertheless, don't ever expect your reasoning to take the place of your faith. If your situation is complicated, then it is time to simplify it through faith, believing that the impossible can and will happen.

The story of the woman with the issue of blood teaches us that to have faith we first need to be willing to hear. It was not until she heard about Jesus that she sought him out to be healed. In this case as well there was no known precedence that by simply touching Jesus' clothes one could be made whole, but that was not on her mind. Instead, tired of having tried every option available, she chose to exercise faith in the impossible. Listen to the Word of the Lord, especially what stirs your faith, because it is the only way to move forward. For twelve years this woman had already gone through the difficult ordeal of trying to find healing. Her only

---

3 Jeremiah 33:3

option now was the easy one: touching the hem of Jesus' garment. Of course, that required faith.

It is not always easy to believe, but this woman did and was healed.[4] Perhaps you might find that the solution to your problem has been right in front of your eyes, but you could not see it because it was so simple that you could not believe it! Jesus never complicates things. To receive your blessing, you just need to believe that no matter how simple or ridiculous it might seem, it will be effective.

Another example is the father who approached Jesus, asking for his son who was tortured by an evil spirit to be delivered, as well as to help him believe.[5] Declare right now, where you are, that no demon, no addiction, and no sin whatsoever will ever place your children in bondage. If you believe this is impossible, then you need to increase your level of faith by drawing close to the Lord, reading his Word and making it a priority to seek him in prayer. Once you are born again into this life of faith, I guarantee that you will be instilled with strength to accomplish all that you desire. You will become a specialist in what I call "holy stubbornness," which means insisting on your miracle until you get it.

If we read the backdrop of this story, we see that the father of this young boy afflicted by supernatural forces first went to Jesus' disciples, but they were unable to do anything. So he then went to the Lord.[6] And Jesus replied, "There is nothing I cannot do if you only believe that by following my simple instructions you will receive what you desire." This father approached Jesus wondering if there was "something" he could do, but Jesus can do "everything"! Don't just have faith for something but for everything. Don't just believe for your healing but also for your prosperity and the restoration of your family and total joy in your generations to follow!

---

4 Mark 5:24–29
5 Mark 9:21–24
6 Mark 9:17-18

That is the level of faith God wants to see in us. So we see two cases here: one is the woman who said, "If I can just touch his robe . . ." and the other is the father who said, "If you can . . ." The woman confessed that it was possible, while the father confessed that he hoped it was possible. Do you see the difference? It is up to you for God to do something. He wants to do it, but you are the one who needs to release the blessing by believing and confessing that even the impossible will be done!

In life, your parents might fail you, a brother or sister might fail you, your husband might fail you, your business partner might fail you, your friends or colleagues might fail you, but Jesus never fails! Forget about your failures, because God can do anything if you show that you believe him with all your heart. Never give up! Be an overcomer and tell the Lord, "I know that you can do mighty wonders in my life." Never doubt it for a second. He will always provide the best option!

19 FOLLOW THEIR FAITH

Learning from others means obeying and humbly recognizing that someone else knows more.

As a pastor, I am continually praying and preparing myself. I am always jotting down ideas that the Lord wants me to share, although my preparation does not begin by scanning two or three books, but in my continual attention to hearing his voice. The message our Lord wants to convey can only be found in his presence.

There is no doubt that you need to know who is worth hearing, following, and obeying. There are people whose faith serves as an example,[1] which also

---

1 Hebrews 13:7–8

implies a great responsibility. The Word of God shared by those whom you wish to follow and obey is much like a small seed designed to produce much fruit if it is cared for and watered. It would be impossible to speak about faith without seeing the results. The Lord's message is not just nice wrapping paper on an empty box, but a priceless gift filled with content that reflects his works. Follow and be like those whose teachings have been proven with visible results. It is in this case that your trust should be based on what you can see and affirm, otherwise they will just be empty words.

You can trust in the Lord wholeheartedly since the results of his Word have been visible since the beginning of time. When the Scriptures talk to us about living by faith and not by sight, the reference is to our future, and not to the lack of reliable precedents, because if anyone could ever say, "The evidence is there," it is God! Don't you think that everything that was created—the universe, your life and all of existence—is more than enough proof of his power? Therefore, why not give him the benefit of your faith as well as your obedience?

Follow and be like those whose teachings have been proven with visible results.

In my experience I can truly say that it is not easy to obey, since that requires humility on our part to recognize that there is always someone who knows more and is in better control of a situation. Relinquishing control is never easy. I have seen many people unable to do just that, perhaps not out of arrogance, but simply because they are used to making their own decisions and getting ahead the best they can. This is why I love seeing Christian businessmen who have become successful due to their faith, which demonstrates a shift in their character by having yielded control to the One who can do all things.

These individuals have chosen to exercise two types of obedience: a vertical one and a horizontal one. Allow me to explain. I usually tell my team that they have the most obedient boss possible because I always surround myself with the best professionals in their fields. Consequently, I listen to them and follow their advice because they are specialists. I am fully convinced that my obedience—first to God, and secondly to my team's great ideas—is the secret to the level of success Casa de Dios has reached. I am like a "talent scout" led by the expert mind of my Father. So I also practice these two types of obedience: the vertical one, listening to and submitting to my supreme authority, and the horizontal one, hearing and heeding the advice of my peers, my colleagues, who are not necessarily my authority, but do have expert knowledge and experience in their respective fields. We have been so creative with our entrepreneurial innovations that we have been able to design and build our own facilities, even producing our own concrete to reduce costs. These are ideas that were birthed with God, who is faithful to provide the necessary people and resources to carry them out.

I can assure you that there is no wiser advice than the one God provides, so we need to follow his instructions even when we find ourselves in the middle of trying situations that we may not understand, such as fraud or embezzlement, a rebellious child, a deceptive partner, or separation in a marriage. I always begin ministry projects according to the instructions I get from the Lord and I am fully convinced that they will work because I get them straight from him. I just focus on putting the best team together to execute those plans. Aligning myself to God's heart is my best guarantee for success. As my children like to say, "It's a win-win situation!"

No one tries to be like someone they do not admire, and I greatly admire my Father, which is why I imitate him. It seems to be the same thing with children under the age of twelve, when they want to be like their parents who are their role models! The expression "actions speak louder than words" has a lot of truth. What better example than the Creator of the universe? This is where the issue of faith becomes a priceless chain, when we see things beyond our circumstances, and we seek to share with others through our results. The works we do out of obedience serve to inspire others to also believe and that is what finally prompts the faith that can move mountains, becomes contagious, and works for the benefit of thousands!

It is now no longer a matter of having faith, but of your life becoming a living testimony for others to follow. Look for leaders you can admire and learn from. Imitate their faith and you also will become a leader others can admire and want to imitate as well. A lady who has been a faithful member of our church for the last twenty years walked up to me one day and gave me a such a warm, emotional hug that it broke me into tears. We had never had the opportunity to talk before, although I would always see her attentively listening in our services, in our conferences, and in every activity we would come up with.

On that particular day, she said, "Pastor, I want to thank you with all my heart for everything you have taught me. My friends know that I came to this church with no family, no finances, no friends, with nothing whatsoever. But throughout these years I have followed your instructions to the letter and I have not one single regret. If you say that it is time to call a person to ask forgiveness, I do it. If you say that it is time to be generous to others, I do it without hesitation and find someone to help. If you say that we need to get better equipped and prepared, I sign up for a class. If you challenge us to go out in the streets and pray for our nation, I join one of the groups. Even if someone says that I am too old for something, I insist anyway and do it. I have reaped such a bountiful harvest, Pastor. Every time I am asked how have I gotten ahead, I always say that obedience is the key." She had unraveled perfectly the mystery of faith!

Be like those priceless examples of individuals who demonstrate their conviction and fortitude in the Lord! I have never imitated those that cave in under the adversity of an economic crisis or an emotional disappointment. Of course, I am also human, and we all face difficult challenges. However, I have made up my mind to always meet them head-on with a positive attitude, full of faith. The Bible bears witness that men and women of God lived in strenuous contexts and the one common denominator they had was faith! They encountered that divine support when they believed. And we today can also be like them by doing the same!

A Blessing for Many

Your projects will have a strong chance of coming to pass when you align them to God's plans, seeking to bless others in the process. Even a healing miracle, which is personal, has a multiplying effect, because that restored life will become a powerful testimony of the love of God. In addition, the individual who received the miracle will also have a new heart willing to help others. That is the power of God working through our lives!

There is no value to a self-centered faith, seeking your own personal benefit. It is true that our Father wants to bless us, since he created us in love and that is our foundation. Still, living by faith is not a matter of selfishly seeking our personal desires because in the end that becomes about me and only me. That cannot happen! Who is the center of the universe? If you believe it is you, then you need to review the foundation of our faith. We were created to have, by our own will and choice, an intimate relationship with God. This is our reason for being, and maintaining it will result in a fulfilling life, together with everything it implies.

Our first focus needs to be on perfecting our relationship with

God. By focusing on the person of God, we'll be more willing to receive what that person has to offer. That is the meaning behind the following advice Jesus gave us: "Seek the kingdom of God above all else, and live righteously, and he will give you everything you need." Of course, God wants us to prosper in all things and to have every need supplied, but it will only be as a direct result of our intimacy with him.

I love my wife. I believe in her; I seek her; I spoil her; I give her my attention and listen to her advice. I obey her instructions, because I respect her opinion. I love the time we spend together and I enjoy everything she gives me as a logical outgrowth of our intimate relationship. Obviously, that is totally different than seeking her only for self-centered purposes, for what she can provide for me. God expects you to seek and love him, beyond anything he can ever give you!

Living by and for Faith

To obey our Father's instructions, we need to follow his instruction manual—his Word—which reveals everything we need to know and do. The gospel is revealed by faith and for faith. In other words, we receive it by faith, and it becomes a testimony of the faith by which to live.[2] Our conviction of the love of God must be fully believed and demonstrated, otherwise, it will just be an abstract concept, void of impact. Faith, however, is tangible and effective, designed to totally transform our circumstances if we become as children who love, admire, believe, and obey him.

God expects you to seek and love him, beyond anything he can ever give you!

---

2 Romans 1:17

When I taught my children how to swim, the first thing I did was dive into the water cannonball style. That simple action broke every uncertainty they were feeling and opened the door to all the fun they could have. Seeing me with that attitude of complete control of the situation gave them confidence, to the point that I almost did not make it back to the edge because they wanted to jump in right on top of me. The same thing would not have happened had I entered cautiously into the pool, step by step, little by little, allowing the water to make me shudder in shock. That is what a life of faith is like, total immersion into a new environment that requires audacity and blind obedience, coupled with the conviction that the instructions we receive come from the One who truly knows what he is doing and has our best interests in mind.

In Hebrew, the word *faith* means faithfulness. Having faith in God means expressing our faithfulness, which in turn makes us just, or in other words, without reproach. No wonder the Word of God mentions more than once that the just shall live by faith.[3] Why is it so important to be totally convinced that living by faith makes us just? Because accepting it implies humility, an acknowledgment that it is not our works, but our attitude of complete trust that grants us salvation and abundant life. We need to be faithful to God and never hesitate in obeying his simple instructions. Everything in his written Word applies to our lives; it is not an archaic, irrelevant book. Take hold of his promises! If the Bible says that those who honor their parents can expect a long life and a wonderful future, embrace that promise and obey it.[4] If it says that life, riches, and honor are the reward for being humble and fearing the Lord, then that is how it is![5] These instructions seem clear and simple, right?

---

3 Habakkuk 2:4
4 Ephesians 6:2–3
5 Proverbs 22:4

Of course, applying them is not so easy, and that is why living by faith requires strength and resolve. It is a life designed for those who want to see great results!

The second meaning of the word *faith* is firmness. Those who believe will remain firm and stable, without wavering. Another word for this is *steady*, just like a steady camera used for taping television programs. These cameras can follow an action scene and record an image with stability, no matter how much movement it might include. These are the cameras we normally use in our Nights of Glory healing crusades, where people leap, run, and dance after receiving their healing. The person who has faith will remain firm and steady, regardless of the force of the storm, because his or her eyes are set firmly on the Lord. That steadiness is what Peter lacked when he walked on water, because in the middle of the storm, he took his eyes off the Lord. Don't ever let your *steady* fail you in your difficult situations.

Trust in the Lord beyond your abilities. All the people in the Bible speak to us about having achieved exploits by faith and for faith. To raise up a nation, Abraham had to leave his homeland in obedience to God's instruction. David became king by following the instructions God gave him. Every person of faith went to God to receive his instructions and counsel. God was their only source and refuge.

For God's work to be fulfilled depends on our trust and obedience. He does not like it when we fall back. On the contrary he wants to see us grow! No matter what situation you might face, always believe because that will fill you with life, courage, and energy to keep on fighting. Faith helps us think better, it uplifts and keeps us from getting too comfortable. When we stop believing, we are more prone to feeling sad, angry, and frustrated. God needs our steadfastness because faith is the substance of things hoped for.[6] For example, a marriage needs more faith than it does weekend seminars. Overcoming circumstances in life requires more faith than knowledge, and incurable sicknesses require more faith than science.

Abraham, Joshua, Isaac, Noah, Sarah, Jacob, Esau, Moses, David, Jephthah, Samson, Barak, and all the other prophets spoken about in the Bible are heroes. If we gathered them in a conference, or invited them to a lecture at a university, they would unanimously say that they had nothing going for them except their trust in the Lord. He was the one who raised them up to be conquerors, the same way he is raising up you and me.

---

6 Hebrews 10:35–39

20 HOW SHALL THIS BE?

Faith leads us to believe in what we are to do, and the Father shows us how we are to do it.

There is a young lady who risked her life by accepting being an instrument of the Lord. Her name is Mary, the mother of Jesus, who, upon receiving news that she was pregnant, shows us that to find God's favor we first need to be humble.[1] It is only God's grace that allows us to discover our purpose and what he wants to do in our lives, just as he did with Mary. Remember that God rejects the proud, but gives grace to the humble.[2]

---

1 Luke 1:30–36
2 James 4:6

Ego should have no place in our hearts, because it can easily ruin every project that we can conceive and realize.

When I decided that I wanted to be a preacher, I laid out an entire plan. However, the Holy Spirit changed it and said, "I don't want you to envision yourself preaching to multitudes, but I do want you to envision the multitudes walking in my presence." At that moment I kneeled, and on that granite floor I told the Lord, "Just like those infinite dots in this granite stone, so shall be the number of people that will come to you, oh Lord." That shift in my life, together with a new way of seeing the ministry, brought a dramatic change that materialized into what is now Casa de Dios. Never minimize those small changes that can result in much greater results.

"How will this be?" Mary asked. There was no way to understand how she could have a child without having known a man in a physical way. It was a valid doubt, especially looking at her situation. However, the attitude she displayed by asking was not arrogant. It is quite difficult to do something if our mind says that it cannot be done. However, the moment you say, "It can be done," the Lord starts giving ideas on how to do it. It is almost like turning on our minds and placing new ideas in them. This is how faith works: first we believe, and then we find the way to do it. It is the opposite of how human reasoning works: first we analyze if it's possible, and then believe in it.

Mary first received the news of what would happen, and then the explanation of how it would happen. The answer she received was quite simple. There was hardly anything she had to do, except boldly make herself available to what was to take place. That is just how the Lord works; his instructions for our lives are always simple.

It Is That Easy

If we look through the Scriptures, we can see that God seldom asks his people to do something difficult. Quite the opposite: his works often appear to be easy, bordering on ridiculous. The miracle of Jesus' conception was to simply happen with a visit by the Holy Spirit. Yes, just that easy! All of creation is a product of his words, that's it. Moses parted the Red Sea by simply raising his hands and believing. And God can do mighty works through those who genuinely believe him. I would rather believe that the sea can part in two than to call God a liar.

We can list many other events such as these in the Bible. For Naaman to be healed of leprosy, he simply had to dip seven times in the river. A blind man simply had to wash himself in a pool. The lepers simply had to go and present themselves to the priest. God's instructions are so simple, they challenge us to believe, even risking ridicule; but faith really is for superior minds.

Sometimes we are ridiculed for believing in miracles, but we are actually quite intelligent if we submit and obey the most intelligent being of all, the King who can do all things, meticulously planning every step for us to obey. Use your God-given intelligence to obey him!

God's instructions are so simple, they challenge us to believe, even risking ridicule; but faith really is for superior minds.

In another passage of the Scriptures we see Zechariah, husband to Elizabeth who was also Mary's cousin, receiving an angelic visitation bearing news that, despite the couple's old age and barrenness, they would conceive a boy.[3] His name would be John, and he would be great before the Lord. He would prepare the hearts of the people for the Lord's coming. However, in Zechariah's case, the unbelief he displayed was all too evident. He was after all a priest, experienced in the things of the Lord, who knew God's will. And still he asks how could it ever happen given the circumstances he was in? That

---

3 Luke 1:5–20

simple doubt literally left him speechless; he was mute until the angel's words came to pass. <u>Our mouths should always declare in faith the fulfillment of God's promises.</u>

So Mary was called blessed and Zechariah was left mute. What is keeping you from using your faith? Is it the fear of making a mistake? If you do make it, start over again! Do not let the doubts of those around you, nor the fear of looking like a fool, limit you. You must act according to the faith you claim to have, because Zechariah ministered wonderfully, but he totally failed when it was time to display his faith.

Abraham was another example of someone who received the promise of a vast number of descendants. In all three cases the message was received, but each one received it in a different way. One was left mute, another became the father of a people, and the last became the mother of our Savior. Since our faith will always determine what we receive, stop doubting!

Faith to Endure, Faith to Break Out

The case of Zechariah deserves further study and assessment. Both he and his wife were servants who were righteous and blameless before the Lord. One might think that a couple like that would never have to suffer any afflictions; however, they were unable to have children. Now another question emerges, "If they served the Lord and were good people, why couldn't they enjoy the blessing of having children?" Nonetheless, when faced with a situation like this, one must have the faith to know that God will surely perform the miracle at the right time.

A friend called me once because his nephew had suffered a stroke and was in the intensive care unit. I arrived as quickly as I could, but was not permitted to see him. So I joined the family in the waiting room, encouraging them and sharing with them about faith. Needless to say, they were devastated and quite saddened. I don't believe they took my words well by the defensive posture they took. "Do you really think we don't have faith after everything we've been through?" Right then the Holy Spirit whispered to me, "They have the faith to endure problems, but not the faith to break out of them." So I returned the following day. The family was not there but I was allowed to see the nephew in the ICU. In that dark, silent room I walked up to his bed, leaned in, and whispered into his ear the words the Holy Spirit told me, "Hi there, I am your friend Cash. You are not going to die, but I came to raise you up in the name of Jesus." A few hours later he awoke and began his recovery process.

We already know that we have a measure of faith,[4] but how are you using yours? To endure pain, or to confront and overcome it? It is much like the target-shooting game at the fairs; you must aim at what you want to hit, according to the prize you want to win. That is what faith is like. You choose what you want to aim at, whether it is to withstand a problem, emerge from it, or even to reach for a new dream. Or you could liken it to a moving car in which you have not decided yet on the route to your destination. Faith will always go where you guide it. Where do you want it to go?

DREAM

EMERGE

ENDURE

---

4 Romans 12:3

If you have had the faith to endure a problem, aim it next at the solution! Achieve what you have always dreamed of. Do not get comfortable with suffering. Of course, when you go through a difficult situation you attract people who love you and want to comfort you, but being the victim is not the best way to draw attention. It only works for a brief time; sooner or later people will tire of it. Challenge yourself! Don't be a conformist, and do not criticize those who do get ahead in faith and achieve their goals. To become the man or woman you were designed to be, look to heal your wounds and rid yourself of all resentment!

Good Ground

I know of people who hear the Word of God a lot, but they are not good ground in which it can be planted. Why? Because they never apply it in their daily lives. God's promises are powerful and reliable, but without the right faith and willing obedience, they fall prey to your problems and inhibitions! Think about my situation. Had I settled with just hearing the Word of God, but never applying it and seeking my promises in it, there would be no Casa de Dios today, nor could we have blessed so many people. If you look at me, I am short, from a small country, and I certainly do not have the typical preacher's voice. I could have been a businessman, but certainly not a pastor. So the message here is: Don't conform! Rise up, trust wholeheartedly in God's Word, and strive to get ahead!

In the case of Elizabeth and Zechariah, who were blameless, virtuous, and just, we see that they had not received their miracle of a child, because it still was not the Lord's time. However, God would give them one, since his plan consisted of making them the proud parents of the man who would prepare the way for the Messiah! The timing had to be flawless because Elizabeth couldn't become pregnant before the exact time to tell Mary that she would be the mother of Jesus. They did not understand it at the time, but God knew exactly what he was doing. It was almost like God telling them, "I can't give you your own child yet, because it's still not time for mine to be born."

Never doubt that everything in life has its right time, and one person's timing can determine another's. Therefore we must not worry or be anxious, but simply trust. Parents, teach this to your children. When young singles become restless in their desire to find their mate, it's best to tell them, "Be patient, your time will come." The angel assured Zechariah and Elizabeth that their child, John, would be great before the Lord. You never have to fear greatness when it comes from the hand of the Lord. Instead, make the most of it in order to bless those around you!

Remember what we mentioned about the faith chain in which one receives and shares with others? I say this to clear up the view of some who claim that humility consists of never attempting great works for God. It is God himself who commands us to extend ourselves to expand his kingdom. It would be the equivalent of telling our soccer team to avoid at all costs scoring as many goals as possible. If they are winning 5-0 and they lower their guard, the other team could tie or even beat them. Break out of your comfort zone and stop seeking the security that failure can provide. Push on to success, because God wants to raise you up!

Virtue and Faith

The passage of Scripture about Zechariah teaches us to see the difference between virtue and faith. We now know that he was a man who was righteous and blameless but was left mute for not believing the angel's message. It is possible to be just and irreproachable and still lack the necessary faith to receive your miracles. These

205

are two areas in which we need to be obedient in order to see our promises fulfilled.

Moral problems are fixed by being just and without reproach, but faith problems can only be fixed with faith! Zechariah was a priest and his job description was intricately connected to speech, yet he was left mute. He was no longer able to carry out his priestly duties throughout that entire time. Talk about a severe lesson in faith!

So will God perform miracles if I am just and without reproach? No. He will only perform them if you show your trust in his love and mercies. Faith can never take the place of a virtuous, grace-filled life, just like being just and virtuous can never take the place of faith! True, we need to strive to be more just, but without faith we will never receive the miracles we need. Your personality could become stunted because of a lack of faith, just like Zechariah's speech. Do you really want to risk losing your ability to work because of a lack of faith?

There is a lady I know who is the most virtuous woman one could imagine. She is a Christian, attends church regularly, has a consistent prayer life, and does much charity work. She has an irreproachable life, but she cannot explain why the Lord has not healed her knees. Could it be a lack of faith? She lives with depression, feeling alone and rejected. She wrestles with forgiving those who have hurt her, including her ex-husband. Her prayers are always, "God, I'm tired. I don't want to live anymore. Please take me to be with you." Actually, I think she could make better use of her faith.

In situations like this we see that for some people it is not so simple to live by faith, because it means having joy and peace in any circumstance. No person who truly trusts in the Lord can live with bitterness. The instruction is simple; but obeying it might not be, especially when it goes against our lifestyle. This kind old lady has achieved a victim mentality and to a certain degree, she is manipulative with her ailment. Her situation indeed is sensitive, and after much prayer and counseling, I have concluded that only God can treat and heal her heart so that her body can also be healed. What she urgently needs is a change of attitude for the miracle to take place. Otherwise, God won't be able to complete his work no matter how much he longs to see her whole.

Help yourself, and allow yourself to be helped. It seems ironic at times to be so worried about the future when we are not even sure we will be around to see it. We do not know with certainty that tomorrow, or the day after tomorrow, we will be opening our eyes, so we need to use our faith today! Ask for your miracle, obey the Lord, and strive hard to reach it! Do not allow your wounds and hurts from the past to hinder your ability to believe today. That was Zechariah's problem: he was blocked by his past, by a barren season of his life. He could not trust for a child, even with God's promise. Trust, and do not be discouraged!

The Handmaiden of the Lord

As we have seen, Mary exhibited more faith than Zechariah, despite being practically a child, thereby justifying the question of how she could have a child if she was still a virgin. She believed and confessed that she was willing to do God's will, even if that obedience meant terrible consequences, including death, if Joseph her fiancé rejected her for being pregnant. Do you see the difference?

Zechariah was aware of the precedent of Abraham and Sarah who also were unable to conceive a child according to this world's norm. Despite his knowledge of the Word, and even being a priest, he still doubted the word from the Lord. Do you want to end up mute with unfulfilled abilities and potential for not believing in the Lord's ability to perform something? Or do you want to be filled with the promise of God and be blessed for having embraced his will, even if it means new challenges in life?

Believing is a source of blessing, in reality it makes us twice as happy.[5] We are all blessed with having the Lord, but when we start believing him, we will receive a double portion of glory, in addition to the fulfillment of what he says in our life! Mary believed and confessed what Zechariah could not because he was left mute. She praised the name of the Lord and honored him with her obedience in this beautiful confession: "Oh, how my soul praises the Lord. How my spirit rejoices in God my Savior! For he took notice of his lowly servant girl, and from now on all generations will call me blessed. For the Mighty One is holy, and he has done great things for me."

Are you willing to say the same, even if that promise in your life might put you at risk? Seek to be blessed and not silent as a mute. Every time we refuse to believe God, something gets stunted in our lives. If you just believe, you will be able to sing a psalm, but if you don't, your heart and mind will weaken.

Faith to Share

We should also remember that sharing with those who cannot pay us back is another way to be blessed. By doing so we clearly demonstrate we have the faith that God is the one who rewards us.[6] In the end, using our faith to get ahead and even more so, using it to share with others in need, will undoubtedly ensure a double blessing!

Seek to be just and blameless before the Lord, but also strive to be obedient and have the faith to excel and share that blessing with others. Be blessed for believing and not weakened because of your doubt. When I discovered this revelation, I could not help but cry out, "Thank you, Father, for always fulfilling your promises when I obey!"

---

5 Luke 1:45–49
6 Luke 14:12–14

At Casa de Dios, the mission has always been to bring greater multitudes to the feet of Jesus. Building a larger sanctuary was just one of the answers to help us fulfill this, since multiplication and growth led us to prepare a place to receive those who are won for his kingdom.[7] We generally ask the Lord to go before us wherever we go. When it comes to challenges of faith, however, we are the ones who need to step out, confident that he will be with us.

I see this also in the people of Israel whom God delivered out of Egypt. Later, however, it was the people who had to arm themselves in faith and courage to conquer the Promised Land, since God clearly told Joshua, "Wherever you go, I will go with you." God expects your initiative and faith to advance toward the conquests he has already assigned to you. So now the question is: When are you going to make up your mind to walk in faith and go to the place he wants you to be? We see again this vertical and horizontal obedience in action. In fact, we could say that, to a certain degree, God also "obeys you." In other words, he is patient and waits to follow you when you choose to move forward. If you advance, he advances. Jesus said, "I will be with you until the ends of the Earth." Don't make him wait any longer!

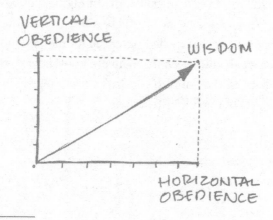

---

7 Isaiah 54:2–3

Stop asking so many questions and seek the courage to start and grow the projects God has placed in your heart. He will go wherever you go. Embrace new challenges! As children of God we were created for challenges, to move forward and make a difference. Even in their old age, Abraham and Moses left their comfort zones, so there is no excuse for you, not your age nor your finances, because we are all called to be leaders who look for growth and multiplication!

Of course, there will also be tense moments. We had our own when building our new sanctuary. There was a time during a trip when I was weeping before the Lord and he reminded me that he was the one who had entrusted me with that project, because he needed a man of courage for the next level of leadership he would pour out. I thanked him and renewed my faith again. On another occasion, someone commented, "Have you seen how many large, empty church facilities there are today?" I went before the Lord and he told me, "They are right, but there are also a number of large sanctuaries that cannot contain the number of people that attend there. What kind of ministry will yours be? Who is teaching you to talk that way? You certainly did not get it from me! I have never taught you to talk in such a discouraging, pessimistic way." Needless to say, that very moment, I began to declare the victory as God reminded me that he had never taught me to doubt but only to believe! Speak faith, even if you do not know how it will happen. Let your trust in the Lord fill you with the courage to always obey his simple, yet powerful, instructions!

VII

THE HUNDRED-FOOT JOURNEY

"I'm not a chef, I'm a cook," young Hassan Kadam told the immigration office interrogating him to allow him entry to France. He was traveling with his father, his elder brother, his teenage sister, and two more siblings: a boy and a girl. A large family that loved cooking! Everyone was piled into an old, run-down station wagon.

They lived in England where "veggies have no life," having moved there from Mumbai, India—their homeland—following the tragic death of their mother at the hands of an angry mob that burned down her restaurant. Talk about a journey! She had been the heart of the family, the heiress of their culinary cuisine, and the one responsible for passing this priceless gift on to her children.

This is the leading family of the film *The Hundred-Foot Journey*, a wonderful choice for those who enjoy great cuisine and a star performance by Helen Mirren. If you still are not interested, let me just say that it's a wonderful production centered around optimism, tenacity, and patience, with a backdrop of beautiful, luminous landscapes in the south of France.

As it turns out, they almost perish when the brakes give out in the French countryside. That is how they meet Marguerite, a young beautiful girl who helps them tow their vehicle and offers them a bountiful feast of vegetables, cheeses, and freshly baked bread in her home. Of course, she falls in love with Hassan, but this love story is also about the passion of culinary history, which brings them together.

The young lady is *sous chef* at *Le Saule Pleureur*, a restaurant owned by Mallory, who is not too pleased with the Kadam family staying in a villa and opening a nearby Hindu restaurant right in front of hers! This short distance gives the movie its name as it was all that separated these two restaurants that quickly gave way to rivalry.

Patience? Yes! Faith? Much! Hassan's composure in every predicament can be likened to that of a monk, always serene and with a good disposition, even when Madame Mallory throws away his delicious pigeon dish with truffle sauce and embarrasses him in front of the staff of her well-equipped kitchen in her elegant restaurant. Patiently he helps his father and brothers set up their restaurant while reading a book on French cuisine given to him by Marguerite. On a beautiful day, by the edge of a river, with the sun glistening, Hassan reflects, "When I read it, all I hear is her voice."

Ever so patiently, he begins experimenting with the recipes, cooking them and even improving them with his own personal seasoning. You cannot help but fancy the omelet he prepares, which even earns him the respect of the lady who had once humiliated him! One takes pleasure in his delicate way of mixing ingredients with so much grace and finesse as he enjoys every moment. That dedication not only made him famous, but also gave Madame Mallory's restaurant a second star. His faith—seasoned with the patience to enhance his good taste—as well as his passion and abilities in the kitchen opened new doors for him.

Our journey of ten, a thousand, or ten thousand steps toward the blessings God has for us is going to require faith seasoned with patience to flavor the life God has destined for us to enjoy.

21 THE BEST SEASONING

> If God has not brought you out of the pit, it is because the situation outside is even worse. Trust in his wisdom and love for you. He will bring you out when the time is right.

There she was! The most beautiful woman he had seen in his seventeen years of life. Graceful in her every movement, she walked into the living room with a couple of her friends. Her blissful gaze and radiant smile seemed to light up the place. This may sound sentimental, but that was exactly how he felt. If that has never happened to you, I guarantee that once it does, you will never be the same.

How could you not fall in love at first sight? How could you not but smile and walk up to her to say hi? That was what he did, with shaking knees, although in the back of his mind he didn't think he had a prayer of a shot. Oddly enough, she turned around and smiled when he said, or better yet, whispered, "Hello." That get-together at his cousin's house became a whole lot easier once it turned into a conversation between two young people who liked each other. Just like that, as natural as their hormones getting the best of them, a love story was born, both unique and like millions of other colorful and diverse relationships throughout the world. Ah yes, true love! Indescribable and elemental, impetuous and desperate. What is your love story?

That's right! Can there be a person more impatient than the one waiting to meet the love of his or her life? Perhaps a soon-to-be mother thirty-seven weeks into her pregnancy, or first-time parents at the pediatrician with their child burning with fever might be more impatient. But a lovesick individual waiting to meet their beloved borders on cruel and inhuman punishment.

This reminds me of the unique story of Jacob, one of Abraham's grandsons and Esau's brother. The genealogy of the people of Israel can be traced back to Jacob, though as it turned out, because of family quarrels, Jacob had to flee his home to the region where his uncle Laban lived. That is where he met his cousin Rachel for the first time and they fell so madly in love that he wasted no time in asking for her hand in marriage. However, there was a condition that had to be met for him to enter nuptials with her, which turned out to be seven years of labor for her father! After those seven years, Laban fulfilled his part of the agreement and gave Jacob his daughter. However, it was not Rachel, but Leah, her older sister. Can you imagine the shock? Laban's excuse was that he could not give his youngest daughter away if the eldest was still single. So they worked out a second deal. Jacob could have Rachel also in exchange for working another seven years for him.[1]

---

1 Genesis 29:16–30

This certainly sounds extreme and even abusive, but those were the customs and the culture of that day. I cannot even begin to imagine Jacob's helplessness during the second set of seven years! But he did complete them out of his deep love for Rachel. (As an aside, some people think that Jacob did not receive Rachel until the fourteen years were up, however they were together after the first seven years.) This lovesick man was patient because he was convinced that the reward was worth it, and he worked hard to deserve her. Now that's the best kind of love!

Desperately Patient

Jacob knew that desperation would wear him out, as well as making the time seem to go by more slowly. How can feeling anxious help us? In nothing! It just constrains us and serves to boycott our plans. An anxious person cannot make good decisions, which greatly increases the risk of mistakes. Therefore the Word of God says that impatience exalts folly.[2] Because of impatience many young people throw away their dreams and projects by engaging in sex before marriage, having to take on responsibilities that they do not know how to manage yet, such as bringing children into the world when they are still children themselves. Indeed, anxiety, impatience, and hastiness get us into some of the worst predicaments. So how do we heal that anxiety?

With humility! That is exactly the attitude that is needed to live by faith, since it is vital to acknowledge that the answers are not in our hands but in God's! He will exalt us at the right time, because he lovingly cares for us.[3] But it is really hard to stay humble! We

---

2 Proverbs 14:29
3 1 Peter 5:6–7

need to be honest and recognize that it is "easier" to go through life with a lofty and arrogant attitude because even a hard appearance can serve as a safeguard against deceptions, though not from pain. Nevertheless, it is simply not the right attitude to have. Whoever thinks he is self-sufficient is digging a well to fall into. What need is there for that when it's such a good thing to know that we can live safely protected by the Lord?

What more can we desire if God clearly says to cast our cares upon him and trust in his wisdom and timing? I would rather be humble, protected by God's mighty hand, than to be arrogant, far away from him! There is no doubt whatsoever that it pays to be humble and get rid of all anxiety, which is a mental state characterized by restlessness, intense agitation, and extreme insecurity. Anyone might say that it is easier said than done, and indeed, it is hard to put aside all anxiety, especially if you are facing a desperate situation such as no food on the table or a debilitating sickness. Therefore, a deep relationship with God is the key to having peace in any situation. As a pastor, one of my job descriptions is to tend to God's sheep; in other words, to instill them with peace. But with tongue in cheek, I tell the Lord, "Some of these desperate people make me really desperate!"

If despite this we still harbor the arrogant attitude of trying to get ahead on our own, without God, and our steps lead us right into a pit of despair, it is never too late to call out for help. However, it is precisely in these situations that we need to be more patient than ever.[4] When I received the call from a software company to apply for a position to head an important project, I got excited because many of the candidates were well-known experts in their field. That excitement escalated when I heard that I had been selected for the position! During that same time I was deciding

---

4 Psalm 40:1–2; Psalm 119:25–28

about my calling to serve the Lord and I found myself at the pro-verbial crossroads.

If I took on the responsibility of the project, it would be much more difficult to dedicate myself to the Lord's work. One night, as I was talking about it with my wife, my head on her lap, she said, "Be patient. Don't decide out of desperation. If God called you to serve him, he will open a way and pull you out of wherever you might be working." Those words of wisdom put me at ease and greatly helped me to choose in faith. I thanked the company for the oppor-tunity and politely turned down the offer, because I knew that God had other plans for me.

He Is with You

When we are facing diverse challenges, it is all too easy to fall into despair and wonder how long we will be there. When I came before the Lord, asking him why it was so difficult to get out when we had been praying about it, he said, "You have to trust me. If you have fallen into a pit and I have not brought you out yet, it is because the situation outside is worse than the one in there." Wow! His reply took my breath away. Sure, we might think it is pretty bad in that pit, but if we insist on getting out before the right time, there are enemies waiting that might have a field day with us.

We need to be confident that the Lord will bring us out of the pit when it is safe to come out. This is why he asks us for the humility to be patient and realize that he knows what the outside is like and when it's the best time to come out. We may not know when that will be, but we can be sure that God is right there with us. Remain with him and make the most of that time by getting to know him better. Facing adversity, we are more willing to seek him because we are more sensitive and we long for consolation. There will be those who mistakenly say, "Well, God sent you this trial so you could meditate and seek him." This is not true because he would never purposely send us problems. These are simply circumstances we need to face in life or the consequences of poor decision-making. The truth is, though, that in those vulnerable moments we are most sensitive to hearing God's voice.

From experience I can safely say that the best remedy for anxiety and hopelessness is spending time with our Lord in praise and worship. The reason I am so sure of this is because it has happened to me. My daily quiet time with God is non-negotiable, but in difficult times I seek him even more, thankful that he is always watching over me. I also ask him for patience and to not allow anxiety to get the best of me. I cry out to him with Psalm 42:5: "Why am I discouraged? Why is my heart so sad? I will put my hope in God! I will praise him again—my Savior and my God!" A downcast soul will always be easy prey for catastrophe, and the cure for that anxiety is the Word of God. Listen to it, read it, meditate on it, and learn it so that it can become the foundation of your life at all times.

> *The cure for that anxiety is the Word of God. Listen to it, read it, meditate on it, and learn it so that it can become the foundation of your life at all times.*

If we learn how to wait, we will undoubtedly reap the benefits. We need to avoid rushing into things and wait under God's mighty hand; in due time he will raise us up. Of course that is not always easy, but that valuable time is essential to shaping our character, and if you pray in faith, I can assure you that you will triumphantly come out of that pit.

Do not allow hopelessness and affliction to control you. Worship the Lord with a humble heart, trusting in his wisdom, protection, and love. Learn to develop a life filled with so much confidence that almost nothing will ever drive you to despair. It is wonderful to hear that the righteous have not been forsaken, nor their seed begging for bread,[5] that is, until you have an empty refrigerator at home. Still, we need to understand that success and failure come in the same package and we need to learn to live through both situations. I encourage you to take a sheet of paper and jot down the things that make you feel most hopeless and desperate. Now fold the page in half, place it in an envelope, and save it. Sometime later when you come across that envelope, you will smile when you realize that whatever had caused your anxiety has been overcome.

One day I was sad over an ordeal I had to face with a person in our ministry. I was so disappointed and frustrated that I even became ill. I thought to myself, *How can I talk about faith when I now doubt the people I should be able to trust?* Then I remembered the Scripture verse that says Jesus Christ is the same yesterday, today, and forever.[6] I was reminded that he never changes, and though some people might let us down, he never will. So our faith in what God has assured us should never waver. Moreover, God sent us a Comforter, his Holy Spirit,[7] because he knew very well that sooner or later we were going to need consolation in trying circumstances. Seek strength in his Word, never outside of it!

Each with His Own Challenges

We need to arm ourselves with courage and patience to use our faith. I often hear people say they regret things they never tried because they lacked the courage to do them. Be bold! We have only one life, one shot at going for our dreams and reaching them. You might have faith, yet lack the patience and boldness to use it.

5 Psalm 37:25
6 Hebrews 13:8
7 John 15:26

Remember that it is one thing to believe and another to act on it, just as it would be one thing to have legs but another to use them to walk somewhere. It is one thing to have a mind, but quite another to use it to think and meditate. We need to always speak and declare things, but it is also necessary to put them in motion. Are you going to go through life seeing what others do, or are you going to do something for others to see? You decide whether you are going to be a spectator or a protagonist of the mighty deeds God has promised us to achieve.

Sometimes we get desperate and do not appreciate our faith, that personal measure God has allotted to us and that we need to develop. After all, it is exactly what God is going to use to bring us out of the pit. When Jesus was about to engage in his passion and death, he spoke to Simon, one of his disciples, about the temptation he was about to face. Jesus told him that he would be sifted as wheat, because that is what Simon's name meant: "a reed blown by the wind."[8] This also reveals to us that Satan can tempt us if we provide the fodder for him. Simon was erratic and that is why Satan could "sift" him. But Jesus knew this and told Simon that he was praying for his faith to not fail him, since it was also that measure of faith that would cause him to overcome that trial, to return and strengthen his brethren. It is faith that turned him into that great apostle we all know as Peter, a name given to him by Jesus,[9] which means "stone," signifying a prophecy regarding his transformation.

When we have faith, not even sin can deter us. Press on! Trust in Jesus who never condemns us but offers us his help and intercedes for us so that our faith will not falter. We are not perfect and we all face temptations, but if we do fall into sin, we never give up. God is faithful to strengthen our faith to overcome every trial. Never despair, because you have the exact measure of faith and the

---

8 Luke 22:31–32
9 Matthew 16:17–18

necessary abilities to overcome every challenge, problem, and trial that might come your way.

Every man and woman in the Bible was given the exact measure of faith needed to overcome their personal challenges. Noah had the faith to build an ark, but not to have a child as did Abraham. Only David needed the faith to defeat Goliath. No one else except Nehemiah needed the faith to rebuild the walls of Jerusalem. You need your own personal faith to overcome that problem you are facing. Activate it now to find the solution you're looking for.

The mind is like a honeycomb, with small hexagonal cells, each with an on-and-off switch. When you say, "It can be done," those cells light up and you start looking for the solution to make that possibility a reality. Remember that once we define the "what," we will find the "how." After Thomas Alva Edison said the electric bulb could be invented, his mind worked unceasingly until he accomplished it. Not only you, but many others will also be blessed when you confess that you can achieve what you set your mind to do! Those with faith are much more creative and successful because they think differently, they challenge reason and focus on solutions to accomplish what they visualize. Faith is the raw energy we need to use to reach our goals.

The Patience That Seasons Faith

Each person the Bible speaks about who had faith also had patience in striving for a goal that was not instantaneous.[10] We know that patience consists of the ability to wait until we get what we have believed for. Noah believed

Faith is the raw energy we need to use to reach our goals.

---

10 Hebrews 6:11–12

and had the patience to build an ark over a period of many years, enduring the taunts and the ridicule of others. Do not think for a moment that his community was behind him. Abraham waited patiently up to his old age to have the child who would make him a father of multitudes. Indeed, he was a man strong in hope. (I always say that heaven must have jumped in joy and admiration when this little, hundred-year-old man chose to believe God.) Joseph was patient, enduring slavery, prison, and dishonor until he became the most influential individual in the Egyptian empire. Promises can only be attained through faith and patience. Season your faith with patience to generate the hope that will never disappoint.

There are times when we have the faith to believe that something can be done, the grit to do it, but not the patience to see it through. We want immediate results because we're drowning in our problems. Patience is to faith what condiments are to typical native foods. In Guatemala, as in any other country, we enjoy an impressive number of local dishes that make us proud. For example, I really enjoy a treat known as "chiles rellenos"—seasoned, meat-filled chiles wrapped in a whisked egg. Other delicacies are "hilachas en arroz blanco" (shredded beef in white rice) and "pepian" (a traditional chicken or beef stew). Thinking about it, there are a lot of dishes I love. As children of God, our faith also has a seasoning, or flavoring, and it is called patience. We believe in prayer to heal the sick. We believe in sowing and reaping. And we believe in the new life that only Jesus can give. Every trial we face moves us toward patience, and together with faith, makes us heirs of our Father's promises.

Embarrassment Is the Risk of Faith

The Bible says that hope does not disappoint.[11] Patience is the seasoning of faith, and embarrassment is the risk. Sometimes we do not risk anything in faith to avoid embarrassment. However, the Bible teaches us that many people believed and risked it all in order to receive the blessing. What would have happened if it had not rained after Noah finished the ark? What would Joshua have done if the walls had not tumbled down after marching around them for seven days? What would have happened to Abraham if there had been no child after announcing it to everyone? Undoubtedly, they would have been seen as fools, but they chose to risk it all in faith. Moses chose shame and rejection over returning to live in Egypt. Jesus suffered shame and pain on the cross to save us. However, when that third day arrived, all that shame was removed. The glory came down, and Jesus became the author and the finisher of our faith.

$$ACCOMPLISHMENT = (FAITH + PATIENCE)^2 - (SHAME + RISK)$$

When we exercise our faith and patience we risk shame, but we must attempt it anyway. All of life is a risk, beginning at birth because we did not know who our parents were. But we survived because we had a purpose to fulfill. Be patient and never be ashamed of your faith. When we organize our healing crusades, we have faith

---

11 Romans 5:2–5

and patience. I do not think about the shame I might experience if miracles were not to happen, because I trust in the Lord's promise. The Bible says that God will not allow those who trust in him to be shamed. Take risks! God will not leave you stranded; he will always be with you. God wanted to tell the story of the people who believed in him so that we could follow their example and trust in the same way. Believe and be patient because your story will also be told as an example of a faith that achieves great things.

22 A NEW SEASON

Hear and obey
his Word.
Everything
else will follow
in due time.

Whenever we are about to enter a rainy season, we prepare for the rain. When we are about to go on vacation, we look forward to rest, and so forth and so on for every season. When we speak about patience, we are obviously referring to a period of time: hours, days, weeks, months, and even years that we must wait and work hard. That is what life is about, times and seasons.

Sometimes we run into really bad seasons, which is where we get the saying "when it rains, it pours"! After learning so much about faith, however, I can assure you that as of this moment a new season of blessing will open up for your life! And there are going to be so many open doors that you will not know which one to go through. The problem will not be your lacking something, but rather what to do with the abundance you will receive. Open your mind and heart to believing in the Lord, and prepare wisely to handle every good thing that will come your way.

Seasons, days, and hours. As human beings we talk about time, worry about time, and often want to make it go by faster, but we must not forget that to everything there is a season.[1] Going through a season is not the same as knowing that your due season has arrived, your time of blessing and harvest. There is a time and a day to be reborn.[2] You have been working on projects, transactions, dreams, and businesses, and the Lord says that it is time for them to be brought to light. The time has come for certain situations to die out and others to be born or resurrected, so be prepared for the harvest.

God does not measure time in a linear manner.[3] He does not see time the way we do. We always want immediate answers, but the Lord moves in different dimensions. One year is like one day to him, and vice versa. Time dwells in God, not the other way around. It is important to understand this, because it helps us visualize this new season opening for us. Seek to understand God's perception of time in order to better manage your anxieties and develop patience. According to our finite vision, we may think that God is taking too long; however, that is not the case because to God a thousand years are like one day. So be willing to wait, even if you don't understand why. Everything will happen as promised! Waiting is not easy, but you need to persist because you might be on the verge of receiving what you have been expecting when you decide to give up.

---

1 Ecclesiastes 3:1–2
2 Matthew 24:22
3 2 Peter 3:8–9

Not the Time to Die

Lazarus's resurrection is a good example of how to understand God's time. In chapter 3 we talked a little about this miracle, highlighting Martha's attitude. Both she and her sister Mary were expecting a miracle of healing, but Jesus knew all along that the plan was about a resurrection to demonstrate God's unquestionable glory. But Martha did not understand this; she thought Jesus had been delayed, which led to her doubt. It was the ideal moment, however, for him to prove to them that he was the resurrection and the life. The Lord's harvest plan for your life will always exceed any possible plan you might have. Never doubt it!

Seek to understand God's perception of time in order to better manage your anxieties and develop patience.

Let's look more closely at some details. When Lazarus first became sick, his sisters sent Jesus a message. You might even say that they tried to pressure him by using the phrase, "the one you love," which was code for, "Can you please hurry! Your good friend is about to die!" But Jesus' response was to extend his stay for two more days.[4] When he did finally arrive at Lazarus's home, Martha did not bother coming out to greet him. Instead, she confronted him and started blaming him for her brother's death, for not making it in time.[5] Those two extra days Jesus took to arrive were indeed decisive, and they continue to be today. That extra time that seems to "delay" the fulfillment of something is sometimes necessary for you to see the glory of God in your own situation. Jesus will change your plans for something better. He knows how to manage pressure and wants to teach us how to manage our impatience.

---

4 John 11:3–6
5 John 11:20–21

Jesus said that Lazarus's sickness was not unto death, but he died anyway. That meant Jesus had gone to resurrect him, and you can't raise what has not yet died.[6] This might sound confusing, but part of life consists of learning from confusing moments and persevering with faith. I have also felt confused at times. I have already shared my experience when God showed me the property on which to build our new sanctuary, and how the negotiations fell through right when we were about to close. It was then that God helped me understand that he had a better plan, and we are so grateful for his help in providing an even better location and building, a wonderful testimony for his glory. He resurrected the project I thought was as good as done, because to him, it was still very much alive. In the same manner, God is about to raise those things that you thought were dead in your life. Just wait on him and bask in this victory.

Time is a mystery. Do not try to unravel it.[7] When we believe the Lord, some things may happen in the twinkling of an eye. Faith in God's timing goes totally against natural intelligence that seeks to glorify our egos. We need to use our spiritual minds to discern God's timing. Let us serve him unconditionally, wholeheartedly, without time constraints, and free of all doubt. Only then will we understand his dimension for our seasons of harvest. He is always faithful to give us way beyond what we ask for or can imagine.

Times and Seasons

The Bible tells of a miracle catch that offers us valuable lessons.[8] Jesus was preaching one day by the seaside, and Peter and the

---

6 John 11:43–44
7 1 Corinthians 15:51–53
8 Luke 5:1–7

others were busy fishing, not paying much attention to the message. Does that sound familiar? Perhaps your anxiety to produce financial results has kept you from seeking the Lord? Then Jesus gave Simon some instructions that he questioned. After all, Simon was a professional fisherman who had just spent all night working. It is possible he was not doing well financially and needed to provide for his family, but his efforts were yielding no results. If your anxiety at work is robbing from your time with God, I can assure you that all worry will leave you and that provision will abound when you put God in first place.

God will bless you, but you have to give him first place in your life. It was their time to fish, even though the results were not in yet. Wait for your due time and your catch will be an abundant one. Your time is coming when those nets are going to break because of the bountiful catch you are going to receive. Your time has come, just as it did with Moses and Joshua. When you seek first his kingdom and his righteousness, all these other things will be added unto you. Peter caught in one moment what he had not been able to catch all night in his own strength.

When we speak about time, we are also referring to "times" and seasons. For example, Samson was a man with God-given supernatural strength. He was destined to be a strong leader in Israel, but was imprisoned after revealing the secret of his strength to Delilah. He was the strongest man on the earth, but even in his best season, he was unable to match what he did in his worse moment when he was all but humanly defeated.[9] A season is one thing, but a day is another. In the end, Samson had his best day during his worst season, while he was at the mercy of his enemies. He went from being a widely popular champion, who could do whatever he wanted, to being the laughingstock of the king.

---

9 Judges 16:30

It was in that dreadful season, however, that Samson experienced his best day for the Lord. He called on the Lord to restore his strength so that he could fulfill his purpose of destroying the enemies of God's people. In your worst season, God can give you the best day of your life! In your worst season of need or worry, in a time of sickness, you can see the Lord at work on your behalf. In the New Testament we see Simon going through his worst season, yet having the best catch of his life. We also see Jesus going through his worst season at the cross . . . betrayed, hurt, humiliated, tortured, but also enjoying the best day of his life, fulfilling his mission and taking that final step of victory. Do not let a bad day ruin your season, and never let a bad season keep you from preparing for your best day, which is yet to come!

Live in expectation of the best day of your season, whether that season is good or bad. Always seek first his Word, then everything else. Without God's Word everything else stops working. Without his Word there can be no catch. This is the year of wonderful surprises for your life! It is going to be the best year for your life, your family, and your dreams. There will be no more anxiety of bad seasons, which will be replaced by the joyful expectation of your best day yet. It is harvest time and your best day is still to come!

In your worst season, God can give you the best day of your life!

The Right Time

We all want to fulfill our time. We are children of a Father who controls space and time. The Bible says that God sent his Son in the fulfillment of time, and it turned out to be the greatest change in the history of mankind. Jesus brought us forgiveness and salvation

YOUR BEST DAY DURING
YOUR WORST SEASON ☺

through grace.[10] And for this to happen, we had to wait. But it did happen, and this same God-given grace allows us to do everything we are called on to do in life. When the Lord's grace is at work, doors open and whoever might be holding back your blessing will be moved aside. Understand that what grace opens for you, no one can shut. Even those who have not accepted you will bless you.

What will activate this grace and favor in your life? The faith and patience we employ during difficult times. After all, God himself urges us to count it all joy when we fall into diverse trials.[11] Who can be joyful in the middle of their problems? No one! One might say, "How can I be joyful with all these issues in my life?" It may sound crazy, but maintaining your joy at all times is an indication of your faith. It shows you are confident that God will fulfill his work. Many times, due to our impatience or eagerness to see quick results, we abort our projects. However, this type of reaction is not in our best interests, since it could easily result in a longer process.

We live in a high-pressure society, which leads to high levels of impatience. People are upset if we do not immediately answer text messages. We could say this is the season of constant interruptions,

10 Galatians 4:4–7
11 James 1:2–4

with everyone in a hurry. You rarely hear a "Good morning" or "Good afternoon" anymore; everyone is direct, demanding immediate responses. When we fall prey to impatience, we become more anxious and nothing is fixed. But God is still the same. He is not affected by our restlessness, and his promises will be fulfilled in his time.

We need to be wise and understand God's timing, as did the sons of Issachar, who was one of Jacob's twelve children from whom the tribes of Israel descended.[12] Of course, that is easier said than done. I was one of those desperate kinds of people. My mother used to say that I had "fourteen solutions for seven problems." I started many things, but the discipline to see them through was a trait I had to develop. January is usually the month when people make new plans, such as dieting. But how many make it to February with the same conviction? To persevere, our emotions need to be at the same level as our faith, not the opposite.

When the Lord called me into the ministry, he gave me a dream. I saw myself on a hilltop and a small white house in the valley below caught my attention. The wood was worn down and the paint was peeling. The window frame next to the door was about to fall off, hanging by one hinge. It was obvious that nobody lived in that old, abandoned cabin in the middle of a forest of sweet-smelling cypress trees.

I wanted to reach it, so I quickly ran trying to find the best way there. I made my way through the brush, carefully walking down the steep terrain. I had chosen the most uneven path, but it was also the quickest, a straight line down. Then I heard a voice that said, "That's not the right way." It was a very quiet voice, barely audible. But despite the instruction, I continued down the path. As I got closer, my heart started beating so fast that when I reached the musty wooden front door, I felt as if I had just run several miles nonstop.

---

12 1 Chronicles 12:32

I pushed on the half-open door, trying not to disturb anything, but the moment I walked in, the floor cracked and my foot became wedged between the floor boards. As I was trying to get my foot loose, I felt someone's presence. I looked up and right by my side was a person dressed in white speaking to me in the most natural way. "Would you like this to happen in the church I am going to give you?" After assuring him that I wouldn't, he continued, "Then learn to take the long path, because the road for your ministry will be long. I am looking for servants with fruit, people willing to dedicate their entire lifetimes to demonstrate that faith can produce results. But this can only be achieved with faith and patience." When I woke up, my heart was still beating fast, as if I had actually run down the steep hill in my sleep.

Sometime later, a poultry company hired me to develop some software. The offices were located at the production farm, in a very country-like, pleasant environment. Lunchtime was like a picnic, with tables for the employees under shade trees. One day I was fasting, which I did once a week, so I did not go out for lunch and instead went for a walk. I found a nice open patch of grass and I lay down, face up. Feeling the sun's rays on my eyes and my cheeks felt quite pleasant. I crossed my hands behind my head and started to pray. I can't explain what happened next, but I felt a presence by my side. For a moment I thought one of my fellow workers was near, but when I opened my eyes I was alone.

I rose and to my utter surprise, about a hundred yards downhill was that little white cottage from my dream. Perhaps not so worn out, but I did recognize it immediately: white wood, neglected, window frame about to fall off and door half open. I immediately tried to find a way to get down there. I could either go straight down through the field, or follow a path around the slope. Then I recalled the instructions I had received in the dream, so I decided to take the path lined with apricot trees. As I started getting closer, my heart began beating faster. When I reached the front door, I pushed it open, taking greater care where I stepped this time. I tried to step on the boards that were more solid. Right there, in the middle of a small open space where there would normally be a small table and chairs, I began to pray with my arms in the air. In that very moment, my mind cleared up as if the sun gently caressing my face a few minutes earlier was flooding every one of my sensory neurons.

My thoughts were clear, and I was able to reach a number of conclusions, making important decisions about my future. I smiled and laughed, feeling joyful, peaceful, and confident with the idea of being patient, focused on the fact that my faith would produce abundant fruit, because my Father would take care of everything else. The project I was developing at the poultry factory only lasted two months, and it seemed as if I had only been hired to experience that spectacular moment that helped determine my attitude toward the future.

There is nothing worse than getting ahead of God's favor. The story of Saul, Israel's first king, did not have a happy ending. He lost his throne, not to adultery or murder, but to impatience. The prophet had been delayed, and out of desperation Saul took matters into his own hands. He did something he was not supposed to do, he presented an offering to God in support of the conquest. We need to ask the Lord for patience, just as he is patient with us. Impatience can ruin so many things. Even in the direst circumstances Jesus was always, calm, serene, and in control. He will never leave you alone.

In 1984, evangelist Luis Palau visited Guatemala. After the event in our National Stadium, I stayed a while longer and remember praying, "Lord, when are *There is nothing worse than* you going to use someone from *getting ahead of God's favor.* Guatemala like this?" Seventeen years later, in 1999, we held our first miracle crusade. Yes, I had to wait, but it did come to pass!

The same thing happened with my ministry as a preacher. I used to be very impatient. I wanted to do things *now*! So I decided to preach at the La Aurora zoo in Guatemala City. Sonia prepared some tracts and we decided to go with a friend who would also sing. When we arrived at the zoo, we looked for an open, busy area. Sonia started handing out tracts to passersby and my friend Arthur began to play some chords on his acoustic guitar, singing a song about the resurrection of Lazarus. Not a single person stopped to listen!

When he finished the song, I prepared to leave, but Arthur quickly looked at me and asked, "Where are you going?" When I said we were leaving because nobody was there, he replied, "Ohhh, no-no-no-no, we'll have none of that. I did my part, I sang. Now it's your turn to preach!" I was both shocked and terrified, but I worked up the courage and started preaching about the parable that compares the kingdom of God to someone who finds a price-less treasure, then sells all that he owns to buy that piece of land where the treasure is buried. Right then and there, I understood how Moses must have felt when he had to overcome his fears and limitations to speak before Pharaoh.

I literally had to preach to the wind, because the only people who showed up were "No-one Smith" and "Not-a-soul Jones." In my desperation to share God's message, I went to the part of the zoo with all the rides and did get some people to listen, those who were sitting around waiting for their children to get off the rides! I zealously urged them to give their hearts to the Lord. One merciful brother did walk up to me and say, "You're doing good. Keep up that passion!"

All my projects have required patience. The same thing happened with my first book in Spanish, *En Honor al Espíritu Santo (In Honor of the Holy Spirit)*. I began writing the first chapter ten years before it was published. Back then, it was fashionable for preachers to publish books. Many of them were already having their books distributed, and I remember different publishers approaching me and asking when I was going to write one. However, I waited patiently with one thought, "I need to be sure that the anointing will stay with me." When the book finally came out, it was the best-selling Christian book by a Hispanic author in the Spanish market for five years in a row. The same thing happened with our television program, our building projects, social media, and radio. I learned to be patient, to serve with love, to identify the right timing, and God has always been faithful to support us.

Let's declare that your season of blessing will no longer be held off.[13] Time always goes by faster for those who wait, and it stretches out for those who are desperate and try to fix everything in their own strength. But don't worry, because things you thought were lost will be recovered, positive situations that seemed to be at a standstill are going to be released, and blessings that seemed all but dead are going to come back to life. However, a word of caution: stay calm. When my mother would see me restless, she would say, "Easy there, bed bug; the night is long." Keep in mind, desperation is the worst counselor.

It is good to repeat what King David asked himself, "Why am I discouraged? Why is my heart so sad? I will put my hope in God!"[14] If you are going through moments of despair, anxious to the point that your muscles tense up, ask God for help. Ask him to speed up his timing. Desperation does not fix anything. When you are drowning, the first thing a lifeguard will tell you is to stop struggling or you both will drown.

Emotions can be deceiving. Didn't Jesus tell his disciples to be calm when the storm hit? Only Jesus can provide us with a peace

---

13 Amos 9:13
14 Psalm 42:5

that surpasses all understanding in the middle of the rain and the wind. If you can learn to be patient, you will be greatly blessed.

All-proof

Patience is when, regardless of how much time has gone by, a person not only continues to wait but also springs into action, not confusing patience with passivity. Patience is one of the factors that most contributes to success.[15] It is applied in sports psychology when coaches teach their players how to strategically think and play the game. They show players how to remain patient and in control to avoid frustration before a possible loss. A basketball player does not throw a fit and march off the court after missing a shot. On the contrary, he concentrates even more and stays in the game until the victory is won.

Patience makes all the difference when you do not immediately get what you want and you need to wait. It is no wonder the Word of God says, "I patiently waited on the Lord to help me, and he turned to me and heard my cry. He lifted me out of the pit of despair." When I first read this verse in Psalm 40, I was confused, because it seemed contradictory. Patiently waiting in the pit of despair? Later I understood that David was right. It is exactly when we have to wait that we usually get impatient, yet it is when we most need to wait and exercise patience. When we take our sick children to the pediatrician, we patiently wait for the doctor to arrive as well as for our turn. We patiently wait amid despair, with a room full of crying children and angry mothers, yet we do not leave until the doctor treats our child. The same principle applies in any situation that requires patience.

---

15 Hebrews 6:12

Those who inherit a promise must never stop waiting to receive it. No matter how desperate they become, they should know that God will never, ever fail them. Sure, sometimes he may delay, but he always arrives on time. With faith and patience, you, too, will be able to face any difficult circumstance. The Lord is faithful to give you the patience if you maintain your belief. Do not be like those who pray, "God give me patience, and I want it now!" We can reach every goal in life through perseverance and patience.

It is in our trials that we reveal what we are made of. I will never tire of repeating this: Never give up during dire or bleak circumstances. Believe the Lord, not what the world says! There will always be obstacles, but keep in mind that there can be no faith without an opposing force to test it.

23 CORPORATE FAITH

*Let us worship
the Father
together,
thanking
him for his
blessings and
praying for
one another's
needs.*

At Casa de Dios, when we embark on a new project, I always seek a consensus because believing for it and developing it takes a group effort. True, God has given every one of us a measure of faith, but it is also possible to combine those "measures" in order to reach one powerful blessing. Of course, we need to be patient and in agreement.

This happened when we first implemented the "Jesus Model," a system for evangelism and discipleship. The Lord had shown me a pattern from Scripture, to win, care for, and consolidate people as he did, but when I first proposed this to the team, they had doubts. Everyone had to read, assess, and contribute for the model to become a reality. We had some marathon meetings for this joint effort that has yielded an abundant amount of fruit and blessing by reaching thousands of people with the love of God. We are now also teaching this discipleship model to churches and ministries in other nations. It has been a direct result of patience and deciding and acting in unity.

There is a miracle in the Bible about a paralytic who was healed, thanks to four friends. They had opened a hole in the roof of the house where Jesus was ministering and then lowered the man so Jesus could heal him.[1] We all need help at times to believe, friends who are willing and patient to be with us through the process we are experiencing. Offer your faith and add it to others', and without a doubt you will see the results. Faith is strengthened and the results are multiplied when two or more come together to reach the same dream. God takes great pleasure when he sees us believing and working together.

It may not have been easy to carry the paralytic on a stretcher. Perhaps it took a little convincing, because there are always going to be arguments along the way, such as "What if you drop me? Look,

---

1 Mark 2:3–12

the place is full, we can't get in!" But a true friend will answer, "Hey, things can't get any worse!" You can be the instrument God uses for someone else to receive their miracle. And other people, in turn, will be used of God to bless you.

In Unity

Jesus saw the faith of the paralytic's friends and he healed him. Let us come together to pray for the needs of others. Pray alone, but also pray together to achieve even more in your business, in your family, and in society. Let us put our corporate faith to work! These four friends weren't priests, they weren't prophets, nor were they prominent leaders. They were simply average people, probably blue-collar workers like most of the others there. Yet, there was a powerful faith at work in them that moved them with a "hunger" to see a healing miracle, even if that meant doing something totally uncommon. They all came into agreement, planned their strategy, and acted to help their friend.

I can picture them now, waiting patiently for the right moment to get through the multitude, hoist their friend to the top of the house, open a hole in the roof, and devise a system to lower him down exactly where Jesus was preaching. Can you think of anything more powerful than that? Perhaps doing the same thing for an enemy? Anyway, this corporate type of faith requires much patience and focus because coordinating joint efforts is always a challenge. Sacrificing to help others is one way of seeking the kingdom of God and putting our convictions into action.

This story of faith displays an urban type of gospel on the

Sacrificing to help others is one way of seeking the kingdom of God and putting our convictions into action.

street, in homes, and in the community. This is a gospel that does not need to be transmitted in another language or with coat and tie for Jesus to manifest himself in power. It is a simple faith shared naturally, free of hype, which can achieve mighty signs, wonders, and miracles. Believe and agree with someone else, and you will see God perform mighty wonders!

Forgive others and seek to live with others peacefully. It is critical to put all strife aside and live humbly in harmony with one another; otherwise, it will be impossible to come together and strengthen our faith and to ask with authority for what we desire. Jesus promised to be wherever two or more gathered in his name.[2] The problem is not about God being present when we come together, but about having a right and willing heart, free of bitterness and resentment.

On a certain December 24, Christmas Eve, a friend of mine called, asking me to pray for her father in the hospital. I drove to the hospital, but he was no longer there. He had been moved to another one, because he was certainly going to die.

When I arrived, they did not want to let me in, but I told the nurse, "If his condition is really that bad, what do we have to lose? Please, let me pray for him." So they let me in. I prayed and rebuked the spirit of death over him. When I stepped out of the ICU, his relatives were waiting. My friend thanked me and said, "Thank goodness they let you in! We have been praying for God to take my father to be with him." I got a little upset, because if they had been praying for him to die, then I could have been at home with my family all that time. I explained to them that our faith should always be used toward life: "We shouldn't be praying for those things that are most likely to happen, but we should pray for healing. And if he dies, it'll be while hearing and believing words of life! So I can't

---

2 Matthew 18:18–22

come into agreement for him to die. Just believe, and don't worry if it doesn't happen. Because you don't owe anyone any explanation!" We prayed together, thanking God for the life he would pour out that moment. And when my friend's father recovered, his family began to call him Lazarus, because the doctors said he had come back to life.

I want to join you now and say, "Thank you, Father, for this corporate faith. Together we are going to do mighty exploits in your name. Hear us, Lord, we have come as one, and we come into agreement to fulfill your work. We declare healing and unity in the family, and we cast out every division that draws us away from your plans."

The Word of God says that we are brothers and that we need to help one another. I thank Jesus that despite our weaknesses he is not ashamed to call us his brothers.[3] And I can also call you brother or sister! We are all part of the same family in Jesus. He loves us just as we are, and he joins us in singing praises, worshipping, and interceding for us before the Father.

Finally, remember that customs turn into habits, so let's make patience and prayer in unity and teamwork a habit with a positive impact on the results. We need an urban faith, a corporate one with a clean heart, pleasing to God, that motivates him to work in power!

---

3 Hebrews 2:11–12

VIII

HOOK

"Think happy thoughts Peter, so you can fly!" That was the wise advice Tinkerbell gave Peter Pan, a child who refused to grow up, living in Never, Never Land along with the lost children, fairies, a tribe of Indians, and in perpetual battle with the pirates. However, it turns out that Peter Pan did grow up, because Steven Spielberg, who directed the movie *Hook*, decided he should. It is a new version with characters from the original story, depicting what would happen had Peter Pan grown up.

In the movie we see the ageless child turned into a cold banker, worried over his marriage to Wendy's granddaughter, with two children he hardly pays any attention to. Life had stolen his identity, causing him to lose his childlike heart! And immersed in all his grown-up responsibilities, he goes back to the place where it all started: Wendy's house. One night, Captain Hook, Peter's archenemy, pays them a visit and kidnaps the children. It seems that Peter Pan has lost his memory, because he could not recognize Tinkerbell, who has to wrap him in a blanket and carry him back to Never, Never Land. The movie shows the whole ordeal of getting his children back, but the first thing he needs to do is recall who he really is in order to get his powers back as Peter Pan.

When the movie first premiered in 1991, I was facing an identity crisis that was causing me to doubt my calling. Someone even told me, "No one is going to give you the time of day as a pastor. Maybe as a preacher, but definitely not as a pastor." Peter Pan had always been one of my favorite heroes as a child. I remember once dressing up as him in school, and I always loved the idea of flying. One Thursday afternoon when I was feeling a little down and gloomy—one of those days when you ask yourself why you even bothered getting up—I called home and said, "Honey, I need some alone time please. I'll be back later. I'm okay, don't worry. Love you!" Without much of a plan of what I was going to do, I headed to a nearby movie theater. And to my wonderful surprise, they were playing that film with Robin Williams as Peter Pan, Dustin Hoffman playing the role of Captain Hook, and Julia Roberts as Tinkerbell. I never imagined that a little more than two hours could be so significant for my destiny.

Every scene spoke to me. I was shocked to see Peter so doubtful, disoriented, scared, and riddled with the worries of life and the deceitfulness of riches, longing to save his children from the negative influence of Captain Hook. That child, now a father, seemed defeated and hopeless, because though he still possessed the ability to fly, fight, and rescue his children, he had lost all confidence in himself. Tinkerbell also spoke powerfully to me, as she interceded for him, wanting more time for Peter to get ready, recall who he is, and recover his courage, his faith, and his power. I literally felt like God was speaking to me in every scene, and it was no coincidence that I happened to be watching this film.

But the crucial moment, the one that totally broke me—to the point that the few people scattered around could hear my sobbing—was when Peter discovers a large, hollow tree trunk where Wendy, John, and Michael had slept in the past. That is where he starts to regain his ability to fly, after talking with Tinkerbell and opening his mind to happy thoughts. In fact, once he removed every doubt from his heart and opened up to faith, without even realizing it, he was already floating in the air, ready to perfrom those incredible stunts. In that scene, God spoke to me and said, "If you don't become like a child, you can't see the kingdom. If you do not have the faith of a child to imagine other wonderful worlds, you will never be able to envision the wonderful plans I have in store for you. There is no point in everyone believing in you, if you doubt in your own abilities. And the opposite is also true, it does not matter if no one believes in you if you are convinced about everything I have prepared for you. Will you finally believe and fly with me?"

My answer was, "Yes, Lord, I'm closing the chapter of every

doubt and I devote myself entirely to the vision you have for me. You know that I am just like a child who believes you. I have a thousand flaws, but I believe in you wholeheartedly. I won't let other people's doubts and insecurities rob me of my faith. I know that you always act on my faith and not my worries, and I can't but smile imagining everything that you will give me the grace to do for your glory and honor. I have decided now more than ever to be happy! Use me, Lord, in anything you want. I am a willing vessel!"

And that is how I rid myself of other people's opinions concerning my calling. In that moment, my spiritual eyes were opened and the rest is history. After serving intensively in my home church of Fraternidad Cristiana, the church where we were born in the faith, my wife and I decided to follow the path the Lord was showing us by accepting an invitation from a few friends, who were not attending any church, to share the Word of God with them. What started in 1994, with a small group of families coming together in a living room, has become what we now know as Casa de Dios.

24 IT'S ALL WORTH IT

Faith can
overcome
every doubt,
fear, and
worry.

I, too, conquered Captain Hook! You cannot tell me that fighting the "pirate" who wanted to strip my vision, my identity, my ability to fly high, and future generations, wasn't worth it! It all depended on the faith God had placed within me and in my ability to hear the Holy Spirit telling me, "I believe in you, I know you can fly!" Without him, I would never have made it anywhere, just as Peter Pan would never have been able to fly without Tinkerbell. The ability to reach our dreams and the vision that God has for us, or in other words our ability to fly, depends on two factors. There is an external one such as Tinkerbell's pixie dust, which for us is the Word of God along with the anointing of the Holy Spirit, and an internal one: our thoughts, our faith, and our decision to focus on the positive and on the blessing that does away with all doubt, deception, worry, and fear.

I invite you to be a child again. Choose happiness; cast aside every negative thought that would choke out your faith; seek the Father; meditate on his Word and make his promises yours, and there will be nothing to keep you bound to this Earth because heaven is your destiny. You will fly ever higher and higher!

In the movie, the pirates are portrayed by children who had grown up and lost their ability to dream and imagine. No wonder Jesus said that to enter the kingdom of heaven we had to be as little children.[1] Put in other words, we have to recover the ability to dream and imagine, with that guileless faith, willing to believe in everything that is wonderful. The wonderful little story *The Little Prince* is about another famous child who never grew up, and whose author is none other than the famous French count, aviator, and writer, Antoine de Saint-Exupéry. This short philosophical, image-filled parable describes human nature in all its splendor and misery, depending on the reader's perspective. The Little Prince, originally from Asteroid B612, has enough imagination to interpret the aviator's drawing, which is the story about a pilot stranded in the Sahara Desert and a young boy he engages in a very enlightening dialogue.

This aviator dreamed of being a painter, but he gave up the idea when he saw that no one understood his drawings, some of which appear in the book. One of them is a large bundle with elongated limbs, which at first sight grownups believe to be a hat, when it is really a large boa constrictor who has just eaten an elephant. "Grown-ups never understand anything by themselves, and it

---

1 Matthew 18:3

becomes tiresome for children to be always and forever explaining things to them," says the disillusioned aviator. Unbelievable! I totally identified with him, because I also have regretted many times drawing things I envisioned for the future but found hard to explain.

Let us return to that naivete we had when we were children, because a vital ingredient required to grow in faith is that capacity to imagine and visualize what is to happen. In fact, I'd go so far as to say that we run the risk of death when that flame and passion to dream and imagine goes out. Allow me to explain how I reached this conclusion: if the just shall live by faith, by the evidence of things hoped for, and the conviction of things not seen, it simply means that they live with the capacity to imagine and envision those things that are still not a reality. We live off dreams, off projecting ourselves into the future, enthusiastic about what we hope to achieve. When we lose that ability, life is over! When we are consumed by daily tasks, we get old! Therefore it is said that youth is not about the number of birthdays but is an attitude or a state of mind. Our Father wants us to be alive. Jesus came to give us life in abundance, which is why he asks us to persevere in the faith, to believe that our future is wonderful, and to act according to that certainty!

When Doubt Pays You a Visit

It may sound strange or contradictory, but when we speak about doubt we are also talking about faith. Just as when we talk about death, we are also talking about life, and when we talk about the color black, we also associate it with the color white, because each one complements the other. What I am trying say is, if you have never had any doubts, how can you know that you have faith? Even the best salesman in the world cannot say that he has never been told no.

Let us use our faith to overcome all doubt, in the same way that we have legs and use them to walk. Living confidently means

If you have never had any doubts, how can you know that you have faith?

believing for something you do not have but that you hope to achieve or obtain. Those with faith do not live in the past, nor are they stuck in the present. Instead, they project themselves toward the future, and once a

project is done, they have the next one in their sights. They never stop, because to do so would be like giving up on life, or having your air supply cut off. This has happened to me. In 2017, when we inaugurated Arrowhead, the ministry team's headquarters in the new sanctuary, in addition to thanking God wholeheartedly, I began to plan the projects that followed and were aligned with what the Lord desires for this ministry in the next couple of decades.

Cash Luna was already fifty-five years old, with thousands of plans circling through his mind. We needed to strategically organize to advance toward the future, to continue innovating with new, emerging generations, and to strengthen ourselves as an institution. There were many decisions to make, and we could not stop nor slow down! Faith always challenges us and when we slow down, we give way to a comfort zone that can lead to doubt and discouragement if we focus more on the past and the present rather than the future.

Trust in the Middle of Chaos

We have already spoken about David who became the king of Israel after Saul's failure. Sometimes it is easy to think that he immediately ascended to the throne after slaying Goliath, but that was not the case. David had to face many battles, including persecution by his father-in-law, Saul, who in fits of jealousy tried to kill him. David's life was quite interesting, although he was weak in many areas. He committed grave sins and suffered the consequences, but God still considered him to be "a man after [his] own heart." "Why?" you might ask. Because David's faith and relentless passion for God was his greatest virtue. He trusted in the Lord to such an extent that he said he could sleep and rest in the thick of war[2] because he trusted in God's divine protection.

Insomnia can often result from a lack of faith, that is, unless the excitement of your dreams and vision of the future is keeping you up. I have always said that the best way to rid yourself of a nightmare is to have a good dream. If you are afflicted because your children are on the wrong path, such as abusing drugs, only the dream of seeing them rehabilitated and renewed will make that nightmare disappear and open the path to a new reality. We need to dream that those things which are to come are so much better than our past.

We need to be like David, able to sleep confidently, not only when everything is going well and we have a secure weekly check, but also when suppliers are overbilling and those who owe have not paid! We need to show our faith even when the business is not doing well, or even if it has gone under. During such times we need to say, "I am going to sleep at ease, because the Lord is with me." That is what I call trust, that bridge we can cross during those moments of faith.

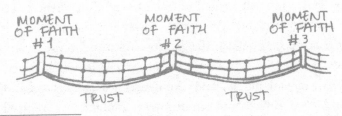

---

2 Psalm 4:8

Some people asked me how could I sleep so well, free of worries, during the building project for the Lord that took us five years to complete. I always reply that I slept in peace because if God told me to build it, then he was responsible to supply the finances and professionals needed to complete it. I was simply obedient. I would tell my family every night, "It's bedtime, nighty-night." Our faith in God allows us to live in trust.

My Cup Overflows

In Psalm 23, David says, "You honor me by anointing my head with oil. My cup overflows with blessings." This means that people who are filled with the Holy Spirit always speak well about their future, because the present turns into the past in a matter of seconds. Everything fades away in an instant. What you saw just a moment ago has already passed and will never come back. So we can only speak about those things that are to come. Anticipate your future with your words of faith!

If your mouth is only filled with complaints about the present and the past, it is because your cup still is not running over and you need to come before his presence to be filled once again. Remember, a person who is filled with the Holy Spirit will always speak well about his future. I have often been criticized for encouraging the congregation and lifting their spirits with the Word of God. People say that I should preach the truth to them, to scare them into conversion. In response, I always say that when it comes to bad news, they get a sufficient dose from the world. Everyone leaves Casa de Dios with a smile because my desire is to lift them up so they can walk in trust and confidence, just as Jesus did. People should weep in hope, not out of sorrow and anxiety. We need to pass on a childlike heart that can dream and imagine.

Jesus was never a grumpy old man. On the contrary, I believe that even his warnings to the Pharisees were with a smile on his lips. Otherwise it is unlikely that the multitudes would have followed him with the desire to be instilled with hope, nor would the children have approached him the way they did. Once my wife Sonia cooked a delicious plate of fish with lots of onions. Each fillet tasted glorious, fresh, and juicy with a few drops of lemon, wrapped in a hot-off-the-grill tortilla. I won't lie to you, every bit of it brought tears of joy and gratitude to God for so much blessing. One of my children, a young boy back then, saw my tears and started to cry as well. I explained to him that I was crying because I was happy and thankful to God, and though he understood, he did not stop crying. We need to be like children, easily affected by the emotion of good things, without complaining about negative ones.

Why Don't You Have What You Want or Need?

The Lord is always attacking our negative thought patterns. When terrified by the storm, the disciples woke him up, and Jesus said to them, "Why do you fear, oh men of little faith?" When they worried about not having anything to eat, right after witnessing the multiplication of the loaves and the fish, Jesus said, "Why do you think you don't have any bread, you men of little faith? Or don't you remember how I fed five thousand with five loaves of bread and four thousand with seven loaves?"

One day my eldest son became sick in the middle of the night, and despite all our efforts he became dehydrated. We saw that

We need to be like children, easily affected by the emotion of good things, without complaining about negative ones.

his eyes were puffy and sunken, and the skin on his little hands, arms, legs, and face was becoming wrinkled. Neither my wife nor I are experts, so we called the doctor immediately. Soon we started feeding him electrolyte liquids, but we gave him so much that the poor child couldn't take another drop. We stopped, since it seemed that the liquids were about to come out of his ears. We thought that everything was going to be okay, but that was not the case. By 3:00 a.m., little Cashito was still burning in fever and things did not look good. Immediately I cried out to the Lord with all my strength and he answered, "You have asked for a miracle, but how can I do it if you think everything is all right?" So I relaxed and said, "You're right, Lord. I am the one going crazy here, because you are in control and I know that my son is going to be made whole." Two hours later, our child was babbling as usual and the fever was gone. I should never have thought my son was not healthy, because he really was. All I needed to do was trust.

The Greatest of the Prophets

We spoke before about Zechariah and Elizabeth, the parents of John the Baptist who would be a prophet from Jesus' maternal family, called to announce the coming of the Messiah. John was used mightily by God: he prepared the way, he was the only one honored with hearing God's audible voice, he baptized Jesus and saw the Holy Spirit descend. How about that? He was also the one who revealed Jesus by declaring that he was "the Lamb of God that takes away the sin of the world."[3]

John's role was unique. He is described as almost a hermit, and he and Jesus had two different preaching styles. Jesus was subtle,

---

3 John 1:29–34

as one can see when he approached the Samaritan woman. John, on the other hand, was a straight-shooter, calling things as he saw them, such as when he called out Herod's adultery.[4] As a prophet, John was so important that even soldiers, publicans, and people in government would consult with him,[5] and he always told them that they needed to change their ways. He was used by God to baptize people and to keep alive the moral condition of both the Jewish and Roman people. Jesus himself stated that of all the men born of women, none compared to John.[6]

Despite his great level of faith and being the greatest of the prophets, even John the Baptist had his moment of doubt when he was imprisoned for telling Caesar's representative in Judea the truth. So John sent his disciples to inquire whether Jesus really was the Son of God, the Messiah everyone waited for, and whom John himself had announced![7] He probably asked himself, "Why would God allow such a grave injustice if I am the one who announced the Messiah? Why is this happening to me? I've been a good servant of God!"

He probably felt the same thing you do at times when you doubt in the face of adversity. Like many of us, his affliction led him to doubt. There are times when you feel you are on the right path and you have all the energy to press on. Then, suddenly, something causes you to stumble and doubt and you ask yourself, "Why is this happening to me if I serve, I worship, I pray, I minister, I'm good, and I give my tithes? Is God really who he says he is?" Upon hearing John's doubts, Jesus proved to him that he really was the Son of God by sending word back with John's messengers. And he says the same thing to you today, urging you not to falter. The issue

---

4 Luke 3:7–8
5 Luke 3:12–14
6 Luke 7:27–28
7 Luke 7:17–23

is not about doubting, but about how we handle those moments of weakness.

Do Not Be Mistaken

Your circumstances need to align with your faith and not the other way around. John, the greatest of the prophets, sat in his prison cell and must have had doubts, questioning God and thinking, "I should get that miracle, but since he doesn't give it to me, perhaps I announced the wrong man." There are many people today who act in a similar manner saying, "I don't believe in miracles, but if it happens to me, then I will." There is no reason in the world for God to choose you among the billions of people in the world to prove he is a mighty God and that he does not lie. We should be humble and say, "I believe in you, Lord, and the miracles that I have seen until now prove that you really are Lord. And even if I still have not received mine yet, my faith will allow me to see your work in my life." Don't be mistaken, life in the faith is simple, but not easy. God needs us to be humble for him to act on our behalf.

When doubt arrives at your doorstep, it does not ring the doorbell, but slips in any way it can. We need to know exactly how to act in those moments. Always speak with faith, even if things are not looking good. The patriarchs believed wholeheartedly that God would give them a land, even though Abraham, Isaac, Jacob, Esau, Joseph, and Moses never got to see it. Joshua was the only one of the great leaders that entered. Still, many people today find it hard to believe for just two months, whereas all these people never stopped believing throughout entire generations.

There are some who say, "I don't know why I went to that prayer meeting because it didn't help me one bit. It has been forty-eight hours and nothing has changed." Joseph had so much faith that

God would fulfill his word, that he told his descendants to carry his bones throughout the wilderness, because he wanted to be buried in the Promised Land. Now that shows an unshakable faith that can cause you to tell your family, "The Lord has promised me a full life and if it does not happen to me, get ready because God does not lie and you are going to receive it. Get ready for a triple blessing!" There is no going back. We are right in the middle of a battle between faith and doubt, and we already know which one needs to win.

A person of little faith is the one who believes that God clothes flowers better than he does his own children. That's right, you need faith to eat and dress! And those who live in fear never reveal their faith in the One who said, "Fear not, for I am with you." Set your eyes on the Lord and persevere through any storm, even when frightened. Draw close to him at every moment, both when things are going well and when you need his help. When you come to God because of cancer or financial distress, you are negatively motivated, but if you seek him when you are well and prosperous, then you are motivated by the positive and you will feel his well-being drawing you into his presence. Free your faith from that prison of doubt and meditate on all the promises that you will one day see fulfilled in your life and family!

25 FROM ANXIETY TO VICTORY

> The Lord will perfect us, affirm us, strengthen us, and establish us.

When we truly believe in God, nothing will ever separate us from him. I want to emphasize the word *nothing*, because no circumstance is worth more than our quiet time with him. That is what is known as faithfulness. In our day and time, it seems a little harder to grasp this concept, because we are so used to "disposable" relationships. If a marriage, a friendship, or a society "doesn't work" the way you expect it to, then it is just tossed out. We seem to be losing the character to persevere and overcome difficulties, and that is why we find it hard to trust in our Father's eternal commitment to us. Nonetheless, he is faithful and he does love us. So nothing should ever be separating us from his presence. Let us learn to love *him* more than anything he could ever give us.

A layoff, a divorce, a rebellious child, anxiety, persecution, hunger, nakedness, danger? Nothing should separate us from God. You will be victorious in every situation if you are convinced that neither life, nor death, nor the present, nor the future, nor things above, nor things below . . . nothing can ever separate you from the love of God.[1] He has promised to love us always and without measure.

As humans we have thoughts, emotions, and a will. All three areas are interconnected and they determine our conduct. We need to learn to manage them properly, especially during difficult times. If we do, God will always lift us up in due time.[2] During this process we need to surround ourselves with people who will instill us with confidence. Haven't you noticed that there is always someone in particular with whom you feel secure? When we are sick, we feel relieved when the doctor says we will be fine. In my case, my wife fills me with peace. When I travel without her, I find it hard to sleep, because I am so used to embracing her and resting by her side. God gives me peace through her, but I find my full security in his Word.

When our relationship with the Lord is strong, there is no need for a prophet to give us a specific word, since when we read God's Word, we will find specific counsel for our current situation. We need to learn to manage our anxiety by reading the Scriptures. Feelings of insecurity can be perilous and lead to making poor decisions.

---

1 Romans 8:35–39
2 1 Peter 5:6–7

Zero Tolerance for Negative Emotions

Don't let your emotions control you: not frustration, not anger, not sorrow. The Bible says that those who act in rage lack understanding, and those who do not control their own moods are weak. There is something wrong in your head if you are quick to anger, and even more so if you are impatient, because you will always be led by foolishness.[3] We have already talked about patience as the best seasoning for our faith. Our spiritual and emotional condition will often determine the advice we hear, but when we have a gentle and affable spirit, we will pay attention to wise counsel. Anxiety, on the other hand, breeds affliction, and we should attempt to control it at all costs.

Many things in life may try to crush your soul and make you feel defeated. The solution for a battered soul is the Word of God.[4] If a harmful emotion takes you captive, your mind needs clarity. The first thing you need to do to solve the problem is to take care of the emotion, because while you remain captive to it, your mind will be unable to find the ideas necessary to come out of the crisis.

---

3 Proverbs 14:29
4 Psalm 129:25

Your distraught and afflicted spirit will increase foolish ideas. A soul overflowing with the Word of God will hardly be cast to the ground, but a badly afflicted soul will only find life again in the Word, being filled with the peace that surpasses all understanding. Then you will begin to capture those God-inspired ideas: everything that is good, pure, honest . . . basically, all the possible workable solutions. When it speaks about the peace that surpasses all understanding, it is referring to remaining calm and focused, even in distressing or heartbreaking situations. Being unemployed, yet still at rest, does not mean that you are being irresponsible, but that you are trying to keep your emotions in check to find better options. If you try to find a job with distress showing on your face, you will have a hard time finding one because no one likes to hire people who are emotionally affected. If you seek the Lord, ask for his intervention, and humble yourself in his presence, his mighty hand will lead you and show you the best ideas for your situation. God is just waiting for you to confess his promises! He wants you to trust in him and turn everything over to him. He is waiting for you to cast your cares on him. Anxiety is like one of those insects in movies that gets under your skin and starts to make its way up your body. Every time I have felt that, I have had to say, "Where do you think you are going? Get out!" Take hold of your victory and ask God to quicken you with his Word and fill you with energy and creativity!

Anxiety has the power to destroy the soul, so we need to meditate on the Word of God; in other words, to envision it as a reality in our lives.[5] Once again, we are talking about becoming as little children and employing their vast imaginations. Fill yourself with his Word, meditate on his wonders, and you will be satisfied. We know that it is possible to meditate on both good and evil. When faced with a doctor's negative report, you can choose to focus on God's

---

5   Psalm 1:2

promise that by his stripes you were healed and envision everything you are going to do once you are whole. Or you can meditate on the sickness, imagine what your funeral will be like, what will happen to your children when you are not around, and how everything is going to be one big mess. It is up to you which word you will meditate on, that is, imagine and think on. God has given you the Scriptures and an imagination to use to secure a glorious and prosperous future for you and your family. His Word is our sustenance, and we need to meditate on it, imagine it, and take it as the only viable option we have to heal our souls and press on toward our future.

Fill your heart with hope, because God's Word says that this present suffering is only for a short time, and it is designed by God to perfect us, affirm us, strengthen us, and establish us.[6] Anxiety does not go away on its own. It is like losing weight: we have to take action for it to happen!

Faith versus Feelings

Worry and affliction should never choke out your faith; they should always open a way for it to grow. God wants us to strengthen our faith and believe him with all our hearts, beyond all reason and knowledge. This is the purpose of the examples he has given us in the Bible. Take, for example, Jesus' dilemma in his hometown of Nazareth, from which we learn that it is impossible to experience the God's work without first showing him honor and faith. In fact, unbelief has the power to neutralize God's desire to bless us. As we saw before, we need to be like the mythical Peter Pan, because by nature children always believe. Knowledge is only good if it doesn't block our faith.

---

6 1 Peter 5:8–10

The Lord is saying to us, "Don't doubt. My Word can produce the results you desire through faith." Strive to become a "believer," not just a member of some religion. Jesus worked for those who believed, even if they were not yet converted, meaning that faith is even more important than conversion. This clearly explains why some people who are not converted to the Lord also receive their miracles.

Remember the father who came to Jesus interceding on behalf of his young son who was afflicted by an evil spirit? Even though the father acknowledged his own unbelief, he still asked the Messiah for help.[7] Without faith, God can never work. This poor man was greatly confused; he believed, but not very much. He was still needing more faith because his affliction and his emotions were keeping him from believing 100 percent. Smith Wigglesworth, known as "the apostle of faith," claimed that it was absolutely impossible for him to understand God through his feelings. That is so true. Quite often how we feel does not fully align with what we believe, and we allow our emotions to dictate our faith. It should be the other way around. We're all emotional beings, and it is challenging to believe during times of depression or anxiety. Therefore the key is learning how to correctly control our emotions.

Strive to become a "believer," not just a member of some religion.

When Moses was trying to convince the Israelites about their freedom, they could not hear what he was saying because they were buried so deep in hopelessness and discouragement. In the process of building the first sanctuary for Casa de Dios, we had trouble negotiating the property for the parking area. Having a beautiful sanctuary is pointless if there is not enough parking space. In the

---

7 Mark 9:14-24

middle of all those concerns, the Holy Spirit spoke to me and said, "I don't move with worry, just with anticipation. Your dream is to build something where people can come to know me; so stop worrying already!" How often God speaks to us but we cannot hear him because we are caught up in our emotions. I can assure you that if Jesus himself were to appear in the flesh during those moments, you probably would not recognize him.

If we go back to Martha's case, we see that Jesus gave thanks to God before raising Lazarus from the dead. That difficult trial of losing a loved one was the vehicle God would use to renew that family's faith and take them to another level. Don't be like the people of Nazareth. May God help us with our unbelief! If we truly want to see miracles, we need to believe they are possible. Every challenge is a new opportunity to use our faith, strengthen it, and keep it from atrophying.

We know that human beings are constantly in search of the supernatural. That is why there are so many witches, psychics, and warlords, not to mention so many movies and literature about fantastic powers. Or don't you make your way to the movies to see the latest releases of *Captain America*, *Iron Man*, and *Wonder Woman*? We love watching Thor defeat enemies with his hammer and superhuman strength. And what about Superman, that powerful alien hero, defender of the weak? I really liked a picture that made the rounds in social media, showing Jesus surrounded by famous superheroes, carefully listening to what he was telling them. One can only imagine that he was saying, ". . . and that's how I saved the world." Jesus is the only one truly able to work miracles today!

Everyone knows Abraham as the father of the faith because he believed God's promise that his offspring would be great, despite that both he and his wife were in their old age. We can believe it now, but it would be very difficult to accept an old man walking up to us today and telling us that promise he had received. Would you believe him? Abraham believed and he experienced the miracle. It wasn't easy to have that faith, especially when everything in his body was shouting that it was ridiculous for him to have a son. Still, he praised God, confident that he would bring it to pass. Everything was possible except doubt in the Lord. Today Abraham would probably be told that he had gone mad, that the church was brainwashing him. I would rather have others think that, than flinch at God's promise to me. It is our faith that makes us righteous and worthy of the blessing, just as it did Abraham.[8]

When your feelings are contrary to what you believe, a battle is unleashed within you that must be overcome with faith. God will always work when you act according to your faith, not according to how you feel. Your ego will try to deter you, because no one likes to suffer humiliation. Faith, on the other hand, moves us forward to carry out great deeds, challenging us to remain humble enough to believe God and allow him to guide us toward the promise. Once you are fully persuaded that God cannot lie, your faith will overcome your feelings and you will begin to thank him for your blessing, even before receiving it. Faith is our greatest asset, because to him who believes, not to him who has, but who believes, everything is possible! Let us choose to please the Lord with our faith!

8 Romans 4:17–24

When he promised Abraham a nation, God caused him to look at the stars in the sky to stimulate his imagination, his ability to dream and visualize. When you are struggling with debt, God's promise is not only that you will pay it in full, but that you will have four times more resources to carry out your dreams. When faced with an infirmity, don't ask him for just one more day of life, but thank him for extending your days to such an extent that you will be enjoying your children and your grandchildren.

When your feelings are contrary to what you believe, a battle is unleashed within you that must be overcome with faith.

Inner Healing

The brain is home to our thoughts, the soul to our will, and the body to all our functions. We are triune beings, just as God is the Father, the Son, and the Holy Spirit. Sometimes we focus on only the body, wanting to be healthy and rid of every cancerous tumor or other disease. In our Nights of Glory healing crusades, we have witnessed countless healing miracles, but sometimes our souls continue to be infected and stand in the way of our faith.

During one of these healing nights, a lady suffering from rheumatoid arthritis walked up to me. The articulations in her hands were swollen and her fingers were bent out of shape. As we prayed and declared her healing, the Holy Spirit whispered into my ear, "Tell her to forgive." When I told her, she started weeping uncontrollably, despite having already received her healing because all the pain was gone. Her hands were no longer swollen and her fingers had straightened out. The relatives who had brought her to the meeting took her back to her seat and stayed with her the rest of the meeting. At the end of the service I walked up to her and to my surprise, her hands were back to their original condition. I was devastated! She apparently had a lot of unresolved issues. Her heart was extremely wounded and it was the first thing she needed to heal. We need to heal our souls! It has been proven that many physical illnesses can trace their origin to an emotion. We often somatize—express emotional pain through physical symptoms—and the body pays the price. In addition to eating well, working out, and taking care of our bodies, we need to look after our souls since they can also debilitate our bodies. In fact, the Bible says that a person's good mood has the power to drive away sickness. It does not say it removes it, but it does keep it far away from your life. So in the face of adversity, smile!

One of God's promises is that he has come to *bind*, to *heal*, and to *console*,[9] three words having to do with our souls. Whenever you bind a wound, you know that it will take time to heal, which is why the Spirit of God heals us through a spirit of comfort. However, until that happens he binds our wounds to keep them from getting infected. But if it is an open wound, like a cut, you can't seal it off entirely because the skin also needs oxygen to rebuild itself. If we are talking about a broken arm, it needs to be immobilized with a cast to help the bone regenerate itself. The same thing happens when God heals your soul; the best thing is to allow it to heal. Do you understand the comparison? We have to stay away from the matter and let it rest for a time.

True, we do need comfort, but I always say it is better to ask for counsel before it is too late. When a woman comes to my wife, Sonia, seeking advice because of her failed marriage, she is seeking comfort in a desperate situation. But had she asked for advice before things went sour, everything could have ended differently.

---

9 Isaiah 61:1–3

Everyone knows that many receive advice that is never applied, but that is a subject for another book. The idea is that we need to be wise in searching for the right advice. Nothing will go wrong if the Word of God is our guide. The first item designed to produce a change in our behavior is gleaning right knowledge to influence our emotions. The Lord said that we would know the truth and the truth would set us free. We possess the ability to find that truth and be truly free!

The Scriptures warn us to not allow any root of bitterness to spring up among us and bring contamination. Have you noticed that attitudes are contagious? If someone laughs, we want to laugh as well. If someone cries, we can be led to shed a tear. Surround yourself with people with the right attitude and you will become someone who radiates a positive attitude and you will be like a magnet that draws things to you, whereas bitterness is like carrying a big skunk on your back . . . no one will want to get close! I tell young people, "Don't fall in love with someone who is bitter, or you could end up the same." That person needs a doctor, a psychiatrist or psychologist, not a marriage partner. My wife, Sonia, for example, was already happy when I met her, as was I. Marriage for us was just the logical development that would lead to our blessing each other.

The Lord wants to heal your soul with the Holy Spirit's anointing, because that joy is also designed to heal relationships. Sometimes, however, we meet people who only want to complain. That should not be so. If you do fall in love with someone like this, you will end up in a codependent relationship. It's best for that person's soul to be healed and restored first. Happiness is an attractive feature, and joy beautifies one's countenance. No one can be ugly when they smile. A humorous expression in Spanish says, "The ugliest weevil gets the best corncob." In other words, sometimes we meet a man who may not be very attractive yet is married to a pretty woman. Could it be that the smile said it all? We know that women always seek men who make them feel protected and who make them smile. It's as if they are searching for a clown-ninja. But the truth is that love is blind when someone confronts life with a good attitude, which is attractive and something that leads to love!

No one likes to be around sad people who are always complaining or angry. But happy people, who smile and look at the positive side of things, now, they are a joy to be around. We need to be those types of people. When our soul is unhealthy, we are easily offended and say things like, "Why did you call me five minutes late?" When something's off on the inside, even something little can irritate you. It is easier to conquer a city than to please a person who is offended.[10] These individuals feel that everyone is against them. If they arrive late to work and someone calls them on it, they quickly say that person is out to get them, that they work in a hostile environment, and that they're always under pressure. If that bitter soul should by chance turn you into crystal, anything can and will shatter you! Does that mean you should welcome those who are late to work with a piece of cake, telling them that if they had been on time there would have been coffee as well? Of course not!

We all get hurt, but we need to forgive to avoid leaving a trail of bitterness and resentment everywhere we go. We are called to build up others. However, if you want to play the victim, go ahead, but all you are going to get is a pity party and that will end up making you sick. Can you imagine a society filled with people with healthy souls, free of bitterness? We would only have fighters, people willing to do whatever it takes to get ahead in life!

Today is the day for your soul to be healed of every bit of resentment that's blocking your faith. When a woman offended by her husband's attitude asked for comfort and advice, Sonia led her in

---

10 Proverbs 18:19

the following prayer, "Father, I ask you to heal my feelings with your anointing. Heal my soul, Father, and let me overcome all anger and sorrow in my life. I choose to forgive and to ask for forgiveness. I declare that I am bad ground for offenses and good ground for reconciliation."

26 FEARLESS

Cast out all fear and recover your spirit of power, of love, and of self-control.

We know that God has always looked for men and women of courage who can overcome their personal fears, who believe, and who are willing to conquer what is in their area of responsibility. This is why the Bible mentions Barak, Samson, Jephthah, David, Samuel, and so many others.[1] The point is to notice that all these men had something in common, and it was not their position, their wealth, nor their education; it was their faith! They believed God whole-heartedly regardless of the size of the challenge. God has also given you faith

---

1 Hebrews 11:32–34

to walk and run, and get out of that "spiritual wheelchair" caused by your laziness!

Paul was a great evangelist who raised up many disciples. One of them was Timothy, who had apparently faced a difficult time because Paul later encourages him to not be ashamed of his faith and to stir it up. When you read what Paul wrote to him, it pretty much sounds like this: "I hope your faith is true, that it is not just lip service, but I have seen how you have quenched the gift of the Holy Spirit, and it is almost as if a spirit of cowardice has taken hold of you. Can you please tell me what is happening? Please explain to me how it is that your mother and grandmother, in their old age, are not ashamed of the Gospel.[2] What are you so afraid of? Since when did you start walking in that spirit of fear? It's time to stir up that fire of God that dwells within you!"

When a spirit of fear takes hold of you, even your God-given gifts and talents can be quenched. Fear can paralyze us and make us pull back. Don't ever fall into that trap. If you allow water to seep through, even if it is just a few drops, sooner or later the whole room is going to get flooded. Don't allow even a single drop of fear, because God is like a plumber who has given us all the necessary tools to fix any leak. These tools are called a spirit of power, of love, and of self-control. We have a saying in Guatemala that loosely translated means, "Don't be afraid of your own shadow." This simply means stop running from your fears and face them head-on!

Go in This Your Strength

Earlier we spoke about Gideon, that young man chosen by God to deliver the people of Israel from the Midianites' abuse. Incidentally,

---

2 2 Timothy 1:3–8

the number of times the Israelites had to be rescued is unbelievable. It is reassuring, however, to know that God still delivers. Time and time again he was there to lift them up, to deliver them, and to rescue them. His love knows no boundaries!

As soon as the Israelites planted their crops, the Midianites would attack and ravage their land. Then when they were ready to harvest their crops, the Midianites would camp nearby, waiting to take the harvest for themselves. You do not have to worry because that is not going to happen to you. It is written that the angel of the Lord camps round about those who fear God! Just face those wicked "Midianite" spirits and say, "Get out of here, leave now! The only one with the right to camp around this house is my heavenly Father!"

With Gideon, however, we see a progression. First, the people cried out and God sent them his word. Then God sent an angel to have a word with the one who would fight it out with the invaders. The same thing will happen in your life. Seek God's will in his Word where you will find the medicine, instruction, and hope to conquer. There is no problem too difficult to solve if you just believe. He has already solved the most difficult problem by cleansing us in the blood of the Lamb and changing our eternal destiny. Is there something he cannot do? Absolutely not!

When facing a difficult circumstance, remember that God has already solved the biggest problem in existence: our salvation! Consequently, he can help you with all the rest. The Bible says that God remains faithful, and even if we are not, he always is. God does not know how to be unfaithful! He has made a covenant with you and he does not know how to betray.

There is no problem too difficult to solve if you just believe.

When the angel arrives to talk with Gideon, he finds him hiding. He was fearful just like many of us are fearful in situations having to do with our family or finances. It is almost as if the angel of the Lord were sitting right by your side while you are dying from fear. It is up to you whether you are going to focus on the Midianites or the angel. God commands you to be strong and courageous. He did not deliver you out of sin and bondage to forsake you now!

If you look closely at this story, the prophet spoke first, then the angel, and then God himself spoke to Gideon, encouraging him and instructing him on how to proceed.[3] He does the same with you. You have his Word and his presence, along with the help of angels. What would you do if he appeared to you? Would you have him hear all your complaints like Gideon did? It does not matter if you are the smallest in your family. What matters is that God already had a plan for you to defeat every one of your enemies. He does not want to talk about your hang-ups. He wants to give you some new instructions to conquer his promises!

The Word of God says that the Midianites were numerous but they seemed like one man. God is about to make those countless problems you have been facing to seem like one, making it easier to knock out. Your debt of thousands of dollars will seem small, because you are going to pay it without the least difficulty. It is time for action. Your business is not going to fail. Put away all pessimism and fear once and for all.

Convinced of his assignment, Gideon asked God to wait for him to bring an offering.[4] It was probably the last bit he had, tucked away somewhere out of the Midianites' prying eyes. Could it be a picture of you, hiding your talents out of fear? Are you afraid of failure or unemployment? No one and nothing deserves your fear except God! Actually, fear is a type of negative worship. Don't hide what you have, but rather, fearlessly invest your talents, your time, and your finances because God is with you every step of the way.

---

3 Judges 6:3–17
4 Judges 6:18

Have faith that these will be multiplied. If something goes wrong, consider it a time of renewal, but stop living in fear, because every decision made out of fear is bound to be wrong. You must face doubt squarely in the eyes, pray, and worship God, and give him thanks for helping you make wise decisions!

So no more fear! Whoever messes with me, messes with him also. Those finances are going to come to you much quicker than you expected, but the Lord wants you to strip away all fear! Juan Manuel Fangio, Formula 1 champion, said that the secret to his success on the race track was in accelerating when everyone else slowed down due to the risk of a crash. He knew it meant putting his life on the line, but it was the way to gain an advantage. Now is not the time to slow down. It is time to speed up and move on fearlessly. Put the pedal to the metal, because there is no turning back!

I know it is not easy to do. In September 2017, Hurricane Maria passed through Puerto Rico leaving enormous losses. A pastor friend of mine was left devastated; more than half of his sanctuary was reduced to rubble. When they walked into his house after the storm, there was a small stream of water coming down the stairs, and he said, "Look! There's the family portrait and my blue socks going out the door," and "Quick, grab that notebook! It has my sermon notes for the next couple of months." Water was coming out of the drawers and cupboards in the kitchen. The material loss was complete, but they continually thanked God because he, his wife, and four children were safe. Of course, his family was not alone, since all the members of the church were in the same situation. Everybody was stunned by the devastation the hurricane had caused in just a few hours.

It is in moments like those that, in addition to unconditional love and support, we need to come together and believe! My wife and I wanted to travel to the island as soon as possible, but it was almost impossible to get a flight. So we made arrangements to bring them here to Guatemala. When we finally sat down and had a cup of coffee, in a not-so-wet environment, we talked for hours. Seeing my friend's fortitude in the face of such adversity was nothing short of admirable!

We need to renew our faith and have the courage to activate it! Often it is fear that is holding us back. I admit that I am afraid of heights, but I have gone through experiences in which I have had to conquer that fear. When I was in Toronto, Canada, we visited one of the highest free-standing towers in the world. The top floor is made of glass, and while others were jumping up and down in the center of the room, I sat down in a corner, dizzy from the altitude, and slowly slid my way over to them.

Something similar happened when someone challenged me to go down a water slide. My friends kept urging me on and joking, "Come on, Pastor, it'll just take a few seconds. We won't tell anyone if you scream." All the meanwhile I was saying to myself, "How did I ever get up here?" Just as I was trying to get out of that predicament with whatever dignity I had left, a young, small boy, not more than seven years old, said, "Excuse me," then with an expression somewhere between worry and amusement, looked me over from head to toe, sat on the water slide with his arms crossed over his chest, and pushed on down to what appeared to me was a bottomless pit. I grew even paler, gulped a few times, and lacking any more arguments in the face of the courage that young child had just displayed, I put my spirit in God's hands and was the first to follow that brave lad's action. Fortunately, I still had my swimming trunks on, because that was about the only sense of dignity I still had remaining. It was without a doubt one of the most terrifying things I had done in a long time.

Thank God my job does not require my overcoming a fear of heights, because that would be quite cumbersome. I probably would be saying each time, "Should I . . . shouldn't I . . . should I . . .

shouldn't I. . . . should I?" However, I do need to focus on those fears that could affect my performance, especially when it comes to new endeavors God entrusts into my hands. The same principle applies to every area of life. An Olympic diver has to conquer his fears of height, and I am sure that in the process some have been able to do it, and others not. Nevertheless, this is what sets champions apart from others: facing and overcoming your fears to achieve the goal you believe in!

Force Yourself to Go Up a Level

God told Moses that his presence would always be with him, and it served as Moses' motivation to lead the people out of the wilderness. Even though it was his calling, Moses still asked God, "Do not bring us out, lest you come with us." At first sight, it would seem as if Moses was evading his responsibility since, after God delivered them out of Egypt, he was the one who was tasked with taking them into the Promised Land. In the same way today, God has promised to be with us always, but it is now up to us to go forward. So the question is, where are you going to take God? He expects you to be strong and reach your goal. When the generation who would finally conquer the Promised Land rose up, God repeatedly told Joshua to be strong and of a good courage.[5] He did not tell him to believe, because it was obvious that Joshua did have faith. In fact, the people of Israel had been believing in the Lord's promise since the time of Abraham! However, they had not been able to enter the land because they lacked the courage to fight for it. With Joshua, the time had now come to do it. They had believed for a long time, but now was the moment to roll up their sleeves to conquer that promise!

---

5 Joshua 1:6

Our faith is designed to grow, even when we are afraid. The faith you use to tell your girlfriend that you love her is not the same as the one that is going to keep your marriage going for a lifetime. David's faith before Goliath had to be greater than the one he used to defeat the lion. That new challenge required a renewed faith! We need to break in a new level of faith each time we take on a new challenge.

When you come out of a crisis, the worst thing you can do is get comfortable, because if you remain next to that pit, you run the risk of falling into it again. Once you are out of that pit, press on and climb your mountain! Step by step, but never get comfortable.

Emerge from your difficulties determined to reach new heights. Demonstrate the confidence in God to heal you, and once you are whole, ask him to fill your body with new vitality and energy. Faith is great to bring us out of the pit, but it is also designed to take us to the summit!

Faith is great to bring us out of the pit, but it is also designed to take us to the summit!

If we owe a great amount of money, we feel free to ask the Lord with all our faith to help us pay for it. However, we think it is vanity to ask for that same amount to build a home for our children, or to provide them a more comfortable lifestyle. What is wrong with us? We need to raise our level of our faith if it is being used only as a life preserver and not as our most powerful weapon.

The faith the Lord gives us is to bring us out of the wilderness, but it is also intended to help us subdue the land. While they were in the desert, the Israelites did nothing but walk in circles and receive their food from heaven, but in the Promised Land, they had to be bold and fight. Why is it that we can pray for restoration of our families if they have fallen apart but not pray to be happier when things are going well?

It's not necessary to be drowning for your faith to be at work. We can also activate it to take us to new heights when everything is going well. During a trip to a lake with a friend, I heard him pray: "Father, I want you to give me a beautiful boat to ski with and enjoy." I was flabbergasted, and asked him: "How can you possibly think about asking for such a thing?" He simply replied: "I'm not asking you. I'll do the asking and he will answer me." Right then I realized he was right. Our Father wants to give to us abundantly, because he is not limited. He wants us to increase our measure of faith to ask for anything.

Resistance to Grow

Out of all the miracles Jesus performed, there is one that can leave us open-mouthed because of the attitude of the woman who requested it. As my granddaughter would say, "You go, girl!" This woman was distressed because an evil spirit was tormenting her daughter. This woman's level of faith was so great that she persisted, unafraid and without shame, until she received an answer to her request. Well, maybe she was a little fearful, maybe even a lot. Remember, women in those days were not supposed to approach a man publicly, but she put aside that fear to receive what she longed for. When we read what happened in this story, it would be easy to assume that Jesus was rejecting her, then reproaching her, looking down on her with arrogance, but that was not the case. What he hoped to do was challenge her faith so that it would rise to the level of what she was asking.

This passage from Scripture challenges our way of thinking because it would seem as if Jesus was rude to someone who was asking him for a miracle. In fact, it's the only time the Bible records him acting this way. We could assume Jesus was too harsh, but really he was acting like a father who wants the best for his children and challenges them in ways that may seem stern. If he made everything easy for them, however, they might not mature. Nor will they develop the necessary character to fight for what they desire.

The woman in the story was obviously distraught, not only by the situation of her daughter, who could have played the lead part in the movie *The Exorcist*, but also by her courage to challenge the status quo and break through the crowd to get noticed. I am sure she was a nervous wreck, and in that state it would normally be hard to believe in deliverance from an evil spirit. Our emotions, however, should never be greater than our faith. Self-control is important and necessary for your faith to surpass your feelings and cause the miracle to happen.

If you need healing, you should focus on health, not the illness or disease. You must show that your faith has reached the level of assurance that you are healthy. But if you are feeling sorry for yourself, if your emotions and affliction control you, and your focus is on the disease, your faith will be drowned out and will not produce the desired results. In our miracle crusades, we see so much sadness and suffering that it is sometimes difficult for me to manage my emotions. However, I force myself to overcome my emotions and declare healing, revealing to God that the level of my faith is greater than any intense feelings. What Jesus wanted from that mother who requested prayer for her daughter was to increase and strengthen her faith so that the miracle would happen.

What was it going to take to make the woman's faith stronger? In addition to her persistence, she needed to be in control of her emotions. In the face of a big problem or crisis, the level of one's will needs to be raised. The Canaanite woman could have been offended and gone away when she was ignored, when she heard the disciples asking Jesus to send her away, or when Jesus himself appeared to reject her. Nevertheless, she was convinced that if she insisted, her daughter would be healed. Had she allowed her feelings of rejection to dominate her, she would have killed her faith and lost her daughter.

Jesus knew that her faith needed some resistance to increase. The same happens with your faith, which needs resistance and perhaps even opposition in order to become stronger and able to overcome obstacles. It is often difficult to value what has not cost effort, and we appreciate success when it is contrasted with failure. Whatever may seem contrary to meeting your need is actually preparation for your victory!

Holy Stubbornness

I can imagine that Jesus, rather than making it difficult for the woman, was praying for her not to give up and to have a sense of holy stubbornness that would allow her faith to reach the level necessary to receive her miracle. In the end, she did show Jesus that she was ready to receive. She knew she would receive the blessing others passed up and that her daughter would be healed. At that moment Jesus told her to let it be done as she desired.[6] There was no more resistance. Her faith had broken through the emotions of fear, confusion, and shame to achieve healing power. Jesus had practically pushed her to receive her answer!

6 Matthew 15:22–29

When a childhood friend heard this story, she said to me: "If Jesus had told me to receive as I desired, I would have asked for healing, a good husband, provision, and happiness for my daughter and myself. I would have even asked for the order in which I wanted my grandchildren to be born!" I could not help but laugh, delighted and satisfied because my friend had understood perfectly Jesus' intent. Indeed, that would be the best way to show God that our faith has reached a level that would take us beyond all our expectations. You can ask him, because he wants to see how great your faith is! Do not be like those who are invited to a banquet and do not take advantage of all that is available by only drinking a glass of water.

Put aside any foolishness that could limit your potential and prevent you from seeing your faith grow. God is not deterred by what you request. What good would so much power be if not to work in your favor? The death of someone close to you is sad, and a great void is left. At the same time, there is regret in thinking about what that person did not get to do and the dreams left unrealized— the bucket list that was not checked off. The Canaanite mother exercised a bold faith and did not allow herself to be intimidated, and your attitude should be one of faith and insistence as well. You don't need to feel embarrassed to ask the Lord with faith. What should embarrass you is asking for so little when he is willing to give you so much. Challenge him with your faith! Change your thinking, because your results will depend on it.

Thank the Lord for his Word, for the challenges you face, and for the will and character he has given you. Promise him that from now on you will have the courage to raise your level of faith and see great results. As your faith becomes more powerful than any fear, anxiety, doubt, or resentment, you will achieve everything on which you set your mind.

IX

THE GREATEST GAME

When superstar golfer Harry Vardon told seven-year-old Francis Ouimet, "Even in difficult situations, do not let them discourage you," Vardon never imagined that thirteen years later his advice would serve his young caddy and golf fanatic to beat him in an unforgettable tournament.

The US Open of 1913 was historic for many reasons. The movie *The Greatest Game Ever Played* recounts it in a very pleasant way. The storyline is about two golfers of humble origins who reached the tournament finals. It is clearly a story about self-improvement, which is why the writers of the film went overboard with memorable phrases like the one the young and doubtful Francis received from his mother: "You have a gift from God, and you have the unique opportunity to prove it."

The story itself presents a contrast between the rich and poor, between aristocrats and commoners. The movie also gives out helpful information such as listening to the right advice and learning self-control. As an inspirational film, it is all well and good. However, what stole my heart and moved me to tears had to do with the honor that is expressed through sentiments of gratitude.

Eddie Lowery is an affable ten-year-old boy who quite by accident, but just at the right moment, becomes Francis's caddy. There could not have been a more unique and out of place pair on that elegant Boston golf course! The jokes were plentiful, because how could a simple former caddy have qualified for the tournament and in turn have a mere child for a caddy?

The mocking gave way to admiration considering Francis's performance. Eventually, between successes and mistakes, he became the only American to reach the final round. It would be a matter of honor for the trophy to remain at home in the United States and unthinkable that the English could take it away. Consequently, before that final round, some "well-meaning" members of the golf club tried to convince young Eddie to give up his place as caddy for

Francis. They offered to pay him very well for doing so, because they felt that at that moment someone with greater experience was needed next to the man who was fighting for the honor of American golf.

When Francis arrived that morning, he found his little friend crying in front of the men who were trying to bribe him. He consoled Eddie and told him not to worry and that everything would be all right. Then he told the boy to go ahead and get everything ready. Alone with the aristocrats, Francis glared at them and said the famous words: "Do not mess with my caddy." Wow! That was the best gesture of honor and gratitude he could have given toward the little boy who had faith in him, who had endured sun and rain, who had turned a deaf ear to mockery and contempt, and who had kept him wisely advised throughout the tournament.

Neither Francis nor Eddie would receive payment for their participation. They were both intruders in a world of people who viewed them out of the corner of their eyes with contempt. These two were marginalized amateurs, but when the moment of glory arrived, the enthusiastic crowd lifted them on their shoulders for achieving a feat that no one had imagined possible. They were not only applauded but were also offered money. Fists full of dollar bills were waved in front of them! Francis began collecting the bills and tucking them inside his beret, all the while shouting: "It's for Eddie, it's for Eddie!" He knew that having kept the boy as his caddy had fulfilled the child's dream, but even more, because Eddie had rejected the temptation of a juicy pay-off that could have met the desperate financial needs of his family.

I was left with this important lesson that I want to share with you: the most extraordinary game ever played, rather, the most extraordinary game you will ever play, and by that I mean everything extraordinary you do in your life, begins and ends with faith, honor, and gratitude.

27 WRITE YOUR OWN PSALM

Thank you, thank you, thank you! Thankfulness is a powerful expression of faith.

One Saturday afternoon, while my wife, one of my sons, my daughter-in-law, and I were watching our favorite series on television, my youngest daughter, Andreita, came into the room and without any explanation threw herself into my arms and said: "Thank you, I love you!" At that moment, the last thing I wanted was a distraction to interfere with the climax of the drama that had us all in suspense. So I reacted on impulse and fleetingly responded, "I love you, too, honey." But immediately I was jolted to reality. She was thanking me and I did not even know why. Nothing could have been more important and significant than my daughter's grateful kiss! In the manner of true confessions, I really wanted to know how the program turned out. Against my own natural inclination, however, I got up from the couch and went into the kitchen to talk with her.

There, sitting in front of a steaming cup of coffee for me and a soda for her, we laughed about the things going on in her life. It was an especially enjoyable time together. She and I seldom see each other, as often happens in families in which each member is passionate about what they do; in my case, the ministry, and in hers, just beginning her university studies. As it turned out, her impulsive act earlier went deeper than I could have imagined. I shared before how Andreita came into our lives after her mother, my cousin, died in an accident. Well, now she was telling me: "You know what? I want to be a Luna." She was thanking me for the decision to welcome her into our family and was now asking me to officially adopt her so she could have our last name. This left me with my mouth open, but speechless out of emotion! It had been something we wanted to do, but had given her the freedom to think about it with no hurry. We wanted to let her tell us what she wanted, when she felt it was the right time.

I did not know what to say or how to act, and I did not want to frighten her by so much excitement in my heart. This was one of those moments in which books about fatherhood are not much help. But I think the expression of love on my face and my tear-filled eyes said it all. There was nothing else I could do but give her a big hug and say, "Thank you for choosing us." As she lovingly put her arms around me, I kissed the top of her head that smelled of flowers, and said quietly, "Thank you, Father, for the blessing that is my family."

Gratefulness is an indispensable virtue and a powerful expression of faith that brings peace to the heart. Even more so when we give thanks in advance, as Jesus did many times before seeing the miracle for which he was asking the Father. It happened that way with the resurrection of his friend Lazarus.[1] Giving thanks just feels good, the way little effervescent bubbles feel in the stomach or heart of the one who gives as well as the one who receives with gratitude. A friend once told me, "My grandmother taught me the habit of starting the day by reading a chapter from Proverbs in the Bible to give me wisdom, and finishing the day by reading a psalm in order to thank the Lord for everything I experienced during the day, whether good or bad, as well as to ask for a restful night's sleep." It seemed to me such wise and practical advice that I applied it to my own life, and I assure you that it is super-effective in strengthening a relationship with God and seeing good results in a life of faith.

Double Blessing

On a certain occasion, Jesus healed ten lepers. We do not know how long they had suffered from that unfortunate disease, but what we do know is that lepers led very difficult lives. They were cursed by others who believed that leprosy was a punishment for previous sins. For a leper to approach healthy people was an act of insolence with the potential of severe punishment, even banishment. However, the suffering of these ten men was such that they dared to cry out to Jesus with a faith much like that of the Canaanite woman.

Although still sick, they obeyed Jesus' instructions to appear before a priest. As they were on their way, they were healed. Imagine what joy they must have felt! Unbelievably, only one, who happened to be a foreigner, returned to give thanks and by doing so earned himself a double blessing. In addition to healing, he also obtained

---

1 John 11:41–44

salvation, as we see in Jesus' words, "Get up and go, your faith has saved you."[2] Could it be possible that the Samaritan was the only one who was grateful? I don't think so, but we do know that his expression of gratitude doubled the blessing he received. You can feel happy because you are healthy and have a job, but if you are not expressing gratitude, you will become ungrateful. Why deprive yourself of the satisfaction that can also change your life?

There are times we have false expectations regarding the life of faith because we just assume that our paths will be free from difficulties.[3] The truth, however, is that we all will go through some form of tribulation. As the apostle Paul says, the power of the Lord dwells in each one, but there are external situations beyond our control that can afflict us. Our faith will produce fruit when we acknowledge the power of God within each of us, with the ability to overcome any external situation that may possibly threaten us. When you feel weak, go to the Lord in prayer and thank him for what he has done, is doing, and will continue to do in your life. You can be sure that your faith will be strengthened.

The Righteous Rise Up

God has given a promise that the righteous may fall and suffer but will rise again and God will deliver them.[4] It's as if our Father sees our problems head-on and boldly declares for everyone to hear: "My son is capable of rising from his defeats, as many times as is necessary." The righteous person can be confident that victory is waiting right around the corner!

Recall how Jesus told Peter that Satan had asked permission to

---

2 Luke 17:11–19
3 2 Corinthians 4:7–9
4 Proverbs 24:15–16;

sift him like wheat, but he had prayed that Peter's faith would not fail him. Both requests asked of Peter were in fact fulfilled. The apostle did fall into temptation, but he also rose up and strengthened his brothers. Our purpose is to rise up each time we fall, stronger than before and, as a result, bear witness to the power of the Lord that dwells within us. When I developed a throat infection and my vocal cords were swollen, I stopped preaching for a few weeks, but I declared, "In the name of the Lord, I am not defeated! I will come out of this preaching better than ever before and to more people." When faced with a difficult situation that could bring us to tears, give thanks to the Lord with faith in the knowledge that he will raise us up and place a song and smile back on our lips.

When I was facing a particular problem, my wife asked me, "Have you prayed about it?" I said, "Not yet, I'm thinking about what I am going to say." Following that, I wept, pouring my heart out and as I meditated before the Lord, I knew that God wanted to show me something and I was ready to hear. Then, just as in a movie, I began to see parts of his story, including Creation, the fall of Adam, Abel's murder, the flood, the Israelites who spent forty years in the wilderness, and King Saul's failure. I realized that God had apparently also "lost" on some occasions, but through these stories he teaches us to rise up and move on. While drying my tears, I jokingly said to the Lord, "Now I see that you also need to be comforted at times."

Our Father was disappointed with the first Adam, but that did not stop him. He sent Jesus, the second Adam, to provide us with the greatest gifts of all, his grace and eternal life. This is how he teaches us to always move toward something better. For God there is no such thing as surrender, and he persists because the victory is his. If King Saul had not been such a great disappointment, then David would not have risen to provide that grand example of faith, not to mention his beautiful psalms of praise and thanksgiving.

It may sound illogical, but we are to give thanks even while going through difficult times, not because we are masochists, but because we know without doubt or reservation that we are overcomers.

Live to Tell About It

In Psalm 103, David writes about how blessing God's name is of great benefit to him and how it rescues him.[5] It is important to note that for him to write it he first needed to experience everything he mentions: iniquities, illnesses, and the sensation of being in a deep pit. It is easy to sing the words of this psalm if we have not had to suffer to write it. However, each person can write his or her own psalm, just as David did, about difficulties that have been faced and how the Lord gave the victory. We should praise the Lord every moment, not only when we cry out for his help and for solutions, but also when we receive them.

Perhaps at this moment you are in the process of "writing" the part of your psalm concerning your trials and ailments, but do not lose faith. Exalt the name of the Lord always, for he will rescue you from the pit and crown you with favor and mercy. In the end you will be able to sing: "I have risen as on the wings of an eagle!"

I will never forget Claudia, a young quadriplegic woman who never gave up. She recovered her mobility little by little, and with a lot of faith, until she was completely healed. The first thing she moved was her little finger and soon after she moved other limbs as well. Her parents persevered for months and took her to our Sunday services to praise and thank the Lord for her recovery process. She had faith to overcome her paralysis and fulfill her dream of becoming a doctor.

---

5 Psalm 103:1–6

I was deeply moved by her testimony when she said, "While I was lying flat on my back without being able to move, there were times when I was left alone and cockroaches would crawl over my body. There was nothing I could do to prevent it, not even scream." As I listened to her, I thought: *How nice it is to give praise now for everything that has happened, but how difficult it must have been to go through that very process that we now are able to see as a wonderful miracle.* Ask God for the strength to write those difficult verses of your psalm and to later pen your joyful ending when he raises you up. Let us write songs of faith and praise with renewed hearts, psalms with which to give thanks for God's love.

Let Us Worship

Perhaps nothing is worse than watching a child suffer. Can you imagine the affliction the Canaanite mother must have felt when she cried for mercy for her daughter who was being tormented by an evil, supernatural force? It was not about a simple fever; it was about a demon! That woman cried out to Jesus, but at first there was no response from him. This part of the story raised questions and doubts in my mind, but the Lord spoke to me, saying that he always answers, but he does not always say when or how. The important thing is that you believe that he will. The Bible says the woman worshipped him, which probably means she knelt, with her forehead on the ground, after kissing his hand. She cried out and worshipped, but the Lord did not heal her daughter until the moment she demonstrated her persistent faith.

We worship God because he is our Lord, worthy of all glory and honor. The Canaanite woman worshipped and then persisted in faith for her miracle. We need to see that faith and worship complement each other. Worship is an act of honor that has meaning in and of itself, independent of everything else we do as believers. There are non-Christians who sing Christian music, but they are not worshipping, just as there are Christians who worship, desiring God to manifest and make his presence known. The reason he manifests is because Jesus Christ shed his blood on the cross of Calvary, and not because we sing and dance. We cannot say that praise opens the doors of heaven because there is no song that can ever take the place of the precious blood of our Lord Jesus Christ, and it is through that sacrifice that we have access to the Father. We adore him because he is our God, simply because of that.

To think that by dancing we will obtain something is to return to the mystical practices of the Apache Indians who danced to bring rainfall. In fact, on the day of Pentecost nobody sang or danced, yet the Spirit was poured out with power. Worship, just like prayer, is not a matter of time but of quality and intensity. It's like the time you spend with your children, your spouse, and others you love. Take time to worship God in intimacy!

We must be worshippers in spirit and truth, not "soulish," meaning we let our mood dictate our worship. God continues to be Lord, regardless of whether we make mistakes, are angry with someone, or feel bad. The Lord's Prayer begins with adoration, and then continues with repentance and forgiveness. Don't condition your worship to your state of mind because God is our Lord and deserves your honor regardless of circumstances.

And If Not . . .

Shadrach, Meshach, and Abednego were three young Israelites, living in captivity in Babylon. They were friends of Daniel, the young man who became famous for choosing to be thrown into a den of lions rather than to deny his faith. Well, these three young men were also faithful worshippers and heroes of the faith who offer us a great example of conviction and courage.

It seems that in those days it was fashionable to devise unique forms of punishment and these three were thrown into a fiery furnace, for the same reason Daniel was thrown to the lions: they were firm in their faith. In their case, they refused to bow down and worship the statue of Nebuchadnezzar, the Babylonian king.[6]

These three young men teach us, many years later, how to respond when faced with the temptation to do what is wrong. In those moments we need to say, "Don't ask me to do that, because the answer is *no*! If you want to sink with the ship, that is your problem, but I'm going to choose what is right." At one point or another we are all bound to receive incorrect or indecent proposals. People are always looking for company, especially when it comes to drugs and alcohol. Don't give in to the temptations of friends who can influence you in the wrong way. We need to stand firm and say that no matter what, we will not compromise our convictions. Like Daniel's friends, we need to boldly declare: "The God whom we serve is able to deliver us."

Shadrach, Meshach, and Abednego set a great example for us, but perhaps the most significant part of their lives was their love for God and their great faith in him. This is evidenced in the words they added to their affirmation about God: "and even if he does not deliver us, we want you to know that we will not serve your gods . . ."[7] The Scriptures say that the Babylonians saw four individuals in the oven, because the Lord himself was with them. Their faithfulness was rewarded with the Lord's own faithfulness. They were not only tested, but approved and exalted. The king ordered that they be removed from the fiery furnace and issued edicts in favor of the God of Israel, and the men were given prominent positions.

---

6 Daniel 3:15–18
7 Daniel 3:25–30

Let us be as faithful and persistent as Shadrach, Meshach, and Abednego. They only saw two options: that God would deliver them from the fire or that he would take them into his presence. Yet, with both options, they were bound to discover his grace and mercy.

Worship Him at All Times

Our love for God is demonstrated when we worship him for who he is, our Father and all-powerful Creator.[8] When Jesus entered Jerusalem, he was received with palms and praises. Some were telling Jesus to shut up the crowd, but he replied that if they did not worship, the very stones would have to cry out. Everything alive worships the Lord, every being, every organism. If you do not do it, the plants will do it, but in the end, God will receive what he deserves. The lion worships the Lord, not because it is asking for permission to hunt giraffes, but because it is God's creature and honors its Creator.

The time is coming when everyone in all places will worship him, since his glory and presence will cover the entire earth![9] You

---

8 Psalm 150
9 John 4:20–24

can worship him anywhere. There are some who come to church only to hear the message, but do not worship. With that attitude they are saying they recognize him as a teacher, but not as their God. Take great care that the message you send to heaven gives honor to the Lord. He will bend his ear to listen to those who selflessly worship him with pure hearts.

Worship God when everything goes well, but also in your difficulties. He is your God in the good times and in the bad. It is easy to worship in nice facilities with comfortable seating and good music. But how about worshipping him in a prison, as Paul and Silas did?[10] With or without supernatural works, with or without music, with or without your mistakes, God is the same yesterday, today, and forever and deserves honor regardless of your personal situation. We do not enter into his presence because of a good heart, but because of the blood of the Lamb, which is pure. Do not even try to compete with that truth. Instead, tell the Lord: "Here I am, weak and imperfect, but I worship you because you are strong and perfect. I acknowledge you as my God, in health or in illness, with or without miracles."

---

10 Acts 16.25

28 GIFTS

Let us enjoy our blessings.

At this point it would seem to me that we have no doubt about God's love and generosity. We are convinced that he has given us everything we are and have. First, he has given us our existence, the opportunity of being, of having a life, and of breathing. But that is not all. He also blesses us with other gifts, one being the capacity to work and earn a living. Even more than that, he has given us the ability to enjoy our work. That is what is important: giving value to everything and not living to work but working to live and enjoy that life.[1] As we have already said, worry is an expression of doubt.

---

1 Ecclesiastes 2:22–24

Of course, we can find it difficult at times to disconnect from all our cares and concerns, but the Word of God calls that vanity,[2] which means it is vain and senseless because work is a blessing and turns into an affliction only when we allow it to rob us of our peace.

Enjoy Your Work

Obviously, work implies a certain level of effort, but we must learn to be thankful and enjoy our work even when it comes with hardships and challenges. If God has given you the chance to be useful where you work, then prove with a good attitude and enthusiasm that you are ready for the next blessing he wishes to give you. I am reminded of a story about a race-car driver who suffered an accident. As he could not go back to racing again, he began to look for a different job. The only job he could find was at a dock, cleaning fish. When asked how it was possible for him to keep such a positive attitude in his circumstances, he replied, "You can't always choose where you work, but you can always choose the attitude with which to perform your work, and I have chosen to be happy." We have to live each moment with joy! Learn to enjoy what you do, find ways to improve yourself, and reach out to where you want to be.

Enjoy everything: your work, your life, all you can do in the company of others![3] Do not allow criticism to affect you, because there will always be someone thinking the worst. Vanity is to receive God's gifts and not enjoy them. If the Lord has blessed you with abilities to get ahead, show him your gratitude through your best efforts and good spirits.[4] Your joy and positive attitude are the best testimonies of your faith. In the book of Ecclesiastes, Solomon

---

2 Ecclesiastes 1:13–14
3 Ecclesiastes 3:12–13
4 Ecclesiastes 3:22

says that God has granted us the ability to lead a good life, since he wants us to fight our battles and then rejoice in our victories. Do not complain, but rather enjoy your work, and turn your "spirit of despair" into a "garment of praise."

When you enjoy your work, your performance is much better. Excellence on the job can cause envy, but that should not worry you. If you were not envied, that would mean there is no excellence in what you do. Of course, it is better to cause envy because that means you are doing things right, the way God wants things done.[5] So focus on pleasing the Lord with your excellence. Don't draw near to the Lord only with requests, but present your results in appreciation for his gifts. The art of being a son and an heir is found in learning to live with a good attitude. Everything we do sends a message to the Lord, and the best message is one of gratefulness and praise, not disappointment and defeat.

In addition to taking full advantage of your talents, make room for rest because it is better to have little with joy than abundance with stress and illness. This is not written in stone, but it should be a conscious decision you make according to your strengths. If you can work hard with joy, do it, but recognize your limits. I thank God for my job, and I enjoy what I do, even though it requires a monumental effort. I am a pastor, I teach the Word, and I encourage and lead a congregation. In addition, I direct an entire organization and manage talent, which is something I do well. What is your dream job? What are you good at? What would you like to be doing even if you were not paid for it? Find out! Use the faith God has given you to work and enjoy the fruit of your labor.

Don't draw near to the Lord only with requests, but present your results in appreciation of his gifts.

---

5 Ecclesiastes 4:4–6

Rewards

After work, enjoy what has cost you so much, because that also is a gift from God. If the Lord blesses you with riches, ask him also for the ability and the character to not only enjoy it, but also to share it with others. The vanity mentioned in the book of Ecclesiastes has to do with the futility of working hard and being unhappy with the results. If you do not enjoy your job or are unsatisfied with what you earn, what is it that would give you real joy? If you work your hands to the bone, when vacation time comes, enjoy it to the fullest because you have earned it.

I cannot help talking about enjoying the fruit of your labor as an expression of faith turning into gratefulness and praise. When I retrace my steps and recall my experience in the process of receiving the anointing of the Holy Spirit, which I wrote about in my first book, *In Honor of the Holy Spirit*, I am moved when I realize it is all about a life of faith. Anointing and faith, love and faith, grace and faith . . . this could be the summary of my life.

I longed with all my heart to receive the anointing of the Holy Spirit. However, that anointing would not come and I became quite frustrated . . . hold on, that is not true . . . I was not frustrated, I was desperate! I was questioning my call, my ability to serve the Lord, as well as how he wanted to use me. In the book I describe how I wept like a baby because I could not receive the powerful anointing that I saw others, including my wife, enjoy. How was that possible if I was a man of prayer, fasting, and holiness?

Then, God confronted my faith! Yes, you read that right. The Lord confronted my faith with the words I shared in my first book:

"Carlos, your problem is faith."
"But I'm considered by others to be a man of faith."
"Look at you, you have money in your bank account and you

cannot buy a good pair of shoes with joy and peace. If you cannot have faith for a pair of shoes, how can you have faith to see my glory? Which is greater? My glory or some shoes?"

Every time I recall it, I feel electricity running through my body because I realize that, as always, God has moved me to talk about logical and illogical faith, faith for material things and spiritual things, faith for the little and the great. Faith is everything! Once again I am led to affirm that without faith it is impossible to please God.

What did I do then? The following day, of course, I put my faith into practice. I woke up excited, with a big smile on my face. I think I may have looked like the Joker in Batman. It was fun, because I even knew which shoes I wanted to buy. So I went to the store, tried them on, asked to see them in different colors, and took the time to walk in them. They felt perfect on my feet. I closed my eyes and enjoyed them. You cannot imagine the pleasure I felt when I paid for them! I was like a child (yes, again). God reminded me I needed to be like a child with an active imagination in order to see my dreams fulfilled; a boy thankful for his dad, with expectations and dreams. In that strange and simple way, God opened my mind and my heart, strengthened my faith, and prepared me for what would take place in the next couple of hours as in the years to come. I will share the end of the story by saying that I indeed received the anointing of the Holy Spirit and it was delightful.

Praise the Lord, give him honor and glory, thank him, enjoy life and what you have achieved because it is a result of his grace and mercy! There are people with nice cars and perfect homes who do not get to enjoy them because nothing can be touched. They want to have everything set up perfectly as if they were to be photographed for a magazine. They focus on material things and not on the purpose for which they were made. When you die, you will not take anything with you, so take advantage of your blessings while you have them. Remember that joy is also a gift from the Lord.

I smile every time I remember those Sundays I would walk in the central park of my city and see happy families enjoying a stroll without any fancy luxuries. It is not uncommon in Guatemala to see people outdoors enjoying some corn on the cob along with a tasty tortilla with beans, sprinkled with cheese and aromatic chopped parsley on top. Others, however, spend their weekends in luxurious beach homes, yet so unhappy and bitter. That should never happen!

It is God who gives riches, honor, and life, but they are of no value when not enjoyed with the right attitudes of thankfulness, humility, and the acknowledgment that everything comes from his hands.[6] So, if you have little, ask him for a good attitude to enjoy whatever you have. What good would it be to prosper with pain? God gives us according to what we have proven to be able to manage well. That is why the parable of the talents reads: "Well done, my good and faithful servant. You have been faithful in handling this small amount, so now I will give you many more responsibilities. Let's celebrate together!"[7] How can he give you more if you show a somber heart incapable of enjoying even what would seem little? Being faithful over few things also means taking what you have and making proper use of it, appreciating and enjoying it.

Be happy, because the simple act of smiling changes any setting. We get nothing out of walking through life cursing as if we were that cartoon character called "Bad Luck Schleprock," who always had a black, stormy cloud over his head.

---

6 Proverbs 22:4
7 Mateo 25:23

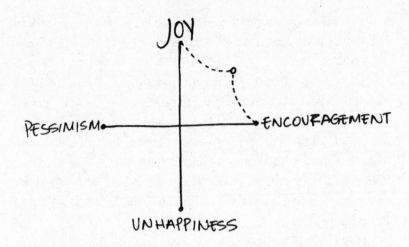

When we are finally able to conquer discouragement and praise God in any circumstance with gratitude, you will see how that good attitude will produce positive changes and everything will improve. Enjoy what you have, and do not put a price tag on your happiness.[8] So, the first gift we must appreciate is our work; the second, enjoying the fruit of our work.

Whom Do We Love?

Family is the third gift we must combine with the first two; that is, enjoying with your spouse and children what you have obtained with effort. Do everything with joy.[9] My wife and I sacrificed a lot during our first years of marriage because we wanted to buy a house. Then, my father-in-law said, "Enjoy life with my daughter. Travel and have fun with her while she can still put on a swimming suit." What wise advice! It is pointless to amass things if you do not

---

8 Ecclesiastes 6:1–3
9 Ecclesiastes 9:7–10

have the time to enjoy them with your family. I know sometimes it is a struggle because it seems as if we were raised to suffer. I do not understand why that is, since our Lord has created a beautiful world and has asked us to enjoy it. Enjoyment is living with faith.

I do not mean that life will always be peaches and cream, but that in both good and bad times everything is better when we are with our families or with those who love us the most. As I write this, I just remembered the case of Kimberly, a young girl whom I admire a lot and who has overcome difficult situations with the support of people who love her. She enjoys the restoring love of a family that received her in their home and treat her as a daughter. "Sandra is like my mom. She received me when no one would give a dime for me," this smiling young lady told me as we talked. There was a time, however, when she had tried on numerous occasions to take her own life.

It was understandable, knowing everything she had gone through. She had been sexually abused by relatives from the time she was eight years old. I don't think anyone can fully imagine such trauma and pain. That situation destroyed her emotionally and psychologically, even to the point of becoming a prostitute in order to pay for the alcohol and drugs she started consuming at the age of ten. Escaping from that monstrous reality in whatever way possible was her only alternative, but each time she tried she just sank deeper and deeper. When she was diagnosed with AIDS at the age of sixteen, she decided it was time to die, but her suicide attempts failed more than once. The situation at home became unbearable and she ran away and ended up living on the streets, at the mercy of everything and everyone.

Sandra was the principal of a school where Kimberly's mom worked. That is how she learned about the young girl's situation and decided to give her the love she needed. When Kimberly finally made it out of the rehab center where she had been secluded, Sandra took the young lady home with her. Getting Kimberly to accept help was a very slow process. Both of Sandra's daughters, who were close to her age, welcomed her as a sister, but Kimberly was incapable of trusting them. And how could she? She was hesitant when they shared their clothes, shoes, or food with her. Finally, unconditional love won the battle. It took time, but her heart began to beat with a new rhythm.

Kimberly had come back to life. She received a new chance at life when during one of our miracle meetings she was healed! She could not believe it was possible because she had come to church full of fear and trepidation, just to see would happen. But Sandra and her daughters did believe, and they were convinced that God had health in store for Kim. That is why, during the meeting, they prayed with such intensity that they passed on their faith, with Kimberly joining in praise as they sang "God of Wonders." She closed her eyes, raised her hands, and asked with all her heart, "Lord, please heal me!"

The Holy Spirit could not resist such a welcome. How would he not heal her given such a demonstration of faith and praise! The fire of the Holy Spirit filled each fiber of her weak and vulnerable body, and there was no room left for HIV. Kim was certain she was healed when she felt the intense fire go through her body. It was not possible to feel something like that and leave the venue in the same condition as when she walked in, and all the medical tests proved her right. The virus was gone. "Kim was healed, she was healed!" Sandra and her daughters asserted with tears of gratitude.

Kimberly received a new identity as the beautiful and talented woman she is. You could say she flourished as she became part of the family that opened its doors to their home and loved her unconditionally. She was encouraged to study and it was not difficult because she enjoyed it. She finished her GED and was excited to get into college. There are no limits to her motivation and drive to live! Beautiful Kim, a beautiful princess who now smiles as she is nurtured and cared for in the new home God has provided for her.

Would it not be a wonderful thing to have every abused or rejected girl receive an opportunity like this? Well, that reality is in our hands! There is no better expression of faith than joyfully sharing the blessings we have received, just as Sandra and her family did. I wish you could see their contagious smiles! Kimberly, Sandra, and the entire family proved that happiness is all about the decisions we make, and not about the decisions made by others, which might affect us in either positive or negative ways. Let's choose to be happy!

Jesus!

All of this is nothing compared to the most beautiful and valuable gift our Father has given us, one for which we cannot be thankful enough: Jesus! Yes, the salvation, grace, mercy, and love given to us through his life, death, and resurrection that open the doors to everything else.[10] How can one talk about faith and a new life without Jesus? It would be impossible! He is the one who gave us that possibility, which we can now enjoy in two ways: One is the eternal life awaiting us, and the other is the abundant life he grants us to enjoy in the present. He defeated the thief that seeks to steal, kill, and destroy.[11] That battle has already been won, so learn to enjoy the victory he has given us.

Don't wait any longer. Fearlessly say: "Jesus, I welcome you into my mind and heart. Today, right now, I take the greatest step of faith. I want to be born again, to learn from you, to be filled with the joy that is beyond understanding. I receive you as my Lord and Savior."

10 John 3:16
11 John 10:10

THE BLIND SIDE

An African American child, alone, homeless, shivering under the rain with an absent look on his face—defeated, marginalized, resigned to his fate as a survivor of a tragic reality. That was Michael Oher when he was found by Leigh Anne Tuohy, a wealthy lady with a beautiful and privileged family in Memphis, Tennessee.

They have no common bond; they are not mother and son, aunt and nephew, or teacher and student. They are not even neighbors! What do they have in common? Actually, nothing! On the contrary, Michael and Leigh Anne are completely opposites, but there is a way for them to bond, a link to connect them. And that is what the movie called *The Blind Side* is about.

Leigh Anne is moved. Despite his great height and weight, which earned him the nickname Big Mike, he seems defenseless and moves her to compassion. She then offers him to spend the night in her home, and he shows up on Thanksgiving Day . . . hmmm, why not ask him to stay for dinner? Little by little, as tough as it may seem, Big Mike becomes part of a family that receives him with love, despite all the criticism from the Tuohy family's social circle.

At first, Big Mike feels uncomfortable because he is not used to being loved (by the way, he does not like to be called Big Mike). The son of a mother addicted to drugs, he has grown up in foster homes where love has not exactly been the main ingredient. However, the simple and easygoing attitude of the Tuohy family finally begins to break down his barriers. Mike is given space, respect, and support without showy displays of affection. You know what I mean: it is not a mushy movie full of hugs and kisses, but a story of real, concrete love that can be seen. This is what touched me! Especially little SJ, the youngest of Leigh Anne's children, who contributes to Big Mike's adjustment by becoming his coach, advisor, and best friend. It is funny to watch them walk together; Mike is so huge and SJ is small, even for his age.

Things move along, and the family decides to adopt him. Perfect! So what is the main point that makes this story exciting and gives the movie its name? It is the true life story of Michael Lewis, the offensive left tackle responsible for protecting the quarterback from his "blind side." Throughout the film we see Big Mike fighting his ghosts through the love he receives from his adoptive family. Leigh Anne sees his potential, believes in him, and opens doors for him with college teams. The first task, however, is getting him to believe in himself so he can focus on overcoming his academic limitations in order to make the most of his talent as a football player.

We know football is an aggressive contact sport, but Big Mike has a peaceful temperament and only shows his strength when he is forced to stand up for those he loves. It was something he had to do during a car accident when his amazing strength keeps SJ from serious injury. Leigh Anne finally solves the problem by telling him during a football practice, "This team is your family, Mike, and you must protect it. This is the quarterback and you have to protect his blind side. When you see him, think of me." And boom! That was all the instruction he needed to release his inner energy. From that point on, nothing could stop him!

Mike enrolls in the university his adoptive parents had attended, graduates with the support of a brilliant tutor, and becomes a successful professional football player, thanks to his faith, encouraged by the love he received. That is the real *blind side*, the one that opens before us and shines through the love that moves us to walk by faith, and not by sight.

29 THE MAIN INGREDIENT

Stop crying, get up, keep walking, recover your sense of purpose, and allow your faith to drive you to success.

Imagine ten fearful, sweaty men hidden in a small chamber with very little illumination. Sad and disappointed with the uncertainty of a plan that was frustrated and a glorious future that turned its back on them. Their master and leader had died: to be precise, he had been cruelly murdered three days before. Slaughtered, humiliated, and crucified as a criminal, why did he not defend himself? Why did he not perform a miracle to save himself? Had it been real, or was it all just a dream they had experienced next to this man who proclaimed himself to be the Son of

God? Did they actually see him heal that many people? But they had seen him raise Lazarus from the grave! What had gone wrong?

"Peace be with you," was the greeting they heard. That voice from outside sounded so familiar. It was him, their master, their friend, their leader! What joy! But—how could that be? This was not a ghost. They touched him, hugged him, saw his scars, and he was giving them instructions. He had risen!

Thomas was the only one missing in the group at the time of the amazing visitation. When he arrived, the other disciples told him Jesus had been there, but he did not believe them. "You're all out of your minds, drunk, or possibly smoked something," I imagine he might have said. "I will not believe until I see him and touch him," Thomas exclaimed. And immediately his wish was granted! Without hesitation, Jesus gave him the evidence he wanted, not without first commenting that it was a greater blessing to believe without having seen that evidence. Not only that, we need to believe in order to see what we hope for.[1] We can all be more blessed if we show God that we believe him, even if what we see is contrary to what we hope for! But we need to talk about the main ingredient, that which moved the life, death, and resurrection of Christ, and which inspired his patience to show Thomas the evidence revealed by his body.

Remember how in the beginning of this journey through the universe of faith we spoke about the difference between the laws of this world and the laws of our Father's kingdom? That conversation prepared us to discover together everything that entails living by faith: renewing our way of thinking, getting to know God's promises, learning to ask for and obey, being patient and perseverant, developing a childlike heart to dream and imagine, and fighting against enemies such as worry, fear, doubt, and resentment. Everything good so far, right?

---

1 John 20:26–31

So, what do you think could be that fundamental ingredient that is implied in everything we have talked about, but have not mentioned explicitly? What do you think is that which moves us to believe blindly? I am personally convinced that it is love. That's right! Everything we have analyzed, discussed, and mentioned makes sense through love. God is the foundation of our faith and he is love.

Because he loves us, he created us; because he loves us, he saved us; because he loves us, he wants to bless us abundantly; because he loves us, he urges us to walk by faith and not by sight,[2] since our human senses can deceive us. For example, if we see a glass with a dark liquid, we might think it is soda or coffee. But to truly know what it is, we must taste it. In many cases we need more than one of our five senses to get to know reality. Faith is much like our sixth sense and the ability to love, our seventh.

Focus

I will not grow tired of saying it, because it has worked for me: if you want to stop worrying about your needs, think of a big dream and focus all your seven senses on reaching it. That is not to say that hardships will disappear, but if you focus on something bigger, what is urgent will be easier to reach. We see that in Erick Barrondo, a Guatemalan track star who despite limited finances managed to train and qualify for the Olympics. If he had been limited in his mind and had only focused on getting the money needed to survive, he would have stayed at home, in Carchá, Alta Verapaz, Guatemala, working on meeting his personal needs. But that was not the case! He focused on a dream, looked into the future, and became a silver medalist in the 2012 London Olympic Games.

---

2 2 Corinthians 5:7

We all have faith, of course, but what makes the difference is what we focus our faith on. Erick used it to sacrifice himself by training for a goal that many said would be impossible to achieve.

If you want to stop worrying about your needs, think of a big dream and focus all your seven senses to get it.

He overcame infinite difficulties, and when I say infinite I am not exaggerating. He endured hunger, faced disappointment when nobody would sponsor him, and considered hanging up his cleats more than once. It was not easy to swim against the current. His first running shoes were the ones his mother had used. He had no money to buy a new pair that would fit him! But his dream was as big as the dreams of many sportsmen, inventors, scientists, businessmen, visionary men and women who have learned to direct their faith toward significant objectives. That is the seed I intend to sow in your heart.

If God came into your room with an iPad and said, "Son, watch this video, this is you, it's your life, it's the plan I have for you," nothing else would ever trouble you again. You would breathe a sigh of relief and just wait for it all to happen. The challenge is in believing that the plan does exist, even if you do not see it. Close your eyes and talk to your Father and I guarantee he will reveal it to you because he loves you. Do not punish yourself if you have stumbled because no one can enter their best season of faith without first going through their worst season of unbelief. However, you cannot remain there, and now is the time to move forward.

Erick's faith and passion were so great that before traveling to the competition he bought his family a flat screen TV so they could see him win! He competed with his eyes set on the gold medal and received the silver. Had he gone there with a limited vision to "maybe earn a bronze medal," perhaps he would not have achieved the results that inspired not only Guatemalans, but also the entire world. If you aim for the stars, perhaps, with luck, you might hit a lightbulb. How hard is it to aim higher if you have to do it anyway?

Our Guide

Not too long ago I watched a documentary about a snowboarder. Part of his performance was doing something call "mirroring," which means following closely the route and performance of someone else. It was amazing to see this person's synchronized movements, but even more fantastic was the fact that he was blind!

Another time I saw a TV show about a blind young man who dreamed of becoming a mountain climber. When he turned seventeen, he decided to do it with his father, who would guide him step by step. Despite being blind, he could climb snow-covered mountains! These examples of courage and determination challenge me to reach for higher goals, especially when I realize that, unlike them, I have no physical limitations. Their testimonies make me think that perhaps it is an abundance of resources that hinders our faith. That is why when we go through times of need we must be thankful so that the problem itself can become the greatest opportunity to fulfill our dreams. Faith must be our guide, our lighthouse in the darkness, and love must be the ship, the vehicle that takes us to our destination.

All the other traits we have talked about that we need to confidently move forward will increase when we keep these two pillars in mind. As you might guess, my advice again is that we become like children, dreaming and insistent. My mother tells me I was like that every time she promised me something. I would not leave her alone until I received what I wanted to get. When she promised me a bike (I share this story in my first book), I would wake her up early in the morning with my face right next to hers, prying open her eyelids, and saying: "Mom, mom! When do I get my bike?"

Does a child want Christmas to be only during the month of December? Of course, not! If you give him a gift any time before December 25, he will insist on opening it and you will need more than just arguments to persuade him to wait. Every child wants things today! In the same way, when God gives me a promise, I look up to heaven every day asking him: "Dad, when will I get what you promised?"

As I read the passage of the blind men who followed Jesus, asking for their healing,[3] I can't help but wonder how they could follow him if they could not see. It's a shame that they, being blind, followed him, while we, being able to see, at times do not. Jesus knew they had faith because they followed him without the ability to see, so sight was the only thing they were missing. If they did not have their sight in order to receive what they wanted, think about how much more they could have achieved after getting their miracle. They showed their faith with acts and facts, just as we should.

Walking by faith and not by sight is like receiving your paycheck and telling the Lord, "Humanly speaking, I know that this money will not be enough, but I have faith that you will provide and all my needs will be met." Let us pay close attention to his voice so our faith may grow, taking us to where we can receive his promises.

---

3 Matthew 9:27–29

The Prophet's Mother

In the Bible we find the story of Hannah, the mother of the prophet Samuel. She suffered because she was barren, so she made a vow and promised the Lord she would give him her son if he allowed her to have one. We later read that Eli, the priest in the temple, approached her and told her to go in peace and to receive what she had asked for.[4] She then did three things that teach us a lot about the right attitude of faith.

The Word says she first went her way. Desperation had misled her, but when she heard that her wish had been granted, she got up and moved on. When you have faith, you get back on the road you were walking on, you pick up where you left off when you became depressed and discouraged. Your Lord says to you, "Get up and walk!"

Second, Hannah ate, which means she recovered her will to live. Sometimes when we fail, we feel as if we don't want to live any longer. Some people commit suicide when they believe they have lost their reason for living. Robin Williams's suicide in 2014 caused me great pain. As the actor who brought Peter Pan to life in *Hook*, anyone would have thought he had an enjoyable life, but we were all fooled by appearances. His roles in movies were usually fun and optimistic: *Jumanji, Mrs. Doubtfire, Dead Poet Society, Good Will Hunting, Patch Adams*, and *Awakenings*. All these presented an image of this genius actor, whose roles, unfortunately, were not a reflection of his real life. Our Father's love leads me to believe there is something beyond what we can see and feel. That love can uphold us to overcome appearances and help us become the real stars in a defiant, yet victorious drama. If we set our faith on him, nothing will strip away our desire to move forward because we will live for

---

4 1 Samuel 1:17–18

what he has promised, with our sights set on him, not on our circumstances. Hannah could do it because when she left the temple she had faith in the word that Eli had given her, even though she had not yet seen the promise fulfilled.

Third, Hannah was no longer sad because faith restored her optimism, even before actually seeing the final results. It may seem strange, but when I see a new challenge or difficulty, I smile. Now don't think I'm as crazy as I look. The truth is, I smile with expectation, curiosity, because I am moved by the idea of witnessing my Father's intervention. When Hannah received her promise, it was as if someone had turned on the light switch, changing her sorrow into joy. God can comfort you when you cry because of a problem, but to fix the situation you need to dry your tears, get up, stay your path, recover your will to live, and improve your attitude. This is the faith process that I recommend because it is the one I have put into practice many times over.

30 THE VEHICLE

Love drives faith; without love, faith falls apart; love and faith are intrinsically related.

The Lord assures us that the faith that operates through love is what has the most value for our lives.[1] He calls our attention toward love because it is vital in order to do his works through faith. Praying for the sick without feeling love would be futile, just as it would be to work hard to help your neighbor without any feeling or interest in their well-being. Love is the engine, the fuel, and the vehicle for faith.

There is no love or human power that can accomplish the supernatural works that occur through the love and power

---

1 Galatians 5:6

of God, just as the apostles demonstrated in the book of Acts.[2] We are just empty vessels to be filled with that love, power, and faith that comes from God, and which we receive so we can share them with others. It can be difficult at times, but it is necessary to persevere with joy and patience[3] because our calling in life is to serve. To have faith without vision or purpose focused on love and God can be a powerful distraction that diverts us to great yet negative results. If you do not believe it, let Hitler, Caligula, Idi Amin, and many other bloodthirsty men who focused their faith in things other than love tell their stories.

If we have gifts, we must ask God for the love with which to share them, because that is why God has given them. Why would you have a gift of revelation if you are only going to boast about what you know? What is the gift of knowledge and the anointing worth if they are used for personal benefit and to receive recognition from others? As human beings in constant search for significance we have been witnesses to the fact that the "void" in our existence is an empty space our Father left in us, ready to be filled with his love, which in turn must be shared with others. Having a concern for others is the only way to reach fulfillment.

What I have just stated has been scientifically proven. Abraham Maslow, a pioneer scholar in human needs and motivation, describes a ladder whose top rung illustrates the culmination in the progression of human beings toward self-realization. However, right after those individual needs have been satisfied, the focus becomes a projection on the needs of others.

Love is part of a divine design! The purpose for the talents God has given us is to love and share, because at no point does the Word talk about selfishness or individualism. When you learn about the gospel and teach it, it is not about satisfying your desire to teach, but rather about fulfilling the desire in others to learn.

2 Acts 3:11, 16
3 Romans 5:3-4

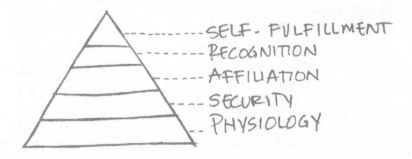

We are blessed for the benefit of others. Our gifts and talents make sense and have purpose only through a spirit of service. The Holy Spirit gives us his gifts for the benefit of all, just as a person who manages well his home not only blesses it but will also be able to bless others who need to move out of the chaos in which they live. What is certain is that we all have gifts and we can develop them to complement each other and work together.[4] Moreover, the Word is clear in stating that without love, we are nothing.[5]

The French philosopher, mathematician, and scientist Descartes said, "I think therefore I am." But our Lord, the Creator of the universe and all that is in it, moves us to say, "I love, therefore I am. Without love, I am nothing. Without love, I am useless." Love is not a feeling or words, but rather action and commitment. Jesus did not walk around saying "I love you," but he taught with love, he cared with love, and he healed out of love. His love moved him to die on the cross for us! He came to break the paradigm that believed fulfilling the law was the same as loving and honoring God. Love is a choice for us to make and as followers of Christ, we must demonstrate it as he did.

---

4 1 Corinthians 12:28–31
5 1 Corinthians 13:1–2.

Our Essence

Love is so essential that we could say not loving is like being dead. If we do not love our brothers, we are not a living society, but a graveyard. The Bible clearly says, "If you do not love your brother you are a murderer!"[6] If we do not love, we remain in death, we have not been born into true life, and we become like zombies.

God is love and he sends us to "perform" acts of love until we "are" love, as he is love. Because we are his children, love is implanted in our DNA.[7] Loving is not always easy. It can be much like working out in the gym; when we reach the level of loving our enemies, it is as if we had already finished three sets of fifty abs in a row. It is difficult, but that is how it should be. Maybe you don't feel so great, but you love nonetheless because it is more than just about feeling good; love is about commitment. Let us remember that negative emotions can only be changed through positive actions; that is the only way to grow in love.

Love implies risks, and God took the greatest risk of all by loving us. We often repay him poorly, but he never gives up nor stops blessing us. Even when we stray from him, as a good Father he would rather see us well and far away than defeated and close. The question is, will we come back in the end, because only in him do we have fullness of life. It is worth taking the risk of loving because we cannot allow evil and indifference to make us cold and to pull us apart from our way.[8] Learn to overcome arrogance, envy, selfishness, and resentment that can do away with love.

The first letter Paul wrote to the Corinthians includes an amazing description of love.[9] If you should ever wonder what it means to

---

6 1 John 3:14–18
7 John 17:20–21
8 Matthew 24:12
9 1 Corinthians 13:4–13

love, you can't find a better description than in this letter. I think we could take that description of love as a description of God: "God is kind and is never envious; God does not parade himself and does not show off; God does not behave rudely and does not put himself first in everything; God does not get easily irritated, and does not think about doing bad things; God never looks at sin as good. God is happy when people live in truth; he puts up with us, believes the best in us, and hopes that we are always well, he is always with us. In fact, God never fails." That is our Father and that is how we should be! In the end, a life of faith is made strong through love.

Keep in mind, dear friend, it is not so complicated. Jesus wrapped up all his teaching in a single word: LOVE.[10] Once again, his instructions are simple: *Love!* Just that easy. When you feel disoriented and do not know which decision to make because the outlook seems confusing, just love and I promise that you will never go wrong. This vehicle, love, has a built-in GPS, and you *will* reach the destination God has set for you. Do not be afraid, because perfect love casts out all fear; it strengthens and guides our faith. So, welcome to your new reality. Welcome home. Live and love by faith!

---

10 John 13:34–35